Emotional Intelligence Habits

Change Your Habits, Change Your Life

Dr. Travis Bradberry

TalentSmartEQ®
11526 Sorrento Valley Road, Suite A-2
San Diego, CA 92121

**For information regarding special discounts for bulk
purchases, please contact TalentSmartEQ® at:**

888-818-SMART (toll free, US & Canada callers) or 858-509-0582

Visit us online at www.TalentSmartEQ.com

ISBN 978-0-9747193-7-5
First printing: 2023

To Maribel,

still and always my aeroplane.

Contents

EMOTIONAL INTELLIGENCE AT WORK

APPENDIX

The Power of Emotional Intelligence

The Burlington Railroad couldn't find a more capable foreman than Phineas Gage. He had a special knack for finding the best route to cut through the rocky terrain, and his men laid track on time and under budget. However, Phineas was more than smart and efficient. He was calm and cool under pressure. The kind of leader you wanted to follow in a crisis—a real port in a storm. Phineas was also fun to be around. He was affable and curious about people. His men simply adored him. Absolutely everyone wanted to work on Phineas Gage's crew.

A fateful day in 1848 was the last time Phineas made it to work on time. It was a cold and damp fall morning, and the crew was short-handed. Phineas was happy to fill in with the tamping iron. A tamping iron is a three-and-a-half-foot-long iron rod about the width of a baseball bat's handle. Phineas' rod weighed 13 pounds, and he used it to compact blasting powder into the bottom of a borehole. The crew would drill a hole into rock, pour in the blasting powder, and top it off with sand, which would allow the tamping iron to pack the powder down without igniting it. This process produced a more precise blast when the time was right. At one point late in the day, as Phineas waited patiently for his assistant to pour in the sand, the men working in the pit behind him overloaded a railcar with boulders, which flipped the car on its side and sent the boulders careening to the ground. Phineas saw that no one was hurt, so he shook his head at the setback and then rammed the iron into the hole.

Phineas wasn't the only one distracted by the racket. It also caught his assistant's attention, who had failed to pour the sand on top of the blasting powder. When Phineas thrust the rod into the borehole, it scraped against the stone walls of the shaft, creating a spark that ignited the blasting powder. The ensuing explosion launched the rod into the air like a rocket. It traveled directly through Phineas' head, entering beneath his left eye and exiting through the top of his skull before landing some 80 feet behind him in the bushes. His men rushed to his side and naturally feared the worst. But just minutes later, Phineas was lucid and talking, even walking with some help from his men. Phineas sat upright in an oxcart for the ride into town, explained to the town doctor what had happened, and even wrote an entry in the logbook describing his exit from the job site.

It took some time, but against all odds, Phineas' physical wounds healed. He was eager to get back to work, and to those who knew him casually, this made perfect sense. Other than his missing left eye, he seemed like the same guy. Phineas was still enamored with building the railroad, and he still had the intellectual capacity to perform his duties as a foreman. But to those who knew him well, some important things about Phineas had changed drastically. These differences were laid bare once Phineas returned to the job site. The once polite, calm, and friendly Phineas was now rude and prone to fits of anger. He was unpredictable and unreliable, and he showed little concern for his men. In the words of his physician, Dr. J. M. Harlow, "He is fitful, irreverent, manifesting but little deference for his fellows, impatient of restraint or advice when it conflicts with his desires, at times pertinaciously obstinate, devising many plans of future operations, which are no sooner arranged than they are abandoned in turn for others appearing more feasible." Naturally, Phineas lost his job with the railroad, but he lived for another 10 years and even found employment driving a stagecoach that was better suited to his temperament.

Phineas changed because the tamping iron robbed him of his capacity for emotional intelligence (EQ). Doctors of his day speculated that the brain regions removed by the tamping iron must be responsible for emotional control, and we now know that's the case. Phineas lost nearly his entire left prefrontal cortex, and a good portion of the right side was damaged or removed. The prefrontal cortex is your brain's emotional intelligence engine. It's where you realize what you're feeling, process this information, and decide what action to take. With most of Phineas' prefrontal cortex gone or damaged, every feeling and impulse that he had exploded unfettered into action.

 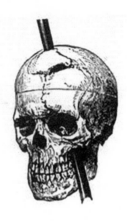

Daguerreotype of Phineas Gage taken after his accident (originally from the collection of Jack and Beverly Wilgus and now in the Warren Anatomical Museum, Harvard Medical School). Illustration of the trajectory of the tamping iron as it passed through Phineas' skull.

Everything you see, smell, hear, taste, and touch travels through your body in the form of electric signals. These signals pass from cell to cell until they reach their ultimate destination—your brain. They enter your brain at the base near your spinal cord but must travel to your prefrontal cortex (behind your forehead) before any rational, logical thinking takes place. The trouble is that they pass through your limbic system along the way—the place where emotions are produced. This journey ensures that you experience things emotionally before your reason can kick into gear. The rational area of your brain (the front of your brain) can't stop the emotion "felt" by the limbic system, but the two areas influence each other and maintain constant communication. The communication between your emotional and rational "brains" is the physical source of emotional intelligence. The more information that flows between these brain regions, the better able you are to understand your emotions, respond to them effectively, and use them to your benefit.

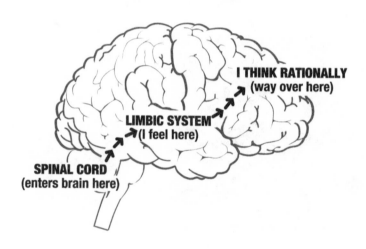

Your primary senses enter at the base of your brain and must travel to the front of your brain before you can think rationally about your experience. First, they travel through the limbic system, the place where emotions are experienced. Emotional intelligence requires effective communication between the rational and emotional centers of your brain.

Because your brain is wired to make you an emotional creature, your first reaction to an event will always be emotional. You have no control over this part of the process. You do control the thoughts that follow an emotion, and you have a great deal of say in how you react to an emotion—as long as you are aware of it. Some experiences produce emotions that you are easily aware of; at other times, emotions may *seem* nonexistent. When something generates an extreme or prolonged emotional reaction in you, it's called a "trigger event." Your reaction to your triggers is shaped by your personal history. As your emotional intelligence skills grow, you'll learn to spot your triggers and practice productive ways of responding that will become habitual.

Your practice of emotional intelligence greatly increases the flow of information between the rational and emotional centers of your brain. Information travels between these brain centers much as cars do on a city street. When you practice EQ skills, the traffic flows smoothly in both directions. Increases in traffic strengthen the connection. Your emotional intelligence is greatly affected by your ability to keep this road well-traveled. The more you think about what you are feeling (and do something productive with that feeling), the more developed this pathway becomes. Some of us struggle with a two-lane country road, while others have a five-lane superhighway. Wherever you stand today, there's always room to add lanes. I like to think that my personal work to add lanes is a small but meaningful way I can honor the legacy of Phineas Gage.

WHY EMOTIONAL INTELLIGENCE IS SO IMPORTANT

Emotional intelligence is your ability to recognize and understand emotions in yourself and others, and your ability to use this awareness to manage your behavior and relationships. It affects how you navigate social complexities and make personal decisions that achieve positive results. And most of us are not particularly good at it. Millions of people have taken the Emotional Intelligence Appraisal® test, and only 36% of us are able to accurately identify our emotions as they happen. This means that the majority of us are not nearly as in tune with our emotions as we should be, and we aren't yet skilled at spotting them and using them to our benefit.

This finding is not surprising. Emotional awareness and understanding are not typically taught in school. So, if you didn't learn them at home growing up, you probably didn't learn them. We move through life knowing how to read and write, but too often, we lack the skills to manage our emotions in the heat of the moment to successfully address the problems we face. This is a shame because emotional intelligence skills are critical to success and happiness. Good decisions require far more than factual knowledge. They are made using self-knowledge and emotional mastery when they are needed most.

Our brains are wired to ensure that our emotions are the primary driver of our behavior. Whether you're aware of them or not, you average about 400 emotional experiences every single day. This makes emotional intelligence a foundational skill. It's central to everything you say and do. When you focus your effort and attention on your emotional intelligence, it impacts so much of your behavior that you see changes in things you didn't even know you were working on. Like a great tree with many branches, emotional intelligence is the trunk. Every time you water it, you grow new branches (skills) and strengthen existing ones.

Researchers have shown that cognitive intelligence, or IQ, is responsible for only about 20% of how you do in life. Much of the rest comes down to your emotional intelligence. Our research has shown that emotional intelligence is responsible for 58% of performance in all types of jobs. It's no wonder then that 90% of top performers are high in EQ. It's the single biggest predictor of performance and the strongest driver of leadership and personal excellence. Naturally, emotionally intelligent people make more money— an average of $29,000 more per year than people who are not emotionally intelligent. The link between EQ and earnings is so strong that every point increase in EQ adds $1,300 to an annual salary.

Emotional intelligence taps into a fundamental element of human behavior that is distinct from your intellect. There is no known connection between IQ and EQ; you simply can't predict EQ based on how smart someone is. This defies the stereotype that really smart people tend to have little emotional intelligence. IQ is also quite inflexible. Your IQ is essentially fixed from an early age and shows little variation across your lifespan. You don't get smarter by learning new facts or information. Intelligence is your *ability* to learn, and it's the same (relative to your peers) at age 15 as at age 50. EQ, on the other hand, is a flexible skill that you can learn because the brain pathway responsible for emotional intelligence is highly malleable. Although it's true that some people are naturally more emotionally intelligent than others, you can develop high EQ even if you aren't born with it.

Increasing your emotional intelligence is also good for your health. Scores of research studies have linked emotional intelligence to susceptibility to disease. The potency of your immune system is tied to your emotional state via neuropeptides, complex chemicals that act as messengers between your mind and body. When your mind is flooded with tension or distress, it signals your body to decrease the energy it's directing at fighting disease. This change increases your vulnerability to an attack.

Research has also suggested that increasing your emotional intelligence may improve your ability to recover from illness. Researchers at Ohio State University studied 227 women diagnosed with breast cancer and saw remarkable effects of teaching emotional coping skills during recovery that aimed to reduce stress, improve mood, promote healthy behaviors, and help patients adhere to their treatment. Women who were randomly assigned to this treatment had reduced levels of stress, maintained a better diet, and built stronger immune systems. Research presented to the American Heart Association revealed a similar outcome for men and women taught emotional intelligence skills while recovering from a heart attack.

Emotional intelligence has a strong influence on health-related outcomes because it reduces your perception of stress in response to trying situations. Emotional intelligence skills strengthen your brain's ability to cope with emotional distress. This resilience keeps your immune system strong and protects you from disease. It's nice to know that working on your emotional intelligence can have benefits in some of the most important areas of your life. A healthy career, a healthy mind, and a healthy body tick a few very important boxes.

WHAT EMOTIONAL INTELLIGENCE LOOKS LIKE

To truly understand emotional intelligence, you need to know how it can be broken down into parts. There are four primary emotional intelligence skills that pair up under two competencies: personal competence and social competence. Personal competence is made up of your self-awareness and self-management skills, which focus more on you individually than on your interactions with other people. Personal competence is your ability to stay aware of your emotions and manage your behavior and tendencies. Social competence is made up of your social awareness and relationship management skills; social competence is your ability to understand other people's moods, behavior, and motives in order to improve the quality of your relationships.

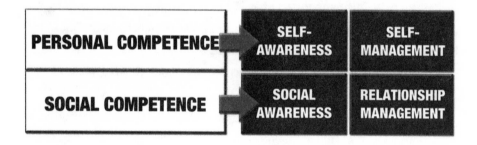

Self-Awareness

Self-awareness is your ability to accurately perceive your emotions in the moment and understand your tendencies across situations. Self-awareness includes staying on top of your typical reactions to specific events, challenges, and people. A keen understanding of your tendencies is important; it helps you quickly make sense of your emotions. A high degree of self-awareness requires a willingness to tolerate the discomfort of focusing on feelings that may be difficult to acknowledge.

The only way to genuinely understand your emotions is to spend enough time thinking through them to figure out where they came from and why they are there. Emotions always serve a purpose. Because they are your re-actions to the world around you, emotions always come from somewhere. Many times, emotions seem to arise out of thin air, and it's important to un-derstand why something gets a reaction out of you. People who do this can cut to the core of a feeling quickly. Situations that create strong emotions always require more thought, and these prolonged periods of self-reflection often keep you from doing something that you'll regret.

Self-awareness is not about discovering deep, dark secrets or unconscious motivations; rather, it comes from developing a straightforward and honest understanding of what makes you tick. People high in self-awareness are re-markably clear in their understanding of what they do well, what motivates and satisfies them, and which people and situations push their buttons. The surprising thing about self-awareness is that just thinking about it helps you improve this skill, although much of your focus initially tends to be on what you do "wrong." Having self-awareness means that you aren't afraid of your emotional "mistakes." They tell you what you should be doing differently and provide a steady stream of information you need to understand as your life unfolds.

Guided by the mistaken notion that psychology deals exclusively with pathology, we assume that the only time to learn about ourselves is when we're facing a crisis. We tend to embrace the things we're comfortable with and put the blinders on the moment something makes us uncomfortable. But it's really the whole picture that serves us. The more we understand the beauty and the blemishes, the better we are able to achieve our full po-tential. Simply put, to be self-aware is to know yourself as you really are. Initially, self-awareness can seem ambiguous. There is no finish line where someone is going to slap a medal on you and deem you "self-aware." Getting to know yourself inside and out is a continuous journey of peeling back the layers of the onion and becoming more and more comfortable with what's in the middle—the true essence of you.

Self-awareness is a foundational skill. When you have it, it makes the other emotional intelligence skills much easier to use. When you're self-aware, you're far more likely to pursue the right opportunities, put your strengths to work, and—perhaps most importantly—keep your emotions from holding you back. Your hardwired emotional reactions to anything come before you even have a chance to respond. As it isn't possible to leave your emotions out of the equation, managing yourself and your relationships means you first need to be aware of the full range of your feelings, both positive and negative. When you don't take time to notice and understand your emotions, they have a strange way of resurfacing when you least expect or want them to. It's their way of trying to bring something important to your attention. They will persist, and the damage will mount until you take notice.

Facing the truth about your feelings can at times be unsettling. Getting in touch with your emotions and tendencies takes honesty and courage. Be patient, and give yourself credit for even the smallest bits of forward momentum.

Self-Management

Self-management is what happens when you act—or don't act. It is dependent on your self-awareness and is the other major part of personal competence. Self-management is your ability to use your awareness of your emotions to stay flexible and to direct your behavior positively. This means managing your emotional reactions to situations and people. Self-management is more than resisting explosive or problematic behavior. The biggest challenge that people face is managing their tendencies over time and applying their skills in a variety of situations. Obvious and momentary opportunities for self-control (i.e., "I'm so mad at that damn dog!") are the easiest to spot and manage. Real results come from putting your momentary needs on hold to pursue larger, more important goals. The realization of such goals is often delayed, meaning that your commitment to self-management will be tested over and over again. Those who manage themselves the best are able to see things through without cracking. Success comes to those who can put their needs on hold and continually manage their tendencies.

Self-management ensures that you use your understanding of your emotions to actively choose what you say and do. On the surface, it may seem that self-management is simply a matter of taking a deep breath and keeping yourself in check when your emotions come on strong. Although it's true that self-control in these situations is a sizeable piece of the pie, there's far more to self-management than putting a cork in it when you're about to blow up. Your eruptions are no different from a volcano—there is all sorts of rumbling beneath the surface before the smoke billows and the lava starts flowing.

Unlike a volcano, there are subtle things you can do every day to influence what's happening beneath the surface. You just need to learn how to pick up on the rumbling and respond to it. Self-management builds directly on a foundational skill—self-awareness. Ample self-awareness is necessary for effective self-management because you can only choose how to respond to an emotion actively when you're aware of it. It's the one-two punch of reading emotions effectively and then reacting to them that sets the best self-managers apart. A high level of self-management ensures that you aren't getting in your own way and doing things that limit your success and happiness. It also ensures that you aren't frustrating other people to the point that they resent or dislike you. When you understand your own emotions and can respond the way you choose to them, you have the power to take control of difficult situations, react nimbly to change, and take the initiative needed to achieve your goals.

When you develop the ability to size yourself up quickly and grab the reins before you head in the wrong direction, you can be flexible and choose positively and productively how to react to different situations. When you don't stop to think about your feelings (including how they are influencing your behavior now and will continue to do so in the future) and manage them, you set yourself up to be a frequent victim of emotional hijackings. Whether you're aware of it or not, your emotions will control you, and you'll move through your day, reacting to your feelings with little choice in what you say and do.

Social Awareness

Social awareness is your ability to accurately pick up on emotions in other people and understand what's really going on with them. This often means perceiving what other people are thinking and feeling, even if you don't feel the same way. It's easy to get caught up in your own emotions and forget to consider others' perspective. Social awareness ensures that you stay focused and absorb critical information. Instead of looking inward to learn about and understand yourself, social awareness is about looking outward to learn about and appreciate others. Tuning into others' emotions as you interact with them will help you get a more accurate view of your surroundings.

Listening and observing are the most important elements of social awareness. To listen well and observe what's going on around us, we have to stop doing many things we like to do. We have to stop talking, stop the monologue that may be running through our minds, stop anticipating the point the other person is about to make, and stop thinking ahead to what we're going to say next. It takes practice to really watch people as you interact with them and get a good sense of what they're thinking and feeling. At times, you'll feel like an anthropologist. Anthropologists make their living by watching others in their natural state without letting their own thoughts and feelings disturb observation. This is social awareness in its purest form. The difference is that you won't be 100 yards away watching events unfold through a pair of binoculars. To be socially aware, you have to spot and understand people's emotions while you're right there in the middle of it—a contributing yet astutely aware member of the interaction.

To build your social awareness skills, you'll find yourself observing people in all kinds of situations. You may be observing someone from afar while you're in a checkout line, or you may be right in the middle of a conversation observing the person to whom you are speaking. You'll learn to pick up on body language, facial expressions, postures, tone of voice, and even things that aren't obvious to most people, such as deeper emotions and even thoughts.

The lens you look through must be clear. Making sure you're present and able to give others your full attention is the first step to becoming more socially aware. Looking outward isn't just about using your eyes; it means tapping into your senses. Not only can you fully utilize your basic five senses, but you can also include the vast amount of information coming into your brain through your sixth sense—your emotions. Your emotions can help you notice and interpret cues that other people send you. These cues help you put yourself in the other person's shoes.

Relationship Management

Although relationship management is the second component of social competence, this skill often taps into your abilities in the first three emotional intelligence skills: self-awareness, self-management, and social awareness. Relationship management is your ability to use your awareness of your own emotions and those of others simultaneously to manage interactions successfully. This ensures clear communication and effective handling of conflict. Relationship management is also the bond you build with others over time. People who manage relationships well can see the benefit of connecting with many different people, even those they are not fond of. Solid relationships should be sought and cherished. They're the result of how you understand people, how you treat them, and the history you share.

Relationship management poses the greatest challenge for most people during times of stress. When you consider that only 11% of the people we've tested manage stress adeptly, it's easy to see why building quality relationships poses a challenge. Conflicts tend to fester when people passively avoid problems because they lack the skills needed to initiate a direct yet constructive conversation. Conflicts explode when people don't manage their anger or frustration, and choose to take it out on other people. Relationship management gives you the skills you need to avoid both scenarios, and make the most out of every interaction you have with another person.

Most people have a spring in their step and put their best foot forward when they're in a new relationship (work or otherwise), but they stumble and lose their footing trying to maintain relationships over the long term. Reality soon sets in that the honeymoon phase is officially over. The truth is, all relationships take work, even the great ones that seem effortless from the outside. We've all heard this, but do we really understand it? Working on a relationship takes time, effort, and know-how. The know-how is emotional intelligence. If you want a relationship that has staying power and grows over time, relationship management is just what the doctor ordered. Use your self-awareness skills to notice your feelings and judge whether your needs are satisfied. Use your self-management skills to express your feelings and act accordingly to benefit the connection. Finally, use your social awareness skills to better understand the other person's needs and feelings. In the end, no man is an island: Relationships are an essential and deeply fulfilling part of life.

WHAT DOES HIGH EQ LOOK LIKE?

By this point, you're probably wondering what level your emotional intelligence is at. The chapter that follows tells you how to go online to take the Emotional Intelligence Appraisal® test and find out. Rest assured that the score you'll receive is simply a snapshot of where your EQ stands now. It can and will improve as you read this book. Taking the test is critical because it gives you an objective view of what you're already good at and what you need to work on. Not everyone you know is going to have access to this test, and you may be wondering whether certain people in your life have high EQ. If they demonstrate many of the following habits, there's a good chance they do.

They have a robust emotional vocabulary. All people experience emotions, but a select few can accurately identify them as they occur. This is problematic because unlabeled emotions often go misunderstood, which leads to irrational choices and counterproductive actions. If you're emotionally intelligent, you master your emotions because you understand them, and you use an extensive vocabulary of feelings to do so. Although many people might describe themselves as simply feeling "bad," emotionally intelligent people can pinpoint whether they feel "irritable," "frustrated," "downtrodden," or "anxious." The more specific your word choice, the better insight you have into exactly how you're feeling, what caused it, and what you should do about it.

They're curious about people. When you're emotionally intelligent, you're curious about everyone around you, whether you're introverted or extroverted. This curiosity is the product of empathy, one of the most significant gateways to high EQ. The more you care about other people and what they're going through, the more curiosity you're going to have about them.

They know their strengths and weaknesses. If you're emotionally intelligent, you don't just understand emotions. You know what you're good at and what you're terrible at. You also know who pushes your buttons and the environments (both situations and people) that enable you to succeed. Having high EQ means you know your strengths, and you know how to lean into them and use them to your full advantage while keeping your weaknesses from holding you back.

They're a good judge of character. Much of emotional intelligence comes down to social awareness: the ability to read other people, know what they're about, and understand what they're going through. Over time, this skill makes you an exceptional judge of character. People are no mystery to you. You know what they're all about and understand their motivations, even those that aren't obvious to most people.

They let go of mistakes. If you're emotionally intelligent, you distance yourself from your mistakes, but do so without forgetting them. By keeping your mistakes at a safe distance, yet still handy enough to refer to, you're able to adapt and adjust for future success. It takes refined self-awareness to walk this tightrope between dwelling on and remembering. Dwelling too long on your mistakes makes you anxious and gun-shy, while forgetting about them completely makes you likely to repeat them. The key to balance lies in your ability to transform failures into nuggets of improvement. This creates the tendency to get right back up every time you fall down.

They embrace change. If you're emotionally intelligent, you're flexible and constantly adapting. You know that fear of change is paralyzing and a major threat to your success and happiness. You look for change that's lurking just around the corner, and you form a plan of action should these changes occur.

They're assertive. Emotionally intelligent people balance good manners, empathy, and kindness with the ability to assert themselves and establish boundaries. This tactful combination is ideal for handling conflict. When most people are crossed, they default to passive or aggressive behavior. If you're emotionally intelligent, you remain balanced and assertive by steering yourself away from unfiltered emotional reactions. This enables you to neutralize difficult and toxic people without creating enemies.

WHAT DOES LOW EQ LOOK LIKE?

What about people who lack emotional intelligence? What sets them apart? People who are low in emotional intelligence have a look all their own. The habits that follow are strong signs that someone's lack of emotional intelligence is holding them back.

They get stressed easily. When you stuff your feelings, they quickly build into the uncomfortable sensations of tension, stress, and anxiety. Unaddressed emotions strain the mind and body. Your emotional intelligence skills help make stress more manageable by enabling you to spot and tackle tough situations before things escalate. If you fail to use your emotional intelligence skills, you're more likely to turn to other, less effective means of managing your mood. You're twice as likely to experience anxiety, depression, substance abuse, and even thoughts of suicide.

They make assumptions quickly and defend them vehemently. When you lack emotional intelligence, you form an opinion quickly and then succumb to confirmation bias, meaning you gather evidence that supports your opinion and ignore any evidence to the contrary. More often than not, you argue, ad nauseam, to support it. Emotionally intelligent people let their thoughts marinate, because they know that initial reactions are driven by emotions. They give their thoughts time to develop and consider the possible consequences and counterarguments. Then, they communicate their developed idea in the most effective way possible, considering the needs and opinions of their audience.

They often feel misunderstood. When you lack emotional intelligence, it's hard to understand how you come across to others. You feel misunderstood because you don't deliver your message in a way that people can understand. Even with practice, emotionally intelligent people know that they don't communicate every idea perfectly. They catch on when people don't understand what they are saying, adjust their approach, and recommunicate their idea in a way that can be understood.

They don't know their triggers. Everyone has triggers—situations and people that push their buttons and cause them to act impulsively. Emotionally intelligent people study their triggers and use this knowledge to sidestep situations and people before they get the best of them. When you don't understand your triggers, you struggle to adjust and adapt to the challenges that life throws your way.

They don't get angry. Although some people who lack emotional intelligence are prone to angry outbursts, just because you don't get angry doesn't mean you're emotionally intelligent. Emotional intelligence is not about being nice; it's about managing your emotions to achieve the best possible outcomes. Sometimes, this means showing people that you're upset, sad, or frustrated. Constantly masking your emotions with happiness and positivity isn't genuine or productive. Emotionally intelligent people intentionally employ negative and positive emotions in the appropriate situations. They feel angry, and they show it. They just do so in a way that's constructive.

They blame other people for how they make them feel. Emotions come from within. It's tempting to attribute how you feel to the actions of others, but you must take responsibility for your emotions. No one can make you feel anything that you don't want to, at least once you've had some time to adjust. Thinking otherwise only holds you back.

They're easily offended. If you have a firm grasp of who you are, it's difficult for someone to say or do something that gets your goat. Emotionally intelligent people are self-confident and open-minded, which creates a pretty thick skin. You may even poke fun at yourself or let other people make jokes about you, because you are able to mentally draw the line between humor and degradation.

INCREASING YOUR EMOTIONAL INTELLIGENCE

"Plasticity" is the term neurologists use to describe your brain's ability to change. When you start to work on new habits, your brain grows new connections in response, much as your biceps might swell if you started curling heavy weights several times a week. The change is gradual, and the weight becomes easier to lift the longer you stick to your routine. Your brain can't swell like your biceps because it's confined by your skull. Instead, your brain cells develop new connections to speed the efficiency of thought without increasing the size of your brain.

As you work to develop the emotional intelligence habits that are the bulk of this book, the billions of microscopic neurons lining the road between the rational and emotional centers of your brain will branch off small "arms" (much like a tree branch) to reach out to other cells. A single cell can grow 15,000 connections with its neighbors. This chain reaction of growth ensures that the pathway of thought responsible for the new habit grows strong, making it easier to kick this new behavior into action in the future. Your brain loves efficiency. When you show your brain that a new habit is here to stay by repeating it, your brain will build the pathway needed to reinforce that behavior. Before long, you're repeating the habit without even thinking about it.

If you typically yell when you feel angry, for example, you have to learn to choose an alternative reaction. You must practice this new habit many times before it replaces the urge to yell. In the beginning, doing something other than yelling when you are angry will be extremely difficult. But each time you succeed, the new pathway grows stronger. Eventually, the urge to yell is so small that it's easy to ignore, and in time, it disappears altogether.

The rest of this book will teach you how to develop powerful new emotional intelligence habits. The 30-plus chapters cover a host of topics, each deeply intertwined with the four emotional intelligence skills. These skills rarely exist in isolation. Therefore, rather than dedicating individual chapters to a particular skill, all of the chapters in this book teach you the habits you need to develop all your emotional intelligence skills. As you develop new emotional intelligence habits (and kick bad ones), you'll increase your emotional intelligence in its entirety. The emotional intelligence skills are so interconnected that there's no point in saying this habit focuses on this emotional intelligence skill, while that habit focuses on that one. The habits in this book increase all of your emotional intelligence skills—often two, three, or all four at a time. You should choose to work on the habits that will give you the results you want to see in your life (such as increased confidence, stress tolerance, dealing with toxic people, great leadership skills, or what have you). In the process of forming the habits that you need to achieve these outcomes, you'll increase every aspect of your emotional intelligence. This book is all about outcomes—real-world results that come from the emotional intelligence habits you demonstrate every day.

In the example of yelling when angry, it would be a completely arbitrary process to try and say that the habit of avoiding yelling is a self-awareness skill or even a self-management skill. It takes self-management not to yell, but that can't happen without self-awareness. Your social awareness and relationship management skills play big roles, too. Effectively reading and responding to the people who are making you angry will affect your desire to yell. So, really, the habit of learning not to yell requires all four emotional intelligence skills to make it happen. This is why you'll see a standalone chapter on anger, including the habits required to manage anger, that isn't categorized under a particular emotional intelligence skill. The whole book works this way.

This book is arranged so that you can pick and choose the habits that you want to develop. It isn't designed to be read straight through. You should start with what's important to you right now, work on that, and then move on to a different chapter once that journey is finished. Not everything in this book will speak to you today. This is by design. I can't stop you from reading straight through, but if you do, just understand that you will be inundated with information. The habits addressing each topical area covered by this book are numerous and thorough. Trying to read straight through and absorb all of this information at once isn't going to be the most effective approach for most people.

As you work to master each of the habits presented in this book, you'll develop an increased capacity to appreciate and respond effectively to your emotions and the emotions of others. This isn't always going to be easy. It takes courage to grow and change. Increasing your emotional intelligence is not for the faint of heart. No matter how skilled you become in managing your emotions, there will always be situations that push your buttons. Your life won't morph into a fairy tale devoid of obstacles, but you will equip yourself with everything you need to take the wheel and drive. To reach your full potential, you must learn to maximize your emotional intelligence skills, for those who employ a unique blend of reason and feeling achieve the greatest results. The remainder of this book will give you the habits you need to make this happen.

02

How to Take the Emotional Intelligence Appraisal® Test

efore you begin working on your emotional intelligence habits, you should go online to take the Emotional Intelligence Appraisal® test. Taking the test first will show you where your emotional intelligence stands right now. This will give you insight into your strengths and weaknesses. You'll learn which skills come easier to you and which skills you need to work on the most. The test will analyze your unique score profile and provide customized results that include suggestions for which chapters of this book you should read first. This way, you'll start by learning habits that address your biggest areas of need.

The Emotional Intelligence Appraisal® is the world's most popular emotional intelligence test. It was created in 2001, and millions of people have taken it to discover their emotional intelligence scores. Rigorously researched and scientifically validated, the test is an accurate and reliable measure of emotional intelligence. Once you take it, you'll receive an overall emotional intelligence score and a score for each of the four emotional intelligence skills.

To take the Emotional Intelligence Appraisal® test, visit:

www.TalentSmartEQ.com/HabitsTest

Once you're there, you'll need your passcode to access the test. Your passcode is printed inside an envelope located in the back of this book. If you're reading the eBook version or listening to the audiobook version, your passcode is provided by the vendor who sold you this book. For eBook and audiobook versions, vendors typically provide the passcode in an email or through your user account on their website. On the test website, click the "TAKE THE TEST" button and enter your passcode. Click "Submit." Then you can take the test. It has 28 questions and takes most people about 10 minutes to complete. Your passcode is good for one person only.

Once you've completed the test, you'll receive access to your results via the TalentSmartEQ assessment portal. You can download your results and print them out or save them to your computer. You can also come back anytime to view your test results. To revisit them, just follow the link emailed to you by the TalentSmartEQ assessment portal and enter the login credentials you used to create your account. You can also revisit your test results by returning to the test website, clicking the "VIEW MY REPORT" button, and entering your email address and passcode from this book.

- Beat Stress and Stay Calm
- Make Yourself Even More Likeable
- Neutralize Toxic People
- Increase Your Happiness
- Increase Your Confidence
- Increase Your Mental Strength
- Know When You're Being Lied To
- Develop a Growth Mindset
- Clean Up Your Sleep Hygiene
- Read Body Language Like a Pro
- Maintain a Positive Attitude
- Be Utterly Authentic
- Increase Your Self-Control
- Control Your Anger
- Unlock the Power of Your Personality
- Increase Your Intelligence
- Make Smart Decisions
- Crush Cognitive Biases
- Make Your Relationships Last

PART ONE

EMOTIONAL INTELLIGENCE AT LARGE

—

03

Beat Stress and Stay Calm

We all know that living under stressful conditions has serious emotional, and even physical, consequences. So why do we have so much trouble taking action to reduce our stress levels and improve our lives? Researchers at Yale University have the answer. They found that stress reduces the volume of gray matter in the areas of the brain responsible for self-control. So, experiencing stress actually makes it more difficult to deal with future stress because it diminishes your ability to take control of the situation, manage your stress, and keep it from getting out of control. A vicious cycle, if there ever was one.

The ability to manage your emotions and remain calm under pressure has a direct link to your performance. Individuals with high EQ are skilled at managing their emotions in times of stress in order to remain calm and in control. The tricky thing about stress (and the anxiety that comes with it) is that it's an absolutely necessary emotion. Our brains are wired such that it's difficult to take action until we feel at least some level of this emotional state. In fact, your performance peaks under the heightened activation that comes with moderate levels of stress. As long as the stress isn't prolonged, it's harmless.

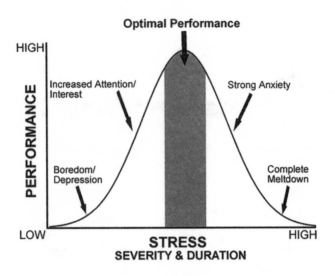

Researchers at the University of California, Berkeley, revealed an upside to experiencing moderate levels of stress. But it also reinforces how important it is to keep stress under control. The study, led by post-doctoral fellow Elizabeth Kirby, found that the onset of stress entices the brain into growing new cells responsible for improved memory. However, this effect is only seen when stress is intermittent. As soon as the stress continues beyond a few moments into a prolonged state, it suppresses the brain's ability to develop new cells.

"I think intermittent stressful events are probably what keeps the brain more alert, and you perform better when you are alert," Kirby says. For animals, intermittent stress is the bulk of what they experience, in the form of physical threats in their immediate environment. Long ago, this was also the case for humans. As the human brain has evolved and increased in complexity, we've developed the ability to worry and perseverate about events, which creates frequent experiences of prolonged stress.

In addition to increasing your risk of heart disease, depression, and obesity, stress decreases your cognitive performance. Fortunately, however, unless a lion is chasing you, the majority of your stress is subjective and under your control. Top performers have well-honed coping strategies that they employ under stressful circumstances. This lowers their stress levels regardless of what's happening in their environment, ensuring that the stress they experience is intermittent and not prolonged.

The sooner you start managing your stress effectively, the easier it is to prevent unexpected stress from causing damage in the future. Luckily, the plasticity of your brain allows it to mold, change, and rebuild damaged areas as you practice new habits. Therefore, implementing healthy stress-relieving techniques can train your brain to handle stress more effectively and decrease the likelihood of ill effects from stress in the future.

While I've run across numerous effective habits that emotionally intelligent people rely on when faced with stress, what follows are 14 of the best. Some of these may seem obvious, but the real challenge lies in recognizing when you need to use them and having the wherewithal to actually do so despite your stress.

Appreciate what you have. Taking time to contemplate what you're grateful for isn't merely the "right" thing to do. It also improves your mood, because it reduces the stress hormone cortisol by 23%. Research conducted at the University of California, Davis, showed that people who worked daily to cultivate an attitude of gratitude experienced improved mood, energy, and physical well-being. It's likely that lower levels of cortisol played a major role in this improvement. The Davis study participants had one simple task: Pause during the day to contemplate what they were grateful for. Lowering your cortisol is that easy.

Stay positive. Positive thoughts help make stress intermittent by focusing your brain's attention onto something that is completely stress-free. You have to give your wandering brain a little help by consciously selecting something positive to think about. Any positive thought will do to refocus your attention. When things are going well, and your mood is good, finding a positive thought is relatively easy. When things are going poorly, and your mind is flooded with negative thoughts, this can be a challenge. In these moments, think about your day, and identify one positive thing that happened, no matter how small. If you can't think of something from the current day, reflect on the previous day or even the previous week. Or perhaps you're looking forward to an exciting event that you can focus on. The point here is that you must have something positive that you're ready to shift your attention to when your thoughts turn negative.

Research from University College London might give you a little extra motivation to stay positive. Researchers there found that negative thinkers have a significantly greater chance of developing dementia over just a four-year period. Dementia wasn't the only problem pessimists faced. Those who ruminated about the past and worried about the future developed more plaque build-up in their brains, had more memory impairment, and experienced greater cognitive decline than those who were positive.

Avoid asking, "What if?" "What if?" statements throw fuel on the fire of stress and worry. Things can go in a million different directions, and the more time you spend worrying about the possibilities, the less time you'll spend focusing on taking action that will calm you down and keep your stress under control. Calm people know that asking "What if?" will only take them to a place they don't want—or need—to go. If you do find yourself having trouble letting go of a particular "What if?," take a moment to consider your plan of action should it come to fruition and move on.

Disconnect. Given the importance of keeping stress intermittent, it's easy to see how taking regular time off the grid can help keep your stress under control. When you make yourself available to your work 24/7, you expose yourself to a constant barrage of stressors. Forcing yourself offline and even—gulp!—turning off your phone gives your body a break from a constant source of stress. Studies have shown that something as simple as an email break can lower stress levels.

Technology enables constant communication and the expectation that you should be available 24/7. It is extremely difficult to enjoy a stress-free moment outside of work when an email that will change your train of thought and get you thinking (read: stressing) about work can drop onto your phone at any moment. If detaching yourself from work-related communication on weekday evenings is too big a challenge, how about the weekend? Choose blocks of time when you cut the cord and go offline. You'll be amazed at how refreshing these breaks are and how they reduce your stress by putting a mental recharge into your weekly schedule. If you're worried about the negative repercussions of taking this step, first try doing it at times when you're unlikely to be contacted—maybe Sunday morning. As you grow more comfortable with these breaks, and as your coworkers begin to accept that you spend time offline, gradually expand the amount of time you spend away from technology.

Limit your caffeine intake. Drinking caffeine triggers the release of adrenaline. Adrenaline is the source of the "fight-or-flight" response, a survival mechanism that forces you to stand up and fight or run for the hills when faced with a threat. The fight-or-flight mechanism sidesteps rational thinking in favor of a faster response. This is great when a bear is chasing you, but not so great when you're responding to a curt email. When caffeine puts your brain and body into this hyper-aroused state of stress, your emotions outrun your behavior. The stress that caffeine creates is far from intermittent, as its long half-life ensures that it takes its sweet time working its way out of your body.

Sleep. I've beaten this one to death over the years and can't say enough about the importance of sleep for increasing your emotional intelligence and managing your stress levels. When you sleep, your brain literally recharges, so that you wake up alert and clear-headed. Your self-control, attention, and memory are all reduced when you don't get enough—or the right kind—of sleep. Sleep deprivation raises stress hormone levels on its own, even without a stressor present. Stressful projects often make you feel as if you have no time to sleep, but taking the time to get a decent night's sleep is often the one thing keeping you from getting things under control. Many of us don't know what appropriate sleep hygiene is or why we have such lousy sleep.

The chapter on cleaning up your sleep hygiene will help you make your sleep top notch.

Reframe your perspective. Stress and worry are fueled by our own skewed perceptions of events. It's easy to think that unrealistic deadlines, unforgiving bosses, and out-of-control traffic are the reasons you're so stressed all the time. You can't control your circumstances, but you can control how you respond to them. So, before you spend too much time dwelling on something, take a minute to put the situation into perspective. If you aren't sure when you need to do this, try looking for clues that your anxiety may not be proportional to the stressor. If you're thinking in broad, sweeping statements such as "Everything is going wrong" or "Nothing will work out," then you need to reframe the situation. A great way to correct this unproductive thought pattern is to list specific things that are actually going wrong or not working out. Most likely, you will come up with only a few things (not everything), and the scope of these stressors will look much more limited than they initially appeared.

Breathe. The easiest way to make stress intermittent lies in something that you have to do every day anyway: breathing. Practicing being in the moment with your breathing will train your brain to focus on the task at hand and get the stress monkey off your back. When you're feeling stressed, take a couple of minutes to focus on your breathing. Close the door, put away all other distractions, and just sit in your chair and breathe. Your goal is to spend the entire time focused on your breathing, which will prevent your mind from wandering. Think about how it feels to breathe in and out. This sounds simple, but it's hard to do it for more than a minute or two. It's all right if you get sidetracked by another thought. This will happen at the beginning, and you just need to bring your focus back to your breathing. If you struggle to stay focused on your breathing, try counting each breath in and out until you get to 20, and then start again from 1. Don't worry if you lose count. You can always just start over.

This habit may seem too easy or even a little silly, but you'll be surprised by how calm you feel afterward and how much easier it is to let go of distracting thoughts that otherwise seem to have lodged permanently inside your brain.

Say no. Research conducted at the University of California, Berkeley, showed that the more difficulty that you have saying no, the more likely you will experience stress, burnout, and even depression. Saying no is indeed a major challenge for many people. "No" is a powerful word that you should not be afraid to wield. When it's time to say no, avoid phrases such as "I don't think I can" or "I'm not certain." Saying no to a new commitment honors your existing commitments and gives you the opportunity to successfully fulfill them.

Neutralize toxic people. Dealing with difficult people is frustrating, exhausting, and highly stressful. You can control your interactions with toxic people by keeping *your* feelings in check. When you need to confront a toxic person, approach the situation rationally. Identify your emotions, and don't allow anger or frustration to add to the chaos. In addition, consider the difficult person's viewpoint and perspective so that you can find solutions and common ground. When things completely derail, take the toxic person with a grain of salt to avoid letting them bring you down. This is easier said than done, which is why there's a separate chapter on techniques and habits for neutralizing toxic people.

Don't hold grudges. The negative emotions that come with holding onto a grudge are actually a stress response. Just thinking about the event sends your body into fight-or-flight mode. When the threat is imminent, this reaction is essential to your survival, but when the threat is ancient history, holding onto that stress wreaks havoc on your body and can have devastating health consequences over time. In fact, researchers at Emory University have shown that holding onto stress contributes to high blood pressure and heart disease. Holding onto a grudge means you're holding onto stress, and emotionally intelligent people know to avoid this at all costs. Letting go of a grudge not only makes you feel better now but can also improve your health.

Practice mindfulness. Mindfulness is a simple, research-supported form of meditation that helps you gain control of unruly thoughts and behaviors. People who practice mindfulness regularly are more focused, even when they are not meditating. It is an excellent technique to help reduce stress, because it helps you reduce the feeling of not being in control. Essentially, mindfulness helps you stop jumping from one thought to the next, which keeps you from ruminating on negative thoughts. Overall, it's a great way to make it through your busy day calmly and productively. There's a separate chapter on how to practice this technique.

STRUCTURING YOUR FREE TIME ALLEVIATES STRESS

Stress has a funny way of sneaking up on you when you least expect it, but how you respond is only half the battle. The secret to winning the war against stress lies in what you do when you aren't working (and presumably aren't stressed). You need to structure your free time wisely. Otherwise, you'll fall into bad habits that can magnify your stress, rather than alleviate it. I structure my time by religiously following seven rules when I'm not working. These rules work wonders, with one limitation: They don't work quite as well if you work too much. Sure, we're all busy, but if you're putting in 80- to 90-hour weeks, you won't have the energy or focus to use your time outside of work wisely. And there's no point in working that much. A Stanford study found that productivity per hour declines sharply when a workweek exceeds 50 hours, and productivity drops off so much after 55 hours that there's no point in working any more. That's right. People who work as much as 70 hours (or more) per week actually get the same amount done as people who work 55 hours. My rules help me shift gears to relaxing and rejuvenating activities during my time off. Try them and see if they help you find balance.

Rule 1: Minimize chores. Chores tend to monopolize your free time. When this happens, you lose the opportunity to relax and reflect. What's worse, doing a lot of chores feels like work, and if you spend all weekend doing them, you just put in a seven-day workweek. To keep this from happening, you need to schedule your chores like you would anything else during the week. If you don't complete them during the allotted time, you move on and finish them the following weekend.

Rule 2: Exercise. No time to exercise during the week? You have 48 hours every weekend to make it happen. Getting your body moving for as little as 10 minutes releases GABA, a soothing neurotransmitter that reduces stress. Exercise is also a great way to come up with new ideas. Innovators and other successful people know that being outdoors often sparks creativity. I know that a lot of my best ideas come to me while I'm surfing. While you're out in the ocean, the combination of invigorating activity and beautiful scenery creates the perfect environment to be creative. Whether you're running, cycling, or gardening, exercise leads to endorphin-fueled introspection. The key is to find a physical activity that does this for you and then to make it an important part of your weekly routine.

Rule 3: Pursue a passion. You might be surprised what happens when you pursue something you're passionate about during your time off. Indulging your passions is a great way to escape stress and open your mind to new ways of thinking. Things like playing music, reading, writing, painting, or even playing catch with your kids can help stimulate different modes of thought that can reap huge dividends over the coming week.

Rule 4: Spend quality time with your family. Spending quality time with your family is essential if you want to recharge and relax. Weekdays are so hectic that the entire week can fly by with little quality family time. Don't let this bleed into your weekends. Take your kids to the park, take your spouse to their favorite restaurant, and go visit your parents. You'll be glad you did.

Rule 5: Schedule micro-adventures. Buy tickets to a concert or play, or make reservations for that cool new hotel that just opened downtown. Instead of running on a treadmill, plan a hike. Try something you haven't done before, or perhaps something you haven't done in a long time. Studies have shown that anticipating something good is a significant part of what makes the activity pleasurable. Knowing that you have something interesting planned for Saturday will not only be fun come Saturday but will also significantly improve your mood throughout the week.

Rule 6: Designate mornings as me time. Getting time to yourself on the weekends can be difficult, especially if you have family. Finding a way to engage in an activity you're passionate about first thing in the morning can pay massive dividends in happiness and cleanliness of mind. Your mind achieves peak performance two to four hours after you wake up, so get up early to do something physical and invigorating, and then save the mental tasks for later in the morning when your mind is at its peak.

Rule 7: Prepare for the upcoming week. The weekend is a great time to spend a few moments planning your upcoming week. As little as 30 minutes of planning can yield significant gains in productivity and reduced stress. The week feels a lot more manageable when you go into it with a plan, because all you have to focus on is execution. Weekly reflection is a powerful tool for improvement. Use the weekend to contemplate the larger forces that are shaping your industry, your organization, and your job. Without the distractions of Monday to Friday busy work, you should be able to see things in a whole new light. Use this insight to alter your approach to the coming week, which improves the efficiency and efficacy of your work.

BRINGING IT ALL TOGETHER

If you're living with high levels of stress, you're probably miserable and are certainly harming your well-being. We all know that stress has serious consequences. However, managing stress effectively is a challenge for most of us.

It requires an ample amount of emotional intelligence. William James said, "The greatest weapon against stress is our ability to choose one thought over another." The habits in this chapter will help you make the right choices and get your stress under control. As simple as the habits in this chapter may seem, they are difficult to implement when your mind is clouded by stress. Force yourself to attempt them the next time your head is spinning, and you'll reap the benefits that come with disciplined stress management.

04

Make Yourself Even More Likeable

T oo many people succumb to the mistaken belief that being likeable comes from natural, unteachable traits that belong only to a lucky few—the good looking, the fiercely social, and the incredibly talented. It's easy to fall prey to this misconception. In reality, being likeable is under your control, and it's a matter of emotional intelligence. In a study conducted at UCLA, subjects rated more than 500 adjectives based on their perceived significance for likeability. The top-rated adjectives had nothing to do with being gregarious, intelligent, or attractive (innate characteristics). Instead, the top adjectives were sincere, transparent, and capacity for understanding (another person). These qualities are not innate characteristics. They are critical components of emotional intelligence.

Likeable people are invaluable and unique. They bring out the best in everyone around them, and generally seem to have the most fun. Being likeable doesn't just feel good. It can also have a dramatic impact on your ability to achieve your goals in life. A University of Massachusetts study found that managers were willing to accept an auditor's argument *with no supporting evidence* if he or she was likeable, and Jack Zenger's research showed that just 1 in 2000 unlikeable leaders are considered effective.

When I speak to smaller audiences, I often ask them to describe the most likeable people they have ever worked with. Just like in the UCLA study, people inevitably ignore innate characteristics (intelligent, extrovert, attractive, and so on) and focus on qualities that are completely under people's control, such as approachable, humble, and positive. So, I did some digging to uncover the key habits that set ultra-likeable people apart. Add these habits to your repertoire and watch your likeability and your emotional intelligence soar.

Ask a lot of questions. Likeable people ask lots of questions. The biggest mistake most people make when it comes to listening is that they're so focused on what they're going to say next or how what the other person is saying is going to affect them that they fail to hear what's being said. The words come through loud and clear, but the meaning is lost. A simple way to avoid this is to ask a lot of questions. People like to know you're listening, and something as simple as a clarification question shows that you are not only listening but also care about what they're saying. You'll be surprised how much respect and appreciation you gain just by asking questions.

Put away your phone. Nothing turns someone off to you like a mid-conversation text message or even a quick glance at your phone. When you commit to a conversation, focus all your energy on the conversation and nothing else. You'll find that conversations are more enjoyable and effective when you immerse yourself completely in them. While you're having more fun, the people you're interacting with will like you all the more, and that's a winning proposition.

Greet people by name. Your name is an essential part of your identity, and it feels terrific when people use it. Likeable people make certain they use others' names every time they see them. However, you shouldn't use someone's name only when you greet them. Research shows that people feel validated when the person they're speaking with refers to them by name during a conversation. If you're great with faces but struggle with names, have some fun with it, and make a game out of remembering people's names. Most people who struggle with names tend to forget the name of the person they're introduced to right after they hear it. When this happens, don't hesitate to ask their name a second time. People won't be offended because they appreciate you making the effort to learn their names.

Smile. People naturally (and unconsciously) mirror the body language of the person they're talking to. If you want people to like you, smile at them during the conversation, and they will unconsciously return the favor and feel good about you as a result. Smiling doesn't just make you look happy; it makes you feel happier, too. Multiple studies have shown that smiling (even when the subjects are instructed to do so) stimulates the release of mood-enhancing endorphins and serotonin. Smiling also lowers your blood pressure and can even boost your immune system.

Don't seek attention. People dislike those who are desperate for attention. You don't need to develop a big, extroverted personality to be likeable. Simply being friendly and considerate is all you need to win people over. When you speak in a friendly, confident, and concise manner, you'll notice that people are much more attentive and persuadable than if you try to show them that you're important. People catch on to your attitude quickly and are more attracted to the right attitude than what—or how many people—you know. When you're being given attention, such as when you're being recognized for an accomplishment, shift the focus to all the people who worked hard to help you get there. This may sound clichéd, but if it's genuine, the fact that you pay attention to others and appreciate their help shows that you're appreciative and humble—two adjectives that are closely tied to likeability.

Know who to touch and when to touch them. When you touch someone during a conversation, you release oxytocin in their brain, a neurotransmitter that makes their brain associate you with trust and a slew of other positive feelings. A simple touch on the shoulder, a hug, or a friendly handshake is all it takes to release oxytocin. Of course, you have to touch the right person in the right way to release oxytocin, as unwanted or inappropriate touching has the opposite effect. Just remember, relationships are built not just from words but also from general feelings about each other. Touching someone appropriately is a great way to show you care.

Follow the platinum rule. We all know the golden rule, and it's pretty easy to follow. The platinum rule is harder to follow because it requires us to treat people the way they want to be treated. Not only does doing so make the other person more comfortable (and therefore more likely to open up and connect with you), but it also proves that you've been listening and have really heard what they've been telling you. That shows valuable extra effort on your part. The trick is that when you're engaged in conversation, you have to focus more on the other person than you do on yourself. Otherwise, you'll never be able to understand what makes them tick and, therefore, how they want to be treated.

Balance passion and fun. People gravitate toward those who are passionate because their zest for life is appealing. That said, it's easy for passionate people to come across as too serious or uninterested because they tend to get absorbed in their passions. Likeable people balance their passion with an ability to have fun. They are serious but friendly. They minimize small talk and gossip and focus on having meaningful interactions with others. They remember what you said to them yesterday or last week, which shows you're just as important to them as anything else they are passionate about.

UNLIKEABLE HABITS

Of course, being likeable isn't just a matter of the likeable things you do. It's also driven by the things you're careful not to do. Likeable people are good at understanding what rubs other people the wrong way. They consciously avoid these habits and reap the benefits of their self-control. The following are habits that likeable people are careful to avoid. It's silly that we often succumb to these temptations, but that's all the more reason to be mindful of them.

Humble bragging. We all know people who like to brag about themselves behind the mask of self-deprecation. For example, the woman who makes fun of herself for being a nerd when she really wants to draw attention to the fact that she's smart or the guy who makes fun of himself for having a strict diet when he really wants you to know how healthy and fit he is. Although many people think that self-deprecation masks their bragging, everyone sees right through it. This makes the bragging all the more frustrating because it isn't just bragging; it's also an attempt to deceive.

Name-dropping. It's great to know important and interesting people, but using every conversation as an opportunity to name-drop is pretentious and silly. Just like humble bragging, people see right through it. Instead of making you look interesting, it makes people think that you're insecure and overly concerned with having them like you. It also cheapens what you have to offer. When you connect everything you know with *who* you know (instead of what you know or what you think), conversations lose their color.

Gossiping. People make themselves look terrible when they get carried away with gossiping. Wallowing in talk of other people's misdeeds or misfortunes may end up hurting their feelings if the gossip ever finds its way to them, and gossiping is guaranteed to make you look negative and spiteful every time.

Emotional hijackings. At TalentSmartEQ, I spent much of my career designing and validating 360 feedback assessments. These tests give co-workers the opportunity to provide anonymous feedback on an employee's behavior in the workplace. We've come across far too many instances of people throwing things, screaming, making people cry, and other telltale signs of emotional hijacking. An emotional hijacking demonstrates low emotional intelligence. As soon as you show that level of instability, people question whether you're trustworthy and capable of keeping it together when it counts. Exploding at anyone, regardless of how much they might "deserve it," turns a huge amount of negative attention your way. You'll be labeled unstable, unapproachable, and intimidating. Controlling your emotions keeps you in the driver's seat. When you're able to control your emotions around someone who wrongs you, they end up looking bad instead of you. This increases your likeability.

Having a closed mind. If you want to be likeable, you must be open-minded, which makes you approachable and interesting to others. No one wants to have a conversation with someone who has already formed an opinion and is unwilling to listen. To eliminate preconceived notions and judgment, you need to see the world through other people's eyes. This doesn't require that you believe what they believe or condone their behavior; it simply means that you quit passing judgment long enough to truly understand what makes them tick.

Sharing too much too early. While getting to know people requires a healthy amount of sharing, sharing too much about yourself right off the bat comes across wrong. Be careful to avoid sharing personal problems and confessions too quickly. Likeable people let the other person guide them as to when it's the right time for them to open up. Oversharing comes across as self-obsessed and insensitive to the balance of the conversation. Think of it this way: If you're getting into the nitty gritty of your life without learning about the other person first, you're sending the message that you see them as nothing more than a sounding board for your problems.

Sharing too much on social media. Studies have shown that people who overshare on social media do so because they crave acceptance, but Pew Research Center research has revealed that this oversharing works against them by making people dislike them. Sharing on social media can be an important mode of expression, but it needs to be done thoughtfully and with some self-control. Letting everyone know what you ate for breakfast, lunch, and dinner will do more harm than good when it comes to likeability.

FORMING STRONG CONNECTIONS

Research conducted by Matthew Lieberman at UCLA showed that being social and connecting with others is as fundamental a human need as food, shelter, and water. For example, Lieberman discovered that we feel social pain, such as the loss of a relationship, in the same part of the brain that we feel physical pain. The primary function of this brain area is to alert us to threats to our survival. It makes you realize how powerful and important a social connection is. We're hardwired to be social creatures. MRIs of the brain show that social thinking and analytical thinking involve entirely different neural networks, and that they operate something like a seesaw. When you engage in analytical thinking, the social part of your brain quiets down, but as soon as you're finished, the social network springs back to life. The social brain is the end of the seesaw where the big kid sits; it's our brain's default setting.

Given that social connection is such a fundamental human need, you'd think that it would be easy to connect with everyone we meet. Unfortunately, that's not the case. Against our own self-interest, we get bogged down by shyness, self-consciousness, cynicism, pride, competitiveness, jealousy, and arrogance. If you can get that baggage out of the way, you can use your likeability to connect with anyone—even those who are still holding on to their own. Here are some habits that will help you form strong connections with everyone you meet.

Leave a strong first impression. Research shows that most people decide whether they like you within the first seven seconds of meeting you. They then spend the rest of the conversation internally justifying their initial reaction. This may sound terrifying, but by knowing this, you can take advantage of it to connect with anyone. First impressions are tied intimately to positive body language. Becoming aware of your gestures, expressions, and tone of voice (and making certain they're positive) will draw people to you like ants to a picnic. Using an enthusiastic tone, uncrossing your arms, maintaining eye contact, and leaning toward the person who's speaking are all forms of positive body language that people with high emotional intelligence use to draw others in. Positive body language can make all the difference in a conversation. It's true that how you say something can be more important than what you say.

Be the first to venture beyond the superficial. Our first conversation or two with a new acquaintance tends to be pretty superficial. We portray a careful picture of ourselves, and we stick to nice, safe topics. We talk about the weather and people we know in common and share the most basic details from our lives. But if you really want to connect with somebody, try upping the ante and revealing the real you. You don't need to get too personal, but it's important to let the other person know what you're passionate about. Most of the time, if you open up, the other person will follow your lead and do the same. You'll find that your conversations have real depth because you're willing to reveal some of what lies beneath the surface.

Ask good questions. Sometimes asking a lot of questions isn't enough, and the conversation feels like it's going nowhere. If the other person seems hesitant to open up, encourage them to do so by asking substantial questions. "What do you do?" doesn't further the conversation nearly as much as, "Why did you choose your profession?" Search for questions that will help you understand what makes the other person tick without getting too personal. Some questions will lead nowhere, and others will open doors that get the conversation going. When you land on a question that really gets the other person talking, ask thoughtful follow-up questions that further this line of thought.

Learn from others. During the course of his research, Lieberman concluded that our educational system would be much more effective if we tapped into the social side of learning, rather than trying to quash it. For example, the best way to help an eighth grader struggling with math is to have him get help from another student. Apply that same principle to your life, and be willing to learn from the person you're trying to connect with. Not only does that make them feel more bonded to you, it also makes them feel important. It also shows that you're willing to be vulnerable and aren't too proud to admit that you have much to learn. This makes you far more interesting than someone who appears to have everything figured out.

Don't make them regret removing the mask. If your new acquaintance does you the honor of opening up, don't make them regret it. Sarcasm, criticism, or jokes that might make the other person feel judged for what they've shared are major faux pas. Instead, empathize with their approach to life, which you can do even if you don't agree with their beliefs, and then reciprocate by revealing more about yourself. This process of reciprocation is quick to create new depth in relationships.

Look for the good in them. Our culture can often predispose us to cynicism. We seem to focus on finding reasons not to like people, instead of reasons to like them. Shut that cynical voice off, and concentrate on looking for the good in a new acquaintance. For one thing, that keeps you from writing someone off too soon, but more importantly, when you expect the best from people, they're likely to deliver it.

Don't make it a contest. We've all seen the stereotypical sitcom scene where two guys in a bar spend the night trying to one-up each other. The same thing happens when you meet someone new. Their accomplishments and life experiences sneak up on you and make you feel the urge to make yourself look just as good (if not better). Doing so may stroke your ego, but it doesn't help you connect with them. It keeps you focused on yourself when you should be trying to learn about others and find common ground.

Turn off your inner voice. One giant thing that keeps us from connecting with other people is that we don't really listen. Instead, we're thinking while the other person is talking. To be clear, we hear what the other person is saying (the words come through loud and clear), but our relentless inner voice ensures the meaning is lost. You must turn off this inner voice if you want to connect deeply with people. So what if you forget what you were going to say or if the conversation moves in a different direction before you have a chance to make your point? If your real goal is to connect with someone, you have to shut off your own soundtrack long enough to focus on what they're telling you.

HAVE A FEW TRICKS UP YOUR SLEEVE

When you're working hard and doing all you can to achieve your goals, anything that can give you an edge is powerful and will streamline your path to success. This is especially true when it comes to your likeability. The human brain is a quirky organ, and knowing something about how it works can have an outsized impact on how people respond to you. I like to refer to the behavior that comes from this knowledge as mind tricks. Mind tricks aren't tricks in a manipulative sense (and they won't make you a Jedi, either), but using the brain's natural quirks to your advantage can have a positive impact on everyone you encounter. As soon as you become aware of these tricks, they start popping up wherever you look. With minimal effort on your part, their unconscious influence on behavior can make a huge difference in your day-to-day life.

Open hands and palms create trust. An employee policy at LEGO-LAND says whenever someone asks where something is, the employee "presents" (open-palm gesture) their directions instead of "pointing" them. This is because the open-palmed gesture conveys trust, making people more likely to agree with what you're saying and to find you friendly and likeable. Pointing, on the flip side, is generally seen as aggressive and rude.

When a group of people laughs, each member of the group can't help but make eye contact with the person they feel closest to. This trick can make you an astute observer of relationships of all types. It can tell you who is bonding and learning to trust one another, just as easily as it can tell you if you might have a shot at landing a date with a certain someone. Of course, you'll learn a lot about how *you* feel about other people just by paying attention to whom you unconsciously make eye contact with.

Silence gets answers. When you ask someone a question and they're slow to respond, don't feel pressure to move the conversation forward. Remaining silent plays to your advantage. Moments of silence make people feel as though they should speak, especially when the ball is in their court. This is a great tool to use in negotiations and other difficult conversations. Just make certain you resist the urge to move the conversation forward until you get your answer.

Nodding during a conversation or when asking a question makes the other person more likely to agree with what you're saying. The next time you need to win someone over to your way of thinking, try nodding as you speak. People unconsciously mirror the body language of those around them to better understand what other people are feeling. When you nod as you speak, you convey that what you're saying is true and desirable and people are more inclined to agree with you.

People remember unfinished things better. The natural tendency to remember unfinished things is called the Zeigarnik effect. Ever notice how some television commercials get cut off early? The company paying for the commercial cuts it off so that it sticks in your head longer than other commercials. The best way to forget unfinished things (commercials or songs) is to finish them in your head. If a song gets stuck in your head, try singing the last lines to yourself. You'll be amazed at how quickly it goes away.

When someone does a favor for you, it actually makes them like you more. When you convince someone to do you a favor, they unconsciously justify why they are willing to do so. Typical justifications include things such as "She's my friend," "I like her," and "She seems like the kind of person who would return the favor." These justifications serve you perfectly. Not only did you just get help with something, but the other party also likes you more than they did before.

People's feet reveal their interest. When talking to someone, pay attention to their feet. If their feet are aimed at you, they're interested and listening to what you're saying. If their feet point away from you, they're most likely disinterested and mentally checked out.

When you meet someone new, working their name into the conversation ensures you'll remember it. The goal is to repeat their name three times in the first five minutes. It works extremely well, but the trick is to do it naturally. When you rattle off their name unnecessarily, it sounds foolish and awkward. Try to use phrases like "Hello, _____," "Nice to meet you, _____," and "Where are you from, _____?"

Showing excitement makes other people like you. This goes back to the idea that we mirror the behavior of those around us. If you show excitement when you see someone, they naturally mirror that excitement back at you. It's easy to make a strong first impression and get people to like you when you show enthusiasm for the encounter.

BRINGING IT ALL TOGETHER

Likeability is a delicate balancing act between expressing yourself and understanding what makes other people tick. It isn't something you're born with, but it's something that you can develop. A little effort goes a long way when it comes to increasing your likeability and, ultimately, your emotional intelligence. Add the aforementioned habits to your repertoire, including being mindful of those you should be careful to avoid, and you can reap the benefits of being even more likeable than you already are.

05

Neutralize Toxic People

Toxic people defy logic. Some are blissfully unaware of their negative impact, while others seem to derive satisfaction from creating chaos and pushing other people's buttons. Either way, they create unnecessary complexity, strife, and worst of all, stress. Studies have long shown that stress can have a lasting, negative impact on the brain. Exposure to even a few days of stress compromises the effectiveness of neurons in the hippocampus—an important brain area responsible for reasoning and memory. Weeks of stress cause reversible damage to neuronal dendrites (the small "arms" that brain cells use to communicate with each other), and months of stress can permanently destroy neurons. Stress is a formidable threat to your success and well-being—when stress gets out of control, your brain and your performance suffer.

Most sources of stress are easy to identify. If your non-profit is working to land a grant that your organization needs to function, you're bound to feel stressed and likely know how to manage it. It's the unexpected sources of stress that take you by surprise that harm you the most. Researchers at the Department of Biological and Clinical Psychology at Friedrich Schiller University in Germany found that exposure to stimuli that cause strong negative emotions—the same kind of exposure you get when dealing with toxic people—caused the subjects' brains to have a massive stress response. Whether it's negativity, cruelty, the victim syndrome, or just plain craziness, toxic people drive your brain into a stressed-out state that should be avoided at all costs.

Toxic people are the ultimate test of your emotional intelligence. The hallmark of a toxic individual is manipulation. We all know what it feels like to be emotionally manipulated. It can be extremely effective, which is why some unscrupulous individuals do it so much. Years ago, Facebook, in conjunction with researchers from Cornell and the University of California, conducted an experiment in which they intentionally played with the emotions of 689,000 users by manipulating their feeds so that some users saw only negative stories, while others saw only positive stories. Sure enough, when these people posted their own updates, they were greatly influenced by the mood of the posts they'd been shown.

Facebook caught a lot of flak over the experiment, primarily because none of the "participants" gave their consent to join the study. Perhaps more frightening than Facebook's experiment was just how easily people's emotions were manipulated. After all, if Facebook can manipulate your emotions just by tweaking your newsfeed, imagine how much easier this is for a real, live person who knows your weaknesses and triggers. A skilled emotional manipulator can destroy your self-esteem and even make you question your sanity.

It's precisely because emotional manipulation can be so destructive that it's important for you to recognize it in your own life. It's not as easy as you might think, because emotional manipulators are typically very skillful. They start with subtle manipulation and raise the stakes over time, so slowly that you don't even realize it's happening. Fortunately, emotional manipulators are easy enough to spot if you know what to look for.

They undermine your faith in your grasp of reality. Emotional manipulators are incredibly skilled liars and gaslighters. They insist that an incident didn't happen when it did, and they insist they did or said something when they didn't. The trouble is, they're so good at it that you end up questioning your own sanity. Insisting that whatever caused the problem is a figment of your imagination is an extremely powerful way of getting out of a jam. Their utter confidence in the lie makes you question your own perception of events.

They are an emotional black hole. Whatever emotional manipulators are feeling, they're geniuses at sucking everyone around them into those emotions. If they're in a bad mood, everyone around them knows it. But that's not the worst part: They're so skillful that not only is everyone aware of their mood, but they also feel it. This creates a tendency for people to feel responsible for the manipulator's moods and obligated to fix them.

They are experts at doling out guilt. Emotional manipulators are masters at leveraging your guilt to their advantage. If you bring up something that's bothering you, they make you feel guilty for mentioning it. If you don't mention it, they make you feel guilty for keeping it to yourself and stewing about it. When you're dealing with emotional manipulators, whatever you do is wrong, and no matter what problems the two of you are having, they're your fault.

They claim the role of the victim. When it comes to emotional manipulators, nothing is ever their fault. No matter what they do (or fail to do) it's someone else's fault. Someone else made them do it—and usually, it's you. If you get mad or upset, it's your fault for having unreasonable expectations. If they get mad, it's your fault for upsetting them. Emotional manipulators don't take accountability for anything.

Their actions don't match their words. Emotional manipulators tell you what you want to hear, but their actions are another story. They pledge their support, but when it's time to follow through, they act as though your requests are completely unreasonable. They tell you how lucky they are to know you, and then act as though you're a burden. This is just another way of undermining your belief in your own sanity. They make you question reality as you see it and mold your perception according to what is convenient to them.

They are too much, too soon. Whether it's a personal relationship or a business relationship, emotional manipulators always seem to skip a few steps.

They share too much too soon—and expect the same from you. They appear vulnerable and sensitive, but it's a ruse. The charade is intended to make you feel "special" for being let into their inner circle, but it's also intended to make you feel not just sorry for them but also responsible for their feelings.

They eagerly agree to help—and maybe even volunteer—and then act like martyrs. An initial eagerness to help swiftly morphs into sighs, groans, and suggestions that whatever they agreed to do is a huge burden. If you shine a spotlight on that reluctance, they'll turn it around on you, assuring you that, of course, they want to help and that you're just being paranoid. The goal? To make you feel guilty, indebted, and maybe even crazy.

They always one-up you. No matter what problems you may have, emotional manipulators have it worse. They undermine the legitimacy of your complaints by reminding you that their problems are more serious. The message? You have no reason to complain, so shut the heck up.

They know all your buttons and don't hesitate to push them. Emotional manipulators know your weak spots, and they're quick to use that knowledge against you. If you're insecure about your weight, they comment on what you eat or the way your clothes fit. If you're worried about an upcoming presentation, they point out how intimidating and judgmental the attendees are. Their awareness of your emotions is off the charts, but they use it to manipulate you, not to make you feel better.

THE NINE TOXIC TYPES

It's often said that you're the product of the five people you spend the most time with. If just one of those five people is toxic, you'll soon find out how capable they are of holding you back. You can't hope to distance yourself from toxic people until you first know who they are. The trick is to separate those who are annoying or simply difficult from those who are truly toxic. The following are nine types of toxic drainers that you should stay away from at all costs.

The Gossip

Eleanor Roosevelt famously said, "Great minds discuss ideas, average ones discuss events, and small minds discuss people." Gossipers derive pleasure from other people's misfortunes. It might be fun at first to discuss somebody else's personal or professional misfortune, but over time, it gets tiring, makes you feel gross, and hurts other people. There are too many positives out there and too much to learn from interesting people to waste your time talking about the misfortunes of others.

The Victim

Victims are tough to identify because you initially empathize with their problems. However, as time passes, you begin to realize that their "time of need" is *all the time*. Victims actively push away any personal responsibility by making every speed bump they encounter into an uncrossable mountain. They don't see tough times as opportunities to learn and grow from; instead, they see them as an out. There's an old saying: "Pain is inevitable, but suffering is optional." It perfectly captures the toxicity of the victim, who chooses to suffer every time.

The Arrogant

Arrogant people are a waste of your time because they see everything you do as a personal challenge. Arrogance is false confidence, and it always masks major insecurities. A University of Akron study found that arrogance is correlated with a slew of problems. Arrogant people tend to be lower performers, be more disagreeable, and have more cognitive problems than the average person. Arrogant people can be completely self-absorbed, and they bring you down through the impassionate distance they maintain from other people. You can usually tell when you're hanging around self-absorbed people because you start to feel completely alone. This happens because as far as they're concerned, there's no point in having a real connection with anyone else. You're merely a tool used to build their self-esteem.

The Envious

To envious people, the grass is always greener somewhere else. Even when something great happens to envious people, they don't derive any satisfaction from it. That's because they measure their fortune against the world's when they should be deriving their satisfaction from within. And let's face it, there's *always* someone out there who's doing better if you look hard enough. Spending too much time around envious people is dangerous because they teach you to trivialize your own accomplishments.

The Manipulator

Manipulators suck time and energy out of your life under the façade of friendship. They can be tricky to deal with because they treat you like a friend. They know what you like, what makes you happy, and what you think is funny. However, they use this information as part of a hidden agenda. Manipulators always want something from you, and if you look back on your relationships with them, it's all take, take, take, with little or no giving. They'll do anything to win you over, just so they can work you over.

The Dementor

In J. K. Rowling's "Harry Potter" series, Dementors are evil creatures that suck people's souls out of their bodies, leaving them shells of humans. Whenever a Dementor enters the room, it goes dark, people get cold, and they begin to recall their worst memories. Rowling said that she based them on highly negative people—the kind of people who have the ability to walk into a room and instantly suck the life out of it. Dementors suck the life out of the room by imposing their negativity and pessimism on everyone they encounter. Their viewpoints are always "the glass is half empty," and they can inject fear and concern into even the most benign situations. A Notre Dame University study found that students assigned to roommates who thought negatively were far more likely to develop negative thinking and even depression themselves.

The Temperamental

Some people have absolutely no control over their emotions. They lash out at you and project their feelings onto you, all the while thinking that you're the one causing their malaise. Temperamental people are tough to dump from your life because their lack of control over their emotions makes you feel bad for them. When push comes to shove, though, temperamental people will use you as their emotional toilet and should be avoided.

The Twisted

There are certain toxic people who have bad intentions, deriving deep satisfaction from the pain and misery of others. They are out to hurt you, to make you feel bad, or to get something from you. Otherwise, they have no interest in you. The only good thing about this type is that you can spot their intentions quickly, which makes it that much faster to get them out of your life.

The Judgmental

Judgmental people are quick to tell you exactly what is and isn't cool. They have a way of taking the thing you're most passionate about and making you feel terrible about it. Instead of appreciating and learning from people who are different from them, judgmental people look down on others. Judgmental people stifle your desire to be passionate and expressive, so you're best off cutting them out and being yourself.

HOW TO PROTECT YOURSELF FROM TOXIC PEOPLE

Toxic people are a challenge that few wish to face. It's no fun, but with the right tools, it can be far more bearable. People with high emotional intelligence are skilled at managing their emotions when the going gets tough. One of their greatest gifts is the ability to neutralize toxic people. They have well-honed coping strategies that they employ to keep toxic people at bay.

I've run across numerous effective habits that emotionally intelligent people employ when dealing with toxic people. The following are the nine best.

Set limits (especially with complainers). Complainers and negative people are bad news because they wallow in their problems and fail to focus on solutions. They want others to join their pity party so that they can feel better about themselves. People often feel pressure to listen to complainers because they don't want to be seen as callous or rude, but there's a fine line between lending a sympathetic ear and getting sucked into their negative emotional spiral. You can avoid this only by setting limits and distancing yourself when necessary. One way to set a limit is to ask complainers how they intend to fix the problem. They will either quiet down or redirect the conversation in a productive direction.

Don't die in the fight. People with high EQ know how important it is to live to fight another day, especially when your foe is a toxic individual. In conflict, unchecked emotion makes you dig your heels in and fight the kind of battle that can leave you severely damaged. When you read and respond to your emotions, you're able to choose your battles wisely and stand your ground only when the time is right.

Stay aware of your emotions. Maintaining emotional distance requires awareness. You can't stop someone from pushing your buttons if you don't recognize when it's happening. Sometimes, you'll find yourself in situations in which you'll need to regroup and choose the best way forward. This is fine, and you shouldn't be afraid to buy yourself some time to do so. Think of it this way—if a mentally unstable person approaches you on the street and tells you he's John F. Kennedy, you're unlikely to set him straight. When you find yourself with a coworker who is engaged in similarly derailed thinking, sometimes it's best to just smile and nod. If you're going to have to straighten them out, it's better to give yourself some time to plan the best way to go about it.

Rise above. Toxic people drive you crazy because their behavior is so irrational. Make no mistake about it; their behavior truly goes against reason. So, why do you allow yourself to respond to them emotionally and get sucked into the mix? The more irrational and off-base someone is, the easier it should be for you to remove yourself from their traps. Quit trying to beat them at their own game. You don't need to respond to the emotional chaos—only the facts.

Establish boundaries. This is the area where most people tend to sell themselves short. They feel like because they work or live with someone, they have no way to control the chaos. This couldn't be further from the truth. Once you find someone's behavior more predictable and easier to understand, you are equipped to think rationally about when and where you have to put up with them and when you don't. For example, even if you work closely with someone on a project team, you don't need to have the same level of one-on-one interaction with them you have with your other team members. You can establish a boundary, but you'll have to do it consciously and proactively. If you let things happen naturally, you're bound to find yourself constantly embroiled in difficult conversations. If you set boundaries and decide when and where you'll engage a difficult person, you can control much of the chaos. The only trick is to stick to your guns and keep boundaries in place when the person tries to encroach upon them—which they will.

Don't focus on problems—only solutions. Where you focus your attention determines your emotional state. When you fixate on the problems you're facing, you create and prolong negative emotions and stress. When you focus on actions to better yourself and your circumstances, you create a sense of personal efficacy that produces positive emotions and reduces stress. When it comes to toxic people, fixating on how crazy and difficult they are gives them power over you. Quit thinking about how troubling your difficult person is, and focus instead on how you're going to handle them. This makes you more effective by putting you in control, and it will reduce the amount of stress you experience when interacting with them.

Don't forget. Emotionally intelligent people are quick to forgive, but that doesn't mean that they forget. Forgiveness requires letting go of what's happened so that you can move on. It doesn't mean you'll give a wrongdoer another chance. Emotionally intelligent people are unwilling to be bogged down unnecessarily by others' mistakes, so they let them go quickly and are assertive in protecting themselves from future harm.

Use your support system. It's tempting but ineffective to try to tackle everything by yourself. To deal with toxic people, you need to recognize the weaknesses in *your* approach to them. This means tapping into your support system to gain perspective on a challenging person. Everyone has someone who is on their team, rooting for them, and ready to help them get the best from a difficult situation. Identify these individuals in your life and seek their insight and assistance when you need it. Something as simple as explaining the situation can lead to a new perspective. Most of the time, other people can see a solution that you can't because they are not as emotionally invested in the situation as you are.

BRINGING IT ALL TOGETHER

Toxic people are inherently challenging, but emotionally intelligent people are well equipped to handle them. To deal with toxic people effectively, you need an approach that enables you, across the board, to control what you can and eliminate what you can't. The important thing to remember is that you are in control of far more than you realize. Before you get the habits from this chapter to work brilliantly, you'll have to pass some tests. Most of the time, you'll find yourself tested by touchy interactions with problem people. Thankfully, the plasticity of your brain allows it to change as you practice new habits, even when you fail. Implementing these healthy, stress-relieving techniques for dealing with toxic people will train your brain to handle them more effectively and decrease the likelihood of ill effects. In the process, you'll form lasting new habits that serve you in the long term.

06

Increase Your Happiness

It's no secret that we're obsessed with happiness. After all, the "pursuit of happiness" is even enshrined in the Declaration of Independence. But happiness is fleeting. How can we find it and keep it alive? When we think of happiness, we typically think of things that bring us immediate pleasure—a decadent meal, a favorite book, or a relaxing day at the beach. These pleasures bring happiness, but only temporarily.

We're always chasing something—be it a promotion, a new car, or a significant other. This leads to the belief that "When (blank) happens, I'll finally be happy." Although these major events make us happy at first, research has shown that this happiness doesn't last. A Northwestern University study measured the happiness levels of regular people and people who had won large lottery prizes the previous year. The researchers were surprised to discover that the happiness ratings of the two groups were practically identical. A University of Illinois study found that people who earn the most (more than $10 million annually) are only a smidge happier than the average Joes and Janes who work for them. The mistaken notion that major life events dictate your happiness and sadness is so prevalent that psychologists have a name for it: *impact bias*. The reality is that event-based happiness is fleeting. Studies have shown that true happiness, or life satisfaction, works a bit differently.

Psychologists at the University of California have discovered fascinating things about happiness that could change your life. Dr. Sonja Lyubomirsky is a psychology professor at the Riverside campus who is known among her peers as "the queen of happiness." She began studying happiness as a grad student and never stopped, devoting her career to the subject. One of her main discoveries is that we all have a happiness "set point." When extremely positive or negative events happen (such as buying a bigger house or losing a job), they temporarily increase or decrease our happiness, but we eventually drift back to our set point. The breakthrough in Dr. Lyubomirsky's research is that you can make yourself happier—permanently. Lyubomirsky and others have found that our genetic set point is responsible for only about 50% of our happiness, life circumstances affect about 10%, and a whopping 40% is completely up to us. The large portion of your happiness that you control is determined by your habits, attitude, and outlook on life.

Aristotle was right when he said, "Happiness depends upon ourselves." Happiness is synthetic—you either create it, or you don't. Even when you accomplish something great, that high won't last. It won't make you happy on its own; you have to work to make and keep yourself happy. Supremely happy people have honed habits that maintain their happiness day in, day out. These habits require emotional intelligence. Indeed, happy people are highly intentional. If you want to follow in their footsteps, learn to incorporate the following habits into your repertoire.

Make an effort to be happy. No one wakes up feeling happy every day, and supremely happy people are no exception. They just work at it harder than everyone else. They know how easy it is to get sucked into a routine where you don't monitor your emotions or actively try to be happy and positive. Happy people constantly evaluate their moods and make decisions with their happiness in mind. Sometimes that includes forcing themselves to do something they aren't in the mood for, such as exercise or socializing.

Don't obsess over things you can't control. It's good to know how inflation might affect your wallet or that your company could merge with its largest competitor, but there's a big difference between understanding these larger forces and worrying about them. Happy people are ready and informed, but they don't allow themselves to fret over things that are beyond their control.

Believe the best is yet to come. Don't just tell yourself that the best is yet to come—believe it. Having a positive, optimistic outlook on the future doesn't just make you happier; it also improves your performance by increasing your sense of self-efficacy. The mind tends to magnify past pleasure to such a great degree that the present pales in comparison. This phenomenon can cause you to lose faith in the power of the future to outdo what you've already experienced. Don't be fooled. Believe in the great things the future has in store.

Surround yourself with the right people. Happiness is contagious. Happiness spreads through people. Surrounding yourself with happy people builds confidence and stimulates creativity, and it's flat-out fun. Hanging around negative people has the opposite effect. They want people to join in their misery so that they can feel better about themselves. Think of it this way: If a person were smoking, would you sit there all afternoon inhaling their secondhand smoke? You'd distance yourself, and you should do the same with negative people because their unhappiness is lethal to everyone around them. Proof in point, the famous Terman study from Stanford followed subjects for eight decades and found that being around unhappy people is linked to poorer health and a shorter life span.

Slow down to appreciate life's little pleasures. By nature, we fall into routines. In some ways, this is a good thing. It saves precious brainpower and creates comfort. However, sometimes you get so caught up in your routine that you fail to appreciate the little things in life. Happy people know how important it is to savor the taste of their meal, revel in the amazing conversation they just had, or even just step outside to take a deep breath of fresh air.

Stay positive. Bad things happen to everyone, including happy people. Instead of complaining about how things could have been or should have been, happy people reflect on everything they're grateful for. Then they find the best solution available to the problem, tackle it, and move on. Nothing fuels unhappiness quite like pessimism. The problem with a pessimistic attitude, apart from the damage it does to your mood, is that it becomes a self-fulfilling prophecy: If you expect bad things, you're more likely to experience negative events. Pessimistic thoughts are hard to shake off until you recognize how illogical they are. Force yourself to look at the facts, and you'll see that things are not nearly as bad as they seem.

Learn to love yourself. Most of us have no problem marveling at our friends' good qualities, but it can be hard to appreciate our own. Learn to accept who you are, and appreciate your strengths. Studies have shown that practicing self-compassion increases the number of healthy choices you make, improves your mental health, and decreases your tendency to procrastinate.

Express gratitude. The real neural antidepressant is gratitude. Gratitude boosts levels of serotonin and dopamine—the brain's happy chemicals and the same chemicals targeted by antidepressant medications. The striking thing about gratitude is that it can work even when things aren't going well for you. That's because you don't actually have to feel spontaneous gratitude in order to produce chemical changes in your brain; you just have to force yourself to think about something in your life that you appreciate. This train of thought activates your brain to make you feel happier. Put a reminder on your calendar each day so that you'll be sure to take a brief moment to pause and appreciate.

Label negative feelings to dilute their power. There is an amazing amount of power in simply labeling, or consciously identifying, your negative emotions. In one study, participants underwent fMRI scans of their brains while they labeled negative emotions. When they named these emotions, their brains' prefrontal cortex took over, and their amygdala (where emotions are generated) calmed down. This effect doesn't just work with your own emotions; labeling the emotions of other people calms them down too, which is why FBI hostage negotiators frequently rely on this technique.

So, the next time you're feeling down, take a moment to contemplate and label what you are feeling. You'll be surprised at the positive impact this has on your frame of mind.

Making decisions feels good. Similar to naming emotions, making decisions engages your prefrontal cortex, which calms your amygdala and the rest of your limbic system. The key is to make a "good enough" decision. Trying to make the perfect decision causes stress. We've always known that, but now there's scientific research that explains why. Making a "good enough" decision activates the dorsolateral prefrontal areas of the brain, calming emotions down and helping you feel more in control. Trying to make a perfect decision, on the other hand, ramps up your ventromedial frontal activity—which basically means your emotions are overly involved in your decision-making process.

Do things in person. Happy people let technology do their talking only when absolutely necessary. The human brain is wired for in-person interaction, so happy people jump at the chance to drive across town to see a friend or meet face-to-face because it makes them feel good.

Spend money on other people. Research shows that spending money on other people makes you much happier than spending it on yourself. This is especially true of small things that demonstrate effort, such as going out of your way to buy your friend a book that you know they'll like.

Get in touch with your feelings. Attempting to repress your emotions doesn't just feel bad; it's bad for you. Learning to be open about your feelings decreases your stress levels and improves your mood. One study even suggested that there was a relationship between how long you live and your ability to express your emotions. It was found that people who lived to be at least 100 were significantly more emotionally expressive than the average person.

Get high-quality sleep. This won't be the last time you see this habit mentioned in this book. There's good reason for that. Happy people make sleep a priority, because it makes them feel great, and they know how lousy they feel when they're sleep deprived. Simply put, if you want to be happy, you need to sleep and sleep well. That means you need to clean up your sleep hygiene. If you haven't read it yet, be sure to read the chapter on sleep hygiene. Cleaning up yours will make you much happier.

Heed your moral compass. Crossing moral boundaries in the name of success or pleasing other people is a surefire path to unhappiness. Violating your personal standards creates feelings of regret, dissatisfaction, and demotivation. Know when to stand your ground and express dissent when someone wants you to do something that you know you shouldn't. When you're feeling confused, take some time to review your values and write them down. This will help you locate your moral compass.

Lend a hand. Taking the time to help other people not only makes them happy but also makes you happy. Helping other people gives you a surge of oxytocin, serotonin, and dopamine, all of which create good feelings. In a Harvard study, employees who helped others were 10 times more likely to be focused at work, and they were the most likely to be happy during times of high stress. As long as you make certain you aren't overcommitting yourself, helping others will have a positive influence on your happiness.

Know the power of touch. As you learned in the likeability chapter, humans are social animals, to the point that our brains react to social exclusion in the same way that they react to physical pain—with activity in the anterior cingulate and insula. Similarly, our brains are hardwired to interpret touch as social acceptance. Touch is one of the primary stimuli for releasing oxytocin, which calms the amygdala and, in turn, calms emotions. Studies even show that holding hands with a loved one actually reduces your brain's response to pain. You might think that's bad news for people who are socially isolated, but studies show that a massage increases serotonin by as much as 30%. So, there are always options. Touch reduces your stress hormones, decreases your perception of pain, improves your sleep, and reduces your fatigue. Most importantly, it's good for your mood.

THE HABITS OF UNHAPPY PEOPLE

UCLA neuroscience researcher Alex Korb has spent a great deal of time studying the effects of different happiness strategies on the brain. His findings teach us what actually works to boost our happiness. Korb's research demonstrated that our thoughts—and the emotions we feel in response to those thoughts—have a profound impact on surprising areas of our brains. Guilt and shame, for example, activate the brain's reward center, which explains why we have such a strong tendency to heap guilt and shame upon ourselves. Likewise, worrying increases activity in the prefrontal cortex (the rational brain), which is why worrying can make you feel more in control than doing nothing at all. I'm not advocating worry, guilt, and shame as the path to happiness. This illustration shows why we tend to succumb to thoughts that fuel these emotions.

Kolb's research focuses on a habit loop that can make or break our happiness. He describes it this way: "Everything is interconnected. Gratitude improves sleep. Sleep reduces pain. Reduced pain improves your mood. Improved mood reduces anxiety, which improves focus and planning. Focus and planning help with decision-making. Decision-making further reduces anxiety and improves enjoyment. Enjoyment gives you more to be grateful for, which keeps that loop of the upward spiral going. Enjoyment makes it more likely you'll exercise and be social, which, in turn, makes you happier."

So much of our happiness is determined by our habits (in thought and deed) that we have to monitor them closely to make certain that they don't drag us down into the abyss. Unhappiness can catch you by surprise. Negative habits break Kolb's feedback loop, which is terrible for your mood. There are numerous bad habits that tend to make us unhappy. Eradicating these bad habits can move your happiness set point in short order. The list of bad habits that follows will help you do just that.

Immunity to awe. Amazing things happen around you every day if you only know where to look. Technology has exposed us to so much and has made the world so much smaller. Yet there's a downside that isn't talked about much: Exposure raises the bar for what it takes to be awestruck. And that's a shame, because few things are as uplifting as experiencing true awe. True awe is humbling. It reminds us that we're not the center of the universe. Awe is also inspiring and full of wonder, underscoring the richness of life and our ability to contribute to it and be captivated by it. It's hard to be happy when you just shrug your shoulders every time you see something new.

Isolating yourself. Isolating yourself from social contact is a pretty common response to feeling unhappy, but a large body of research says it's the worst thing you can do. This is a huge mistake, as socializing, even when you don't enjoy it, is great for your mood. We all have those days when we just want to pull the covers over our heads and refuse to talk to anybody, but the moment this becomes a tendency it destroys your mood. Recognize that when unhappiness is making you antisocial, you need to force yourself to get out there and mingle. You'll notice the difference right away.

Waiting for the future. Telling yourself, "I'll be happy when ..." is one of the easiest unhappy habits to fall into. How you end the statement doesn't really matter (it might be a promotion, more pay, or a new relationship) because it puts too much emphasis on circumstances, and improved circumstances don't lead to happiness. Don't spend your time waiting for something that's proven to have no effect on your mood. Instead, focus on being happy right now, in the present moment, because there's no guarantee for the future.

Blaming. We need to feel in control of our lives in order to be happy, which is why blaming is so incompatible with happiness. When you blame other people or circumstances for the bad things that happen to you, you've decided that you have no control over your life, which is terrible for your mood.

Controlling. It's hard to be happy without feeling in control of your life, but you can take this too far in the other direction by making yourself unhappy by trying to control too much. This is especially true for trying to control people. The only person you can control in your life is you. When you feel that nagging desire to dictate other people's behavior, it will inevitably blow up in your face and make you unhappy. Even if you can control someone in the short term, it usually requires pressure in the form of force or fear, and treating people this way won't leave you feeling good about yourself.

Criticizing. Judging other people and speaking poorly of them is a lot like overindulging in a decadent dessert; it feels good while you're doing it, but afterward, you feel guilty and sick. Sociopaths find real pleasure in being mean. For the rest of us, criticizing other people (even privately or to ourselves) is just a bad habit that's intended to make us feel better about ourselves. Unfortunately, it doesn't. It just creates a spiral of negativity.

Complaining. Complaining is troubling, as is the attitude that precedes it. Complaining is self-reinforcing behavior. By constantly talking—and therefore thinking—about how bad things are, you reaffirm your negative beliefs. Although talking about what bothers you can help you feel better, there's a fine line between complaining being therapeutic and it fueling unhappiness. Beyond making you unhappy, complaining drives other people away.

Leaving the present. The past and the future are products of your mind. No amount of guilt can change the past, and no amount of anxiety can change the future. Happy people know this, so they focus on living in the present moment. It's hard to be happy if you're constantly somewhere else, unable to fully embrace the reality of the very moment. To live in the moment, you must do two things:

1) Accept your past. If you don't make peace with your past, it will never leave you, and it will create your future. Happy people know that the only good reason to look at the past is to see how far you've come.

2) Accept the uncertainty of the future, and don't worry about it. Worry has no place in the here and now. As Mark Twain once said, "Worrying is like paying a debt you don't owe."

Blowing things out of proportion. Bad things happen to everybody. The difference is that happy people see them for what they are (a temporary bummer), whereas unhappy people see anything negative as further evidence that life is out to get them. A happy person is upset if they have a fender bender on the way to work, but they keep things in perspective: "What a hassle, but at least it wasn't more serious." An unhappy person, on the other hand, uses it as proof that the day, the week, the month, maybe even their whole life, is doomed.

Comparing your life to the lives people portray on social media. The Happiness Research Institute conducted the Facebook Experiment to find out how our social media habits affect our happiness. Half of the study's participants kept using Facebook as they normally would, while the other half stayed off Facebook for a week. The results were striking. At the end of the week, the participants who stayed off Facebook reported a significantly higher degree of satisfaction with their lives and lower levels of sadness and loneliness. The researchers also concluded that people on Facebook were 55% more likely to feel stressed. The thing to remember about social media in general is that it rarely represents reality. Social media provides an airbrushed, color-enhanced look at the lives people want to portray. I'm not suggesting that you give up social media; just use it sparingly and with a grain of salt. Jealousy and envy are incompatible with happiness, so if you're constantly comparing yourself with others, it's time to stop.

Numbing yourself with technology. You deserve the opportunity to binge-watch a TV show now and then or switch on your Kindle and get lost in a book. The real question is how much time you spend plugged in (to video games, the TV, the tablet, the computer, the phone, etc.) and whether it makes you feel good or simply makes you numb. When your escape becomes a constant source of distraction, it is a sure sign that you've fallen into the trap of too much of a good thing.

Seeing yourself as a victim. Unhappy people tend to operate from the default position that life is both hard and out of their control. In other words, "Life is out to get me, and there's nothing I can do about it." The problem with that philosophy is that it fosters a feeling of helplessness, and people who feel helpless aren't likely to take action to make things better. While you're entitled to feel down every once in a while, it's important to recognize when you're letting this affect your outlook on life. You're not the only person to whom bad things happen, and you have control over your future as long as you're willing to take action.

Neglecting to set goals. Because unhappy people are pessimistic and feel a lack of control over their lives, they tend to sit back and wait for life to happen to them. Having goals gives you hope and the ability to look forward to a better future, and working toward those goals makes you feel good about yourself and your abilities. It's important to set goals that are challenging, specific (and measurable), and driven by your personal values. Without goals, instead of learning and improving yourself, you just plod along, wondering why things never change.

Holding your feelings in. One of the great misconceptions concerning emotional intelligence is that it is about repressing our feelings and holding them in. Although it's true that there are feelings that people with high EQ do not allow to erupt on impulse, that does not mean those feelings are not expressed. Emotional intelligence means honoring your feelings and allowing yourself to experience the catharsis that comes from embracing them for what they are. Only then can you express them in a manner that helps rather than hinders your happiness.

SPEND YOUR MONEY ON EXPERIENCES, NOT THINGS

When you work hard every single day, and there's only so much money left after your regular expenses, you have to make certain it's well spent. Spend your limited funds on what science says will make you happy. A 20-year study conducted by Dr. Thomas Gilovich, a psychology professor at Cornell University, reached a powerful and straightforward conclusion: Don't spend your money on things. The trouble with things is that the happiness they provide fades quickly. There are three critical reasons for this:

1) We get used to new possessions. What once seemed novel and exciting quickly becomes the norm.

2) We keep raising the bar. New purchases lead to new expectations. As soon as we get used to a new possession, we look for an even better one.

3) The Joneses are always lurking nearby. Possessions, by their nature, foster comparisons. We buy a new car and are thrilled with it until a friend buys a better one—and there's always someone with a better one.

"One of the enemies of happiness is adaptation," Gilovich said. "We buy things to make us happy, and we succeed. But only for a while. New things are exciting to us at first, but then we adapt to them." The paradox of possessions is that we assume that the happiness we get from buying something will last as long as the thing itself. It seems intuitive that investing in something we can see, hear, and touch on a permanent basis delivers the most value. But it's wrong.

Gilovich and other researchers have found that experiences—as fleeting as they may be—deliver longer-lasting happiness than things. Here's why:

Experiences become a part of your identity. You are not your possessions, but you are the accumulation of everything you've seen, the things you've done, and the places you've been. Buying an Apple Watch isn't going to change who you are; taking a break from work to hike the Appalachian Trail from start to finish most certainly will. "Our experiences are a bigger part of ourselves than our material goods," said Gilovich. "You can really like your material stuff. You can even think that part of your identity is connected to those things, but nonetheless, they remain separate from you. In contrast, your experiences really are part of you. We are the sum total of our experiences."

Comparisons matter little. We don't compare experiences in the same way that we compare things. In a Harvard study, when people were asked if they'd rather have a high salary that was lower than that of their peers or a low salary that was higher than that of their peers, many weren't sure. However, when they were asked the same question about the length of a vacation, most people chose a longer vacation, although it was shorter than that of their peers. It's hard to quantify the relative value of any two experiences, which makes them that much more enjoyable.

Anticipation matters. Gilovich also studied anticipation and found that anticipation of an experience causes excitement and enjoyment, while anticipation of obtaining a possession causes impatience. Experiences are enjoyable from the very first moments of planning, all the way through to the memories you cherish forever.

Experiences are fleeting (which is a good thing). Have you ever bought something that wasn't nearly as cool as you thought it would be? Once you buy it, it's right there in your face, reminding you of your disappointment. And even if a purchase does meet your expectations, buyer's remorse can set in: "Sure, it's cool, but it probably wasn't worth the money." We don't do that with experiences. The fact that they last for only a short time is part of what makes us value them so much, and that value tends to increase as time passes.

Gilovich and his colleagues aren't the only ones who believe that experiences make us happier than things do. Dr. Elizabeth Dunn at the University of British Columbia has also studied the topic, and she attributes the temporary happiness achieved by buying things to what she calls "puddles of pleasure." In other words, that kind of happiness evaporates quickly and leaves us wanting more. Things may last longer than experiences, but the memories that linger are what matter most.

BRINGING IT ALL TOGETHER

Although we all have a genetic happiness set point, it isn't the end of the story. Much of how happy you are is dictated by your emotional intelligence, not by your genes or your circumstances. You just have to build the right habits to maintain a mindset that enables happiness. Changing your habits in the name of greater happiness is one of the best things you can do for yourself. But it's also important for another reason—taking control of your happiness makes everyone around you happier, too. You can't control your genes, and you can't control all of your circumstances, but you can rid yourself of habits that serve no purpose other than to make you miserable. Happiness can be tough to maintain, but investing in the right habits pays off. Adopting even a few of the habits from this chapter will make a big difference in your mood.

07

Increase Your Confidence

———

True confidence—as opposed to the false confidence people project to mask their insecurities—has a look all its own. One thing is certain: Truly confident people always have the upper hand over the doubtful and the skittish because they inspire others and make things happen. Emotionally intelligent people often exude confidence—it's obvious that they believe in themselves and what they're doing. It isn't their success that makes them confident, however. Their confidence was there first. Think about it:

- Doubt breeds doubt. Why would anyone believe in you, your ideas, or your abilities if you don't believe in them yourself?

- It takes confidence to reach for new challenges. People who are fearful or insecure tend to stay within their comfort zones. However, comfort zones rarely expand on their own. That's why people who lack confidence get stuck in dead-end jobs and bad relationships, and they let valuable opportunities pass them by.

- Unconfident people often feel at the mercy of external circumstances. Emotionally intelligent people aren't deterred by obstacles, which is how they rise up in the first place.

Henry Ford famously said, "Whether you think you can, or you think you can't—you're right." Ford's notion that your mentality has a powerful effect on your ability to succeed is evident in the results of a study conducted at the

University of Melbourne, which showed that confident people earn higher wages and are promoted more quickly than anyone else. Their confidence in what they can accomplish ensures that their goals become their reality.

Confident people have a profound impact on everyone they encounter. Yet they achieve this only because they exert so much influence internally. We see only their outside. We see them innovate, speak their minds, and propel themselves forward toward bigger and better things. Yet we're missing the best part. We don't see the habits they develop to become so confident. It's a labor of love that they pursue behind the scenes, every single day. And while what people are influenced by changes with the season, the unique habits of truly confident people remain constant. Their focused pursuit is driven by habits that you can emulate and absorb. With proper guidance and hard work, anyone can become more confident. Embracing the following habits will help get you there.

Take an honest look at yourself. Johnny Unitas said, "There is a difference between conceit and confidence. Conceit is bragging about yourself. Confidence means you believe you can get the job done." In other words, confidence is *earned* through hard work, and confident people are self-aware. When your confidence exceeds your abilities, you've crossed the line into arrogance. You need to know the difference. True confidence is firmly planted in reality. To grow your confidence, it's important to honestly and accurately assess your abilities. If there are weaknesses in your skill set, make plans to strengthen these skills and find ways to minimize their negative impact. Ignoring your weaknesses or pretending they're strengths won't make them go away. Likewise, having a clear understanding of your strengths enables you to shake off some of the more groundless feedback and criticism you can get—and that builds confidence.

Listen more than you speak. Confident people listen more than they speak because they don't feel as though they have anything to prove. Confident people know that by actively listening and paying attention to others, they are much more likely to learn and grow. Instead of seeing interactions as opportunities to prove themselves to others, confident people focus on the interaction itself, because they know that this is a far more enjoyable and productive approach to people.

Speak with certainty. You rarely hear the truly confident utter phrases such as "Um," "I'm not sure," and "I think." Confident people speak assertively because they know that it's difficult to get people to listen to you if you can't deliver your ideas with conviction. However, there's a big difference between being assertive and being aggressive. Aggressiveness isn't confidence; it's bullying. When you're insecure, it's easy to slip into aggressiveness without intending to. Practice asserting yourself without getting aggressive (and trampling over someone else in the process). You won't be able to achieve this until you learn how to keep your insecurities at bay. This will increase your confidence.

Seek out small victories. Confident people like to challenge themselves and compete, even when their efforts yield only small victories. Small victories build new androgen receptors in the areas of your brain responsible for reward and motivation. The increase in androgen receptors increases the influence of testosterone, which further increases your confidence and eagerness to tackle future challenges. When you have a series of small victories, the boost in your confidence can last for months.

Get your happiness from within. Happiness is a critical element of confidence, because to be confident in what you do, you have to be happy with who you are. People who brim with confidence derive their sense of pleasure and satisfaction from their own accomplishments instead of what other people think of their accomplishments.

Exercise. A study conducted at the Eastern Ontario Research Institute found that people who exercised twice a week for 10 weeks felt more competent socially, academically, and athletically. They also rated their body image and self-esteem higher. Best of all, rather than the physical changes in their bodies being responsible for the uptick in confidence, the immediate endorphin-fueled positivity from exercise made all the difference.

Don't be afraid to be wrong. Confident people aren't afraid to be proven wrong. They like putting their opinions out there to see if they hold up because they learn a lot from the times they are wrong, and other people learn from them when they're right. If you're self-assured, you know what you're capable of and don't treat being wrong as a personal slight.

Celebrate other people's successes. Insecure people constantly doubt their relevance, and because of this, they try to steal the spotlight and criticize others in order to prove their worth. Confident people, in contrast, aren't worried about their relevance because they draw their self-worth from within. Instead of insecurely focusing inward, confident people focus outward, which allows them to see all the wonderful things that other people bring to the table. Praising people for their contributions is a natural result.

Get right with the boss. A troubled relationship with a boss can destroy even the most talented person's confidence. It's hard to be confident when your boss is constantly criticizing you or undermining your contributions. If this applies to you, try to identify where the relationship went wrong and decide whether there's anything you can do to get things back on track. If the relationship is truly unsalvageable, it may be time to move on to something else. In the next section, the chapter "Survive a Bad Boss" will help you navigate this process.

Dress for success. Like it or not, how we dress has a huge effect on how people see us. Things like the color, cut, and style of the clothes we wear—and even our accessories—communicate loudly. But the way we dress also affects how we see ourselves. Studies have shown that people speak differently when they're dressed up than when they're dressed casually. To boost your confidence, dress well. Choose clothing that reflects who you are and the image you want to project, even if that means spending more time shopping and more time getting ready in the morning.

WHAT CONFIDENT PEOPLE WON'T DO

In *The Empire Strikes Back*, when Yoda is training Luke to become a Jedi, he demonstrates the power of the Force by raising an X-wing fighter from a swamp. Luke mutters, "I don't believe it." Yoda replies, "That is why you fail." As usual, Yoda was right—and science backs him up. Numerous studies have proven that confidence is key to success. For example, studies exploring the performance gap between men and women in math and spatial skills have found that confidence plays a huge role. Women who were asked to identify their gender before taking a spatial skills test performed more poorly than those who weren't. Women also performed better when they were told to envision themselves as men, and both genders performed better when they were told that their gender was better at the task. What's even more interesting is that the gender gap practically disappeared when participants were required to answer every question. Apparently, when the women were allowed to skip questions, they did so not because of a lack of knowledge but because of a lack of confidence.

True confidence is very different from egotistical swagger. When people believe in themselves and their abilities without bravado, there are certain things they simply won't do. The following nine "don'ts" are habits that will only improve your confidence.

Don't make excuses. If there's one trait confident people have in spades, it's self-efficacy—the belief that they can make things happen. It's about having an internal locus of control rather than an external one. That's why you don't hear confident people blaming traffic for making them late or an unfair boss for their failure to get a promotion. Confident people don't make excuses because they believe they're in control of their own lives.

Don't quit. Confident people don't give up the first time something goes wrong. They see problems and failures as obstacles to overcome rather than impenetrable barriers to success. That doesn't mean, however, that they keep trying the same thing over and over. One of the first things confident people do when something goes wrong is to figure out why it went wrong and how they can prevent it from happening again.

Don't wait for permission to act. Confident people don't need somebody to tell them what to do or when to do it. They don't waste time asking themselves questions like "Can I?" or "Should I?" If they ask themselves anything, it's "Why wouldn't I?" Whether it's running a PTA meeting when the chairperson doesn't show up or going the extra mile to solve a customer's problem at work, it doesn't even occur to them to wait for somebody else to take care of it. They see what needs to be done, and they do it. Fear doesn't hold them back, because they know that if they never try, they will never succeed.

Don't seek the spotlight. Confident people know that being yourself is much more effective than trying to prove that you're someone important. When the spotlight shines on them, it doesn't inflate their ego. They are masters of attention diffusion. When they're receiving attention for an accomplishment, they show gratitude for everyone who helped them along the way. They don't crave approval or praise because they draw their self-worth from within.

Don't need constant praise. Have you ever been around somebody who constantly needs to hear how great they are? Confident people don't. It goes back to that internal locus of control. They don't think that their success is dependent on other people's approval, and they understand that no matter how well they perform, there will always be somebody out there offering nothing but criticism. Confident people also know that the kind of confidence that's dependent on praise from other people isn't really confidence at all; it's narcissism.

Don't put things off. Why do people procrastinate? Sometimes, it's simply because they're lazy. A lot of times, though, it's because they're afraid—that is, afraid of change, failure, or maybe even success. Confident people don't put things off. Because they believe in themselves and expect that their actions will lead them closer to their goals, they don't sit around waiting for the right time or the perfect circumstances. They know that to-day is the only time that matters.

Don't sit in judgment. Confident people don't waste time sizing people up and worrying about whether they measure up to everyone they meet. They don't pass judgment on others because they know that everyone has something to offer, and they don't need to take other people down a notch to feel good about themselves. Comparing yourself to other people is limiting, and confident people have few limitations.

Don't avoid conflict. Confident people don't see conflict as something to be avoided at all costs; they see it as something to manage effectively. They don't go along to get along, even when that means having uncomfortable conversations or making unpleasant decisions. They know that conflict is part of life, and that they can't avoid it without cheating themselves out of the good stuff, too. In the next section, the chapter "Mastering Conflict" will help you manage conflict effectively.

Don't get too comfortable. Confident people understand that getting too comfortable is the mortal enemy of achieving their goals. That's because they know that comfort leads to complacency, and complacency leads to stagnation. When they start feeling comfortable, they take that as a big red flag and start pushing their boundaries again so that they can continue to grow. They understand that a little discomfort is a good thing.

BRINGING IT ALL TOGETHER

Confidence and emotional intelligence go hand in hand. Having confidence gives you a massive advantage in life, and true confidence can only be achieved through emotional intelligence. Your confidence is your own to develop or undermine. It's the steadfast knowledge that goes beyond simply "hoping for the best." It ensures that you'll get the job done—that's the power of true confidence. Building confidence is a journey, not a destination. To become more confident, you must be passionate in your pursuit of a greater future. Embracing the habits of confident people is a great way to increase your odds of success, which, in turn, will lead to more confidence.

08

Increase Your Mental Strength

D espite West Point Military Academy's rigorous selection process, one in five students drop out by graduation day. A sizeable number leave the summer *before* freshman year, when cadets go through a rigorous program called "Beast." Beast consists of extreme physical, mental, and social challenges designed to test cadets' perseverance. University of Pennsylvania psychologist Angela Duckworth conducted a study in which she sought to determine which cadets would make it through the Beast program. The rigorous interviews and testing that cadets underwent to get into West Point in the first place told Angela that IQ and talent weren't the deciding factors. So, she developed her own test to determine which cadets had the mental strength to conquer the Beast. She called it the "grit scale," and it was a highly accurate predictor of cadet success.

Duckworth's grit scale was inspired by something she saw very early in her career when she was teaching seventh grade (long before she became a psychologist). She noticed that the material wasn't too advanced for her students, although some of them did poorly. They all had the ability to understand the material if they put in the time and effort. Her highest-performing students weren't those who had the most natural talent; they were the students who had that extra something that motivated them to work harder than everyone else. Angela grew fascinated by this "extra something" in her students, and as she had a fair amount of it herself, she quit her teaching job so that she could study the concept while obtaining a graduate degree in psychology. Her studies have produced some very interesting findings. She's analyzed a bevy of people to whom success is important: students, military personnel, salespeople, and spelling bee contestants, to name a few. Over time, she has concluded that the majority of successful people share one critical quality—grit.

Grit is mental strength, a unique combination of passion, tenacity, and stamina that enables you to stick with your goals until they become a reality. You can't have mental strength if you don't have emotional intelligence. Developing mental strength is all about habitually doing things that no one else is willing to do. There are quite a few signs that you have mental strength, and if you aren't engaging in the following habits on a regular basis, you should be. These habits are the hallmarks of mental strength.

Fight when you already feel defeated. A reporter once asked Muhammad Ali how many sit-ups he did every day. He responded, "I don't count [all] my sit-ups. I only start counting when it starts hurting, when I feel pain, cause that's when it really matters." The same applies to success. You always have two choices when things get tough: You can overcome an obstacle and grow in the process or let it beat you. Humans are creatures of habit. If you quit when things get tough, it gets that much easier to quit the next time. However, if you force yourself to push through a challenge, the strength begins to grow in you.

Delay gratification. There was a famous Stanford experiment in which an administrator left a child in a room with a marshmallow for 15 minutes. Before leaving, the experimenter told the child that she was welcome to eat it, but if she waited without eating it until he returned, she would get a second marshmallow. The children who were able to wait until the experimenter returned experienced better outcomes in life, including higher SAT scores, greater career success, and even lower body mass indexes. The point is that delaying gratification and being patient are essential to success, and they can't be achieved without mental strength. People with mental strength know that results materialize only when you wait and forego instant gratification.

Make mistakes, look like an idiot, and try again—without flinching. In a study conducted at the College of William and Mary, researchers interviewed more than 800 entrepreneurs and found that the most successful among them tended to have two critical things in common: They were terrible at imagining failure, and they tended not to care what other people think of them. In other words, the most successful entrepreneurs put no time or energy into stressing about their failures, as they see failure as a small and necessary step in the process of reaching their goals.

Keep your emotions in check. Negative emotions challenge your mental strength every step of the way. While it's impossible not to feel your emotions, it's completely in your power to manage them effectively and keep yourself in control of them. When you let your emotions overtake your ability to think clearly, it's easy to lose your resolve. A bad mood can make you lash out or stray from your chosen direction, just as easily as a good mood can make you overconfident and impulsive.

Make the calls you're afraid to make. Sometimes, we have to do things we don't want to do because we know they're for the best in the long run: fire someone, approach a stranger, or scrap a project and start over. It's easy to let the looming challenge paralyze you, but the most successful people know that in these moments, the best thing they can do is get started right away. Every moment spent dreading the task subtracts time and energy from actually getting it done. People who learn to habitually make tough calls stand out like flamingos in a flock of seagulls.

Lead when no one else follows. It's easy to set a direction and to believe in yourself when you have support, but the true test of strength is how well you maintain your resolve when nobody else believes in what you're doing. People with mental strength believe in themselves, no matter what, and they stay the course until they win people over to their ways of thinking.

Meet deadlines that are unreasonable and deliver results that exceed expectations. People with mental strength find a way to say yes and still honor their existing commitments. They know that the best way to stand out from everyone else is to outwork them when the time is right. For this reason, they tend to overdeliver, even when they overpromise. If they overcommit themselves, they adjust their future schedule to maintain balance, but they don't let their overcommitment keep them from getting the job done now.

Focus on the details, even when it makes your mind numb. Nothing tests your mental strength like mind-numbing details, especially when you're tired. The more people with mental strength are challenged, the more they dig in and welcome that challenge. Numbers and details are no exception.

Be kind to people who are rude to you. When people treat you poorly, it's tempting to stoop to their level and return the favor. People with mental strength don't allow others to walk all over them, but that doesn't mean they're rude to them, either. Instead, they treat rude and cruel people with the same kindness they extend to everyone else, because they don't allow another person's negativity to bring them down.

Be accountable for your actions, no matter what. People are far more likely to remember how you dealt with a problem than they are to recall how you created it in the first place. By holding yourself accountable, even when making excuses is an option, you show that you care about results more than your image or ego.

THINGS MENTALLY STRONG PEOPLE DON'T DO

We all reach critical points in our lives when our mental strength is tested. It might be a toxic friend or colleague, a dead-end job, or a struggling relationship. Whatever the challenge, you have to see things through a new lens, and take decisive action if you want to move through it successfully. It sounds easy, but it isn't. When Thomas Edison's factory burned to the ground in 1914, destroying one-of-a-kind prototypes and causing $23 million in damage, Edison's response was simple: "Thank goodness all our mistakes were burned up. Now we can start fresh again." Edison's reaction is the epitome of mental strength—seeing opportunity and acting when things look bleak.

Your mental strength is under your control, and it's a matter of emotional intelligence (EQ). Mental strength isn't just about what you do when faced with adversity but also the things you're careful to avoid. Emotionally intelligent and mentally strong people won't do the following 11 things. You should consciously avoid these bad habits because they erode mental strength and are tempting and easy to fall into if you're not careful.

Don't stay in your comfort zone. Self-awareness is the foundation of EQ, and increasing your self-awareness isn't comfortable. You can't increase your EQ without pushing yourself to discover what you need to work on and what you should be doing differently. This is hard because when you take a really good look at yourself, you aren't going to like everything you see. It's more comfortable to keep the blinders on, but they make certain that you'll never have a high EQ or the mental strength you need to succeed.

Don't give in to fear. They say that bravery is being scared to death to do something and doing it anyway. Many times, that's true. The fear doesn't have to come from something as extreme as rushing into a burning building. It can be a fear of speaking in front of groups or going out on a limb to ask someone out on a date. If you use fear as an excuse not to do something, you've already lost. It's not that emotionally intelligent people aren't afraid—they simply pick themselves up and fight on, regardless of the fear.

Don't stop believing in yourself. Emotionally intelligent people persevere. They don't give up in the face of failure, and they don't give up because they're tired or uncomfortable. They're focused on their goals, not on momentary feelings, and that keeps them going, even when things are hard. They don't take failing to mean that they're a failure. Likewise, they don't let the opinions of others keep them from chasing their dreams. When someone says, "You'll never be able to do that," they regard it as one person's opinion, which is all it is.

Don't beg for attention. People who are always begging for attention are needy. They rely on the attention of other people to form their self-identity. Mentally strong people couldn't care less about attention. They do what they want to do and what needs to be done regardless of whether anyone is stroking their ego.

Don't sweep problems under the rug. Emotionally intelligent people are accountable for their actions. When they make a mistake, they own it. People who aren't emotionally intelligent, however, find problems and mistakes threatening, so they try to hide them. Problems tend to get bigger when they're ignored. The more you don't do anything about a problem, the more it starts to feel as though you can't do anything about it. Then you're right back to feeling like a victim.

Don't wait for an apology to forgive. Mentally strong people know that life goes a lot smoother once you let go of grudges and forgive even those who never said they were sorry. Grudges let negative events from your past ruin today's happiness. Hate and anger are emotional parasites that destroy your joy in life.

Don't close your mind. When people close their minds to new information or opinions, it's typically because they find them threatening. They think admitting that someone else is right means that they're wrong, and that's very uncomfortable for people who aren't emotionally intelligent. Emotionally intelligent people aren't threatened by new things; they're open to new information and new ideas, even if it means admitting that they are wrong.

Don't limit the joy of others. Jealousy and resentment suck the life right out of you; they're massive energy-stealers. Emotionally intelligent people don't waste time or energy sizing people up and worrying about whether they measure up. They understand that others' happiness and success don't take away from their own, so jealousy and envy aren't an issue for them. Instead of wasting your energy on jealousy, funnel it into appreciation. Emotionally intelligent people see success as being in unlimited supply, so they can celebrate others' successes. When you celebrate the success of other people, you both benefit.

Don't fight change. Change is an inevitable part of life, and those who fight it do so because they're struggling to remain in control. The problem with this approach is that fighting change actually limits your control over the situation by putting up a barrier between you and the actions you need to take to improve your situation. The idea is to prepare for change. This is not a guessing game where you test your accuracy in anticipating what comes next; rather, it means thinking through the consequences of potential changes so that you are not caught off guard if they surface. The first step is to admit that even the most stable and trusted facets of your life are not completely under your control. When you allow yourself to anticipate change (and understand your options if changes occur), you prevent yourself from getting bogged down by strong emotions like shock, surprise, fear, and disappointment when changes actually happen. Although you are still likely to experience these negative emotions, your acceptance that change is an inevitable part of life enables you to focus and think rationally, which is critical to making the most out of an unlikely, unwanted, or otherwise unforeseen situation.

THE TOXIC THOUGHTS MENTALLY STRONG PEOPLE QUARANTINE

Your self-talk (the thoughts you have about your feelings) can make or break you. When you make a mistake, they either magnify the negativity or help you turn that misstep into something productive. Negative self-talk is unrealistic, unnecessary, and self-defeating. It sends you into a downward emotional spiral that is difficult to pull out of. All self-talk is driven by the important beliefs that you hold about yourself. It plays an understated but powerful role in your success because it can spur you forward to achieve your goals and hold you back. There's nothing wrong with feeling bad about how things are going, but your self-talk can either intensify the negativity or help you move past it.

When it comes to self-talk, some common refrains tend to hold otherwise sensible people back. Mentally strong people are wary of these toxic thoughts, and they quash them as soon as they surface. Be mindful of your tendencies to succumb to the following thoughts so that they don't erode your mental strength.

My destiny is predetermined. Far too many people succumb to the highly irrational idea that they are destined to succeed or fail. Make no mistake about it: Your destiny is in your own hands, and blaming multiple successes or failures on forces beyond your control is nothing more than an excuse. Sometimes life will deal you difficult cards to play, and other times you'll be holding aces. Your willingness to give your all in playing any hand you're holding determines your ultimate success or failure in life.

I "always" or "never" do that. There isn't anything in life that you always or never do. You may do something a lot or not do something enough, but framing your behavior in terms of "always" or "never" is a form of self-pity. It makes you believe that you have no control over yourself and will never change. Don't succumb to it.

My past equals my future. Repeated failures can erode your self-confidence and make it hard to believe you'll achieve a better outcome in the future. Most of the time, these failures result from taking risks and trying to achieve something that isn't easy. Just remember that success lies in your ability to rise in the face of failure. Anything worth achieving is going to require you to take some risks, and you can't allow failure to stop you from believing in your ability to succeed.

My emotions equal my reality. Emotionally intelligent people know how to look objectively at their feelings to separate fact from fiction. If you fail to do this, your emotions will continue to skew your sense of reality, making you vulnerable to the negative self-talk that can hold you back from achieving your full potential.

I succeed when others approve of me. Regardless of what people think of you at any particular moment, one thing is certain—you're never as good or bad as they say you are. It's impossible to turn off your reactions to what others think of you, but you can take people's opinions with a grain of salt. That way, no matter what people think about you, your self-worth comes only from within.

BRINGING IT ALL TOGETHER

You have more mental strength than you can imagine. You just have to push yourself outside of your comfort zone to realize it. Mental strength is as rare as it is important. The good news is that any of us can get stronger with a little extra focus and effort. Improving your mental strength requires emotional intelligence and it's one of the most important things you can do to advance your path to success and achieve what you want in life. You can make it happen with a little determination, effort, and a good model to follow.

09

Know When You're Being Lied To

How many people have you spoken with today? Chances are that most of them lied to you—and that they did it more than once. It's hard to accept, but even your closest friends and coworkers lie to you regularly. University of Massachusetts psychologist Robert Feldman has studied lying for more than a decade, and he has reached some startling conclusions. Most shocking is that 60% of people lie during a typical 10-minute conversation, and that they average two to three lies during that short timeframe. Most of the people in Feldman's studies didn't even realize how often they had lied until the conversation was played back to them on video. People lie in everyday conversation to appear more likeable and competent. Although men and women lie equally as often, they tend to lie for different reasons. "Women were more likely to lie to make the person they were talking to feel good, while men lied most often to make themselves look better," Feldman said.

Research by Dr. Leanne ten Brinke at the Haas School of Business suggested that although most of us have pretty good instincts when it comes to recognizing liars, we tend to talk ourselves out of believing (or at least acting on) what our instincts are telling us. We hesitate to call liars out because we feel guilty for being suspicious. Calling someone a liar for no good reason is a frightening proposition for most people. Thankfully, Dr. Brink's research points to objective, well-documented physiological and behavioral changes—or "tells"—that we can use to accurately assess other people's truthfulness. Keep an eye out for the following signs, and you can use your emotional intelligence to ensure you won't be taken advantage of by a liar.

They repeat themselves and provide too much detail. Liars hate silence, so they often try to fill it up by talking more than they need to. They provide far more information than needed or asked for. Sometimes, the longer you stay quiet, the more details liars throw in to support their story as they try to convince you and themselves of their deception. Liars also repeat phrases over and over again as they struggle to buy time to gather their thoughts.

They cover their mouths. People often cover their mouths when lying. A hand on the mouth or even a touch of the lips shows you that they may be lying, because this unconscious body language represents a closing off of communication. When lying, people also instinctively cover vulnerable body parts, such as the head, neck, or abdomen, because lying makes them feel exposed, vulnerable, and open to attack.

They prepare for an escape. In an unconscious attempt to find an escape route, people who are lying often angle their bodies toward the door if they're sitting, and they may even move closer to the door if they're standing. They may also change their posture from relaxed to erect or guarded as their bodies perk up in unconscious preparation for an escape.

They fidget. Fidgeting is a clear sign of nervous energy. Even practiced liars worry that you won't believe them, so they release that nervous energy by playing with their hair, tapping their feet or fingers, pulling on their ears, and more. Shuffling the feet is a common expression of nervous energy associated with lying. Their feet start moving because the liar feels vulnerable, and their body wants to flee.

Their breathing changes. People reflexively start breathing more heavily when they lie, as lying causes changes in their heart rate and blood flow. Sometimes, liars even have trouble speaking, as the mucous membranes in their mouth dry out as part of their body's response to lying.

Their words and body language don't match. It's easy to lie with words, but our bodies know (and show) the truth. A clear sign that some- one is lying to you is when their words are saying one thing, and their body language is saying something entirely different. For example, someone is telling you a sad story about the personal struggles that made them miss work, yet they're smiling while they're talking, and their hand gestures and body posture are animated and excited.

They change their typical eye movement patterns. They say that the eyes are the "windows to the soul." That's especially true when someone is lying. But there's a catch: It's not where the person is looking that matters, but the change in direction. Some people, for instance, look up and to the right when they're remembering information, but down when they're lying. For other peo- ple, it's the opposite. A change in eye movement can be a very strong indicator of lying, but you have to know the person's typical pattern first. That makes this tactic more suitable to use with people you know well, or at least interact with regularly. However, one eye movement "tell" is pretty universal: People who are lying often look toward the door, their unconscious escape route.

They get aggressive. Liars often get aggressive in a conversation for no apparent reason. Sometimes, they become hostile and point aggressively in your direction. Other times, liars maintain excessive eye contact without blinking, in an abrasive attempt to appear truthful. If someone's aggression is making you uncomfortable, and they seem to be lying, they probably are.

Before rushing to conclusions about someone you think might be lying, be certain to consider what constitutes normal behavior for them. The indi- cators I've mentioned have meaning only in the context of a person's typical behavior. If your friend has ADHD and fidgets constantly, you can't take their fidgeting as a sign of lying. Some people, such as psychopaths, don't demonstrate these behaviors because they don't feel nervous or guilty about lying. A British study showed that the incidence of psychopathy among CEOs is four times that of the general population, so it's not as unlikely as you might think.

WHAT TO DO WHEN YOU CATCH A LIAR

Although most people lie frequently, you don't catch them nearly as often as you might think. Researchers at the University of California system analyzed the results of 253 studies and found that we spot only about half the lies we're told (53% to be exact). In other words, we're about as likely to identify a lie as we are to win a coin toss. The scary thing is that people who are trained in detecting deception—judges, customs agents, law enforcement officers, and even CIA agents—don't fare much better. They can spot a lie only about 60% of the time.

As hard as it is to accept that your friends and coworkers lie to you regularly, the real challenge lies in how you respond once you catch someone in the act. When you catch someone lying to you, it's usually a real whopper. These are the kinds of lies that are so insulting to the recipient that it's hard to think straight. In these moments, you want to keep the conversation constructive without letting the liar off the hook, which is difficult to pull off.

What about the times when you have a nagging sense that you're being lied to but aren't certain and don't want to come across as paranoid or accusatory? Although too much skepticism is never healthy, a small dose can be very good, especially because we're so bad at recognizing lies. The question always becomes, what do you do with a lie? If you think someone is lying to you, do you call them on it? Do you tell someone else? Or do you just go along to get along? There are several things you can do, and the right one, or the right combination, depends on the situation.

First, make certain you understand the rules. Before you decide what course of action to take, consider the recent history of similar situations. If you're going to call someone out, you need to know what you're getting yourself and the liar into. Know the severity of the consequences for lying (if in a setting such as the workplace), and make certain you follow the proper protocol for addressing it, or calling the liar out could backfire on you.

Option 1: Do nothing. Nobody likes being lied to, and the natural reaction is to call the liar out, but that's not always the smartest thing to do. Before you do anything, ask yourself, "What's at stake besides my ego?" Carefully weigh the pros and cons before you act. Consider who, if anyone, should know about the lie and the implications for them. Sometimes, the animosity you avoid by staying silent is worth more than the satisfaction you receive from speaking out. This is especially true with smaller lies. At other times, the lie is serious enough that people have to know.

Option 2: Deflect with humor. Some lies are too big to ignore completely but too small to make a big deal out of. When this happens, you can always make a joke about it. Playful comments that acknowledge the lie usually do the trick: "Hey, I think I just saw your nose grow a little bit" or "I need to get my prescription checked. When I looked at the scorecard, it said you shot 112." This strategy gives the liar a chance to admit their slip-up without fear of reprisal. The key to making this tactic work is to give the impression that the other person was kidding around or intentionally exaggerating and never expected to be believed.

Option 3: Play dumb. Another way to let someone save face—and this is particularly appropriate for group settings—is to play dumb. Pretend you suddenly suffered a memory lapse or are confused about the facts. Ask lots of follow-up questions. The more details you request, the more likely the truth will come out. Drawing it out gives the liar a chance to admit that they "misspoke" and correct themselves without being called a liar.

Option 4: Call them on it. In situations where doing nothing isn't a good option, you can always call the liar out. You just need to think carefully about the best way to do this. Impulsively bashing them is never a smart move. You may choose to have a private conversation with the liar or with others affected by the lie. In either case, it's important to have evidence that backs up your claim, or you may be called a liar. Make certain you are honest and direct with the person who lied. Don't go to others with the lie when you know it's better handled privately between you and the liar.

Many times, calling out a lie is the right thing to do, both ethically and practically. Sometimes, not reporting a lie can cost you your job. However, you need to think about a few things before you take that step. First, question your motives. Are you thinking about telling someone about the lie out of concern that they or someone else could be harmed, or are you just mad? If it's the latter, you run the risk of making yourself look petty. If it's the former, stick to the facts. Don't offer any hypotheses about why the person may be lying, because that's just supposition on your part. Stick to what the person said, what the truth is, and any proof you've collected.

Not optional: Protect yourself. Whether you decide to call out a lie or to let it go, once you know you're dealing with a liar, take steps to protect yourself, especially at work. One way to do this is to have a witness attest to what the liar said. Failing this, interact with the liar via email or text, both of which create a written record. However, if you're dealing with a particularly savvy liar, they're not going to commit to anything in writing. In that case, document the conversation yourself: who, what, when, where, etc. Cap it off by sending your lying colleague an email summarizing the conversation. That's not as good as having proof in the other person's words, but at least you'll be able to make the argument that your colleague had the opportunity to correct you.

BRINGING IT ALL TOGETHER

Research shows that lying is far more common than most people think. Mark Twain was right when he said, "A man is never more truthful than when he acknowledges himself a liar." Most of the lies people tell are small and inconsequential, but others carry serious consequences. Some people tell infrequent lies to make themselves look good or to protect themselves. Others are pros. They've been doing it their whole lives; they're good at it, and they've learned how to avoid getting caught. That's why there's no single solution that works in every situation. The best thing to do with a liar is carefully consider your options, thinking through the pros and cons of each course of action. Using your emotional intelligence skills will help you to navigate this difficult process.

10

Develop a Growth Mindset

W hen it comes to success, it's easy to think that people blessed with brains are inevitably going to leave the rest of us in the dust. However, research from Stanford University will change your mind (and your attitude). Psychologist Carol Dweck has spent her entire career studying attitude and performance, and her research shows that your attitude is a better predictor of success than your IQ. Dweck found that people's core attitudes fall into one of two categories: a fixed mindset or a growth mindset. If you have a fixed mindset, you believe you are who you are, and you cannot change. This creates problems when you're challenged because anything that appears to be more than you can handle is bound to make you feel hopeless and overwhelmed. People with a growth mindset believe that they can improve with effort. They outperform those with a fixed mindset, even when they have a lower IQ, because they embrace challenges, treating them as opportunities to learn something new. People with a high degree of emotional intelligence always have a growth mindset.

Common sense suggests that having ability, like being smart, inspires confidence that gets results. It does, but only when the going is easy. The deciding factor is how you handle setbacks and challenges. According to Dweck, success comes down to how you deal with failure. She described that people with a growth mindset approach failure in the following way: "Failure is information—we label it failure, but it's more like, 'This didn't work, and I'm a problem solver, so I'll try something else."

In the end, there are two kinds of people in this world: those who believe they can make things happen and those who believe things happen to them. The first group is convinced that the outcomes of their lives and careers are more or less in their own hands, and they wouldn't have it any other way. The second group takes more of a Forrest Gump approach—they sit around and wait for the bus to take them somewhere.

University of Florida psychologist Tim Judge and his colleagues have shown overwhelmingly that people who feel they control the events in their lives (more than the events control them) do better on nearly every important measure of performance. This feeling of control is an important component of a growth mindset. In Judge's studies, these individuals were found to do the following:

1. Sell more than other employees.
2. Give better customer service.
3. Adjust better to new assignments.
4. Take home an average of 50% to 150% more in annual income.

Of course, when the good times are rolling, nearly all of us believe we have the world by the tail. What makes people with a growth mindset special—whether they work on the shop floor or in the C-suite—is that they don't get overwhelmed when the going gets tough. They feel intense stress and anxiety when hard times strike, but they use this anxiety differently. Because they believe that they can control the outcomes in their lives, their anxiety fuels passion instead of pity, drive in lieu of despair, and tenacity over trepidation. Whether they're presiding over a division with tanking revenues, on the receiving end of a scathing performance review, or staring at yet another job-hunting rejection in the face, they refuse to wave a white flag. They redouble their efforts.

With concerted effort, you can develop and harness a growth mindset, which will increase your emotional intelligence exponentially. As your growth mindset grows, so will your emotionally intelligent thoughts and behavior. What follows are some of my favorite habits to fine-tune your mindset and help make it as growth oriented as possible. Just remember that life is uncertain—the outcome of your future has not been decided. And your mindset is up to you.

Don't stay helpless. We all have moments when we feel helpless. The test is how we react to that feeling. We can either learn from it and move forward or let it drag us down. There are countless successful people who would have never made it if they had succumbed to feelings of helplessness: Walt Disney was fired from the *Kansas City Star* because he "lacked imagination and had no good ideas." Oprah Winfrey was fired from her job as a TV anchor in Baltimore for being "too emotionally invested in her stories." Henry Ford started two failed car companies before succeeding with Ford, and Steven Spielberg was rejected by USC's Cinematic Arts School multiple times. Imagine what would have happened if any of these people had a fixed mindset. They would have given up hope. People with a growth mindset don't feel helpless because they know that in order to be successful, you need to be willing to fail hard and then bounce right back.

Take action. It's not that people with a growth mindset are able to overcome their fears because they are braver than the rest of us; it's just that they know fear and anxiety are paralyzing emotions, and that the best way to overcome this paralysis is to take action. People with a growth mindset are empowered, and empowered people know that there's no such thing as a truly perfect moment to move forward. So why wait for one? Taking action turns your worry and concern about failure into positive, focused energy.

Then go the extra mile (or two). Empowered people give it their all, even on their worst days. They're always pushing themselves to go the extra mile. One of Bruce Lee's pupils ran three miles every day with him. One day, they were about to hit the three-mile mark when Bruce said, "Let's do two more." His pupil was tired and said, "I'll die if I run two more." Bruce's response? "Then do it." His pupil became so angry that he finished the full five miles. Exhausted and furious, he confronted Bruce about his comment, and Bruce explained it this way: "Quit and you might as well be dead. If you always put limits on what you can do—physical or anything else—it'll spread over into the rest of your life. It'll spread into your work, into your morality, and into your entire being. There are no limits. There are plateaus, but you must not stay there; you must go beyond them. If it kills you, it kills you. A man must constantly exceed his level."

If you aren't getting a little bit better each day, then you're most likely getting a little worse. What kind of life is that?

Be passionate. Growth-minded people pursue their passions relentlessly. There will always be someone who's more naturally talented than you, but what you lack in talent, you can make up for in passion. Growth-minded people's passion drives their unrelenting pursuit of excellence. To find your truest passions, Warren Buffet recommends using what he calls the 5/25 technique: Write down the 25 things that you care about the most. Then cross out the bottom 20. The remaining five are your true passions. Everything else is merely a distraction.

Be flexible. Everyone encounters unanticipated adversity. People with an empowered, growth-oriented mindset embrace adversity as a means for improvement instead of something that holds them back. When an unexpected situation challenges an empowered person, they adjust until they get results.

Don't complain when things don't go your way. Complaining is an obvious sign of a fixed mindset. A growth mindset looks for opportunities in everything, so there's no room for complaints. Plain and simple.

Expect and prepare for change. People change, and businesses go through ebbs and flows. Even the growth-minded in Judge's study couldn't control that. They found themselves out of work. Their companies have fallen on tough times. The difference is that they believe they are fully capable of dealing with changes and making something positive happen. In other words, they are mentally prepared for change—and you can be, too. If you don't anticipate change naturally, you need to set aside some time regularly to create a list of important changes that you think could *possibly* happen.

The purpose of this task is not to predict every change you'll face. Instead, it will open your mind to change and sharpen your ability to spot and respond to impending changes. Even if the events on your list never happen, the practice of anticipating and preparing for change will give you a greater sense of command over your future.

Rewrite your script. This one is the hardest, because it requires you to change the mode of thinking that you're accustomed to. Over time, we all develop mental scripts that run through our heads and influence how we feel about our circumstances and what we do in response. These scripts go so far as to tell us what to say and how to act in different situations. To develop a growth mindset, you need to rewrite your script. To do this, recall a tough time you went through recently. What was it you *believed* about your circumstances that prevented you from making the most of your situation or responding more effectively? Write this script down, and label it your *hard-luck* script. As hindsight is 20/20, go ahead and write a more effective and empowered mental script that you wish you had followed next to it. This is the *empowered* script you will use to replace your *hard-luck* script.

File them away so that you can pull them out and study them whenever you're feeling stressed or very anxious. When you pull your scripts out, compare your present thinking to your *hard-luck* and *empowered* scripts. This will keep you honest and enable you to adjust your thinking so that you're operating from an *empowered* script. These periodic reminders will eventually rewrite your script completely, enabling you to operate from an *empowered* script at all times.

GROWTH-MINDED EXPECTATIONS

Your expectations, more than anything else in life, determine your reality. If you don't believe you'll succeed, you won't. Research from LSU shows that people who believe in themselves use more metacognitive functions than those who don't. This means that they use more of their brains and have more brainpower to solve problems. Metacognition is especially important for achievement, as it ensures that you approach problems from many different angles and adapt your approach as needed.

The tricky thing about your expectations is that they affect other people. As far back as the 1960s, Harvard research demonstrated the power of our beliefs in swaying other people's behavior. When teachers in the studies were told that certain (randomly selected) children were smart, those kids performed better, not only in the classroom but also on standardized IQ tests. We get the most out of other people when we believe in them. Research has shown that this happens because when we believe in someone, we treat them better than people we think will fail, we give them more opportunities to succeed than we give those we think will fail, we give them more accurate, helpful feedback than we give others, and we do more teaching because we believe it's time well spent.

Letting your doubts cloud your belief in someone (or something) practically ensures their failure. Medical professionals call this the "nocebo" effect. Patients who have low expectations for medical procedures or treatments tend to have poorer results than those who expect success, even for well-established treatments. If a doctor uses a treatment with a clinically verified high rate of success but presents it in a negative light, the probability of a negative outcome increases.

The most important person you can believe in is yourself. Your beliefs and expectations shape your reality. They can change your life, emotionally and physically, and they are critical to maintaining a growth mindset and increasing your emotional intelligence. You need to be extra careful about (and aware of) the expectations you harbor, because the wrong ones make life unnecessarily difficult. Be especially wary of the following expectations—they give people trouble and work against a growth mindset.

Life should be fair. We've all had the old mantra *life isn't fair* beaten into our brains since we were young. We've been told a million times (and likely told other people) that life isn't fair, but despite what we know about the intricacies of injustice, it doesn't quite sink in in practice. A surprising number of us subconsciously expect life to be fair, and we believe that any unfairness that we experience will somehow be balanced, even if we don't do anything about it. If you're stuck in that mindset, it's time to get over it. It's a mindset of despair, anxiety, and passive inaction. Although it's true that we sometimes have a limited ability to stop negative events from occurring, we are always free to choose our response. When something "unfair" happens, don't rely on outside forces to get you back on your feet. Sometimes there isn't any consolation prize, and the sooner you stop expecting there to be, the sooner you can take actions that will actually make a difference. You'll surprise yourself with how much control you can wield in response to seemingly uncontrollable circumstances.

Opportunities will fall into my lap. One of the most important things a person can do is stick their neck out and seek opportunities. Just because you deserve a raise, a promotion, or a company car doesn't mean it's going to happen. You have to make it happen. You have to put in the hard work and then go and get what's yours. If you limit yourself to what's given to you, you're at the mercy of other people. When you take action, think, "What steps do I need to take?" "What obstacles are in my way, and what do I need to do to remove them?" and "What mistakes am I making that take me away from my goals rather than toward them?"

Everyone should like me. People have hangups, and that means all sorts of decent, kind, respectable people are not liked by (some) others for no good reason at all. When you think that everyone should like you, you end up feeling hurt when you shouldn't. You can't win them all. When you assume that people are going to like you, you take shortcuts; you start making requests and demands before you've laid the groundwork to really understand what the other person is thinking and feeling. Instead of expecting that people will like you, focus on earning their trust and respect.

People should agree with me. This one can be tough. Sure, you know what you're talking about, and for that reason, people should take you seriously, but expecting people to agree with you out of courtesy or because your ideas are so incredibly sound is another story. Something that's obvious to you might not be to someone with different experiences and a different agenda, so don't be offended when people disagree with you, and don't assume there's only one right answer (yours). Instead, focus on how you can find solutions that give everyone what they need.

People know what I'm trying to say. People can't read your mind, and what you're trying to say is rarely what other people hear. You can't expect people to understand you just because you're talking—you have to be clear. Whether you're asking someone to do something without providing the context or explaining a complex concept behind a big project, it's easy to leave out relevant information because *you* don't think it's necessary. Communication isn't anything if it isn't clear, and your communication won't be clear until you take the time to understand the other person's perspective.

I'm going to fail. If you expect to fail, you have a higher chance of creating the very outcome you're worried about. If you fail, accept that sometimes you'll fail, and sometimes you'll succeed, but if you pursue an endeavor, believe with all your being that you're going to succeed in that endeavor. Otherwise, you'll limit the chances of that happening.

I can change them. There's only one person in this world you can truly change—yourself—and even that takes a tremendous amount of effort. People change only when they want to and have the ability to change themselves. Still, it's tempting to try to change someone who doesn't want to change, as if your sheer will and desire for them to improve will change them (as it has you). You might even actively choose people with problems, thinking that you can "fix" them. Let go of this faulty expectation.

LEARNING FROM MISTAKES

Everybody makes mistakes (that's a given), but not everyone learns from them. Some people make the same mistakes over and over again, fail to make any real progress, and can't figure out why. In the words of Bruce Lee, "Mistakes are always forgivable if one has the courage to admit them." When you make a mistake, it can be hard to admit it because doing so feels like an attack on your self-worth. This tendency poses a huge problem because research has shown what common sense has told us for a very long time— fully acknowledging and embracing errors is the only way to avoid repeating them. Yet many still struggle with this.

Researchers at the Clinical Psychophysiology Lab at Michigan State University found that people with a growth mindset tend to learn from their mistakes ("What a wake-up call! Let's see what I did wrong so I won't do it again"), whereas those with a fixed mindset allow their mistakes to define them ("Forget this. I'll never be good at it"). According to study author Jason Moser, "By paying attention to mistakes, we invest more time and effort to correct them. The result is that you make the mistake work for you."

People with a growth mindset land on their feet because they acknowledge their mistakes and use them to get better. People with a fixed mindset are bound to repeat their mistakes because they try their best to ignore them. Growth-minded people are by no means immune to making mistakes; they simply have the tools in place to learn from their errors. In other words, they recognize the roots of their mix-ups quickly and never make the same mistake twice. Some mistakes are so tempting that we all make them at one point or another. Here are 11 mistakes that almost all of us make, but growth-minded people only make once.

Mistake 1 – Believing in someone or something that's too good to be true.

Some people are so charismatic and confident that it can be tempting to follow anything they say. They speak endlessly of how successful their businesses are, how well liked they are, who they know, and how many opportunities they can offer you. Although, of course, it's true that some people really are successful and really want to help you, growth-minded people only need to be tricked once before they start to think twice about something or someone who sounds too good to be true. The results of naivety and a lack of due diligence can be catastrophic. Growth-minded people ask serious questions before getting involved because they realize that no one, themselves included, is as good as they look.

Mistake 2 – Failing to delay gratification.

We live in a world where books instantly appear on our e-readers, news travels far and wide, and just about anything can show up at our doorsteps in as fast as a day. Growth-minded people know that real gratification doesn't come quickly, and hard work comes long before the reward. They also know how to use this as motivation during every step of the arduous process that amounts to success, because they've felt the pain and disappointment that come with selling themselves short.

Mistake 3 – Losing sight of the big picture.

It's so easy to become head-down busy, working so hard on what's right in front of you that you lose sight of the big picture. However, growth-minded people learn how to keep this tendency in check by weighing their daily priorities against a carefully calculated goal. It's not that they don't care about small-scale work. They just have the discipline and perspective to adjust their course as necessary. Life is all about the big picture, and when you lose sight of it, everything suffers.

Mistake 4 – Surrounding yourself with toxic people.

Growth-minded people believe in a simple notion: You are who you associate with. Think about it. Some of the most successful companies in recent history have been founded by brilliant pairs. Steve Jobs and Steve Wozniak of Apple lived in the same neighborhood, Bill Gates and Paul Allen of Microsoft met in prep school, and Sergey Brin and Larry Page of Google met at Stanford. Just as great people help you reach your full potential, toxic people drag you down with them. Toxic people create stress and strife that should be avoided at all costs. If you're unhappy with where you are in your life, take a look around. More often than not, the people you've surrounded yourself with are the root of your problems. If you need help with toxic people, there's a whole chapter for you.

Mistake 5 – Not doing your homework.

Everybody's taken a shortcut at some point, whether it was copying a friend's biology assignment or strolling into an important meeting unprepared. Growth-minded people realize that, while they may occasionally get lucky, that approach will hold them back from achieving their full potential. They don't take chances, and they understand that there's no substitute for hard work and due diligence. They know that if they don't do their homework, they'll never learn anything—and that's a surefire way to bring your growth to a screeching halt.

Mistake 6 – Trying to be someone or something you're not.

It's tempting to try to please people by being who they want you to be, but no one likes a fake, and trying to be someone you're not never ends well. Growth-minded people figure that out the first time they get called out for being a phony. Other people never seem to realize that everyone else can see right through their act. They don't recognize the relationships they've damaged, the jobs they've lost, or the opportunities they've missed as a result of trying to be someone they're not. Growth-minded people, however, make that connection right away and realize that happiness and success demand authenticity.

Mistake 7 – Trying to please everyone.

Almost everyone makes this mistake at some point, but growth-minded people quickly realize that it's simply impossible to please everybody, and trying to please everyone pleases no one. They know that, in order to be effective, you have to develop the courage to call the shots and to make the choices that you feel are right (not the choices that everyone will like).

Mistake 8 – Playing the victim.

News reports and our social media feeds are filled with stories of people who seem to get ahead by playing the victim. Growth-minded people may try it once, but they quickly realize that it's a form of manipulation, and that any benefits disappear as soon as people see that it's a game. But there's a more subtle aspect of this strategy that only truly growth-minded people grasp: To play the victim, you have to give up your power, and you can't put a price on that.

Mistake 9 – Giving in to fear.

Fear is nothing more than a lingering emotion fueled by your imagination. *Danger* is real. It's the uncomfortable rush of adrenaline you get when you almost step in front of a bus. Fear is a choice. Growth-minded people know this better than anyone, so they flip fear on its head. They are addicted to the euphoric feeling they get from conquering their fears. Don't ever hold back in life just because you feel scared. People often say, "What's the worst thing that can happen to you? Will it kill you?" Yet death isn't the worst thing that can happen to you. The worst thing that can happen to you is you allow yourself to die inside while you're still alive.

Mistake 10 – Letting your age define you.

Age really is just a number. Growth-minded people don't let their age define who they are and what they are capable of. Just think of the latter years of Betty White's career or any young, thriving entrepreneur. I remember a professor in graduate school who told our class that we were all too young and inexperienced to do consulting work. He said we had to go work for a company for several years before we could hope to succeed as independent consultants. I was the youngest in the class, and I sat there doing work for my consulting clients while he droned on (he found out and almost failed me, although my grades were great). Without fail, people feel compelled to tell you what you should and shouldn't do because of your age. Don't listen to them. Growth-minded people certainly don't. They follow their hearts and allow their passion—not the body they're living in—to be their guide.

Mistake 11 – Focusing on things you can't control.

Follow the news for any length of time, and you'll see it's just one endless cycle of war, violent attacks, fragile economies, failing companies, and environmental disasters. It's easy to think the world is heading downhill fast. And who knows? Maybe it is. But growth-minded people don't worry about that because they don't get caught up in things they can't control. Instead, they focus their energy on directing the two things that are completely within their control—their attention and their effort. They focus their attention on all the things they're grateful for, and they look for the good that's happening in the world. They focus their effort on doing what they can every single day to improve their own lives and the world around them because these small steps are all it takes to make the world a better place.

BRINGING IT ALL TOGETHER

Some people believe they can make things happen, while others believe things happen to them. The former have a growth mindset, one of the hallmarks of emotional intelligence. A growth mindset is more than just a frame of mind. It's an unwavering belief in your ability to reach your goals. Success is largely driven by your mindset. Believing that you'll succeed really does make it more likely that you will. With discipline and focus, you can ensure that you maintain a growth mindset so that nothing holds you back from reaching your full potential.

The ability to rise from failure is also a product of your mindset. What one person considers a crushing defeat, another sees as a minor setback.

If you have a growth mindset, you learn from failure and use it to better yourself. You don't let failure discourage you from pursuing important objectives, because in the end, everyone makes mistakes. It's what you do with your mistakes that really matters.

11

Clean Up Your Sleep Hygiene

The next time you tell yourself that you'll sleep when you're dead, realize that you're making a decision that can make that day come much sooner. Pushing late into the night is a health and productivity killer. According to the Division of Sleep Medicine at Harvard Medical School, the short-term productivity gains from skipping sleep are quickly washed away by the detrimental effects of sleep deprivation for days to come on your mood, ability to focus, and access to higher-level brain functions. The negative effects of sleep deprivation are so great that people who are drunk outperform those who lack sleep.

We've always known that sleep is good for your brain, but researchers at the University of Rochester have provided the first direct evidence for why your brain cells need you to sleep (and sleep the right way—more on that later). The study found that when you sleep, your brain removes toxic proteins from its neurons, which are by-products of normal neural activity when you're awake. These toxic proteins accumulate in your neurons throughout the day as you use your brain. Unfortunately, your brain can remove them adequately only while you're asleep, and the higher the quality of your sleep, the better your brain does at removing these toxic proteins. So, when you don't get enough quality sleep, the toxic proteins remain in your brain cells, wreaking havoc by impairing your ability to think—something no amount of caffeine can fix. Skipping sleep impairs your brain function across the board, including your emotional intelligence. It slows your ability to process information and problem solve, kills your creativity, and raises your stress levels and emotional reactivity.

Sleep deprivation is also linked to a variety of serious health problems, including heart attack, stroke, type 2 diabetes, and obesity. It stresses you out because your body overproduces the stress hormone cortisol when it's sleep deprived. While excess cortisol has a host of negative health effects that come from the havoc it wreaks on your immune system, it also makes you look older because cortisol breaks down skin collagen, the protein that keeps skin smooth and elastic. In men specifically, not sleeping enough reduces testosterone levels and lowers sperm count.

Too many studies to list have shown that people who get enough sleep live longer, healthier lives, but sometimes this isn't enough motivation. So, consider this—not sleeping enough makes you fat. Sleep deprivation compromises your body's ability to metabolize carbohydrates and control food intake. When you don't sleep enough, you eat more and have more difficulty burning the calories you consume. Sleep deprivation makes you hungrier by increasing the appetite-stimulating hormone ghrelin and makes it harder for you to feel full by reducing levels of the satiety-inducing hormone leptin. People who sleep less than six hours a night are 30% more likely to become obese than those who sleep seven to nine hours a night. If increasing your emotional intelligence isn't enough motivation to clean up your sleep hygiene, perhaps these health effects will do the job.

SIDE EFFECTS FROM MISSING SLEEP

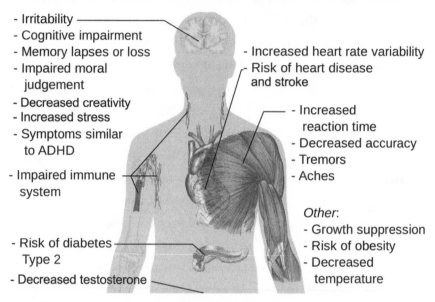

- Irritability
- Cognitive impairment
- Memory lapses or loss
- Impaired moral judgement
- Decreased creativity
- Increased stress
- Symptoms similar to ADHD
- Impaired immune system

- Increased heart rate variability
- Risk of heart disease and stroke
- Increased reaction time
- Decreased accuracy
- Tremors
- Aches

- Risk of diabetes Type 2
- Decreased testosterone

Other:
- Growth suppression
- Risk of obesity
- Decreased temperature

Most people need seven to nine hours of sleep a night to feel sufficiently rested. Few people are at their best with less than seven hours, and few require more than nine without an underlying health condition. And that's a major problem, because more than half of Americans get less than the necessary seven hours of sleep each night, according to the National Sleep Foundation. For go-getters, it's even worse. A survey of Inc. 500 CEOs found that half of them sleep less than six hours a night. And the problem doesn't stop at the top. According to the Centers for Disease Control and Prevention, a third of U.S. workers get less than six hours of sleep each night, and sleep deprivation costs U.S. businesses more than $63 billion annually in lost productivity.

Beyond the obvious benefits of thinking clearly and staying healthy, quality sleep improves your ability to manage your emotions and remain calm under pressure, both of which have a direct link to your performance. Emotionally intelligent individuals know it's not just how much you sleep that matters, but also how you sleep. When life inevitably gets in the way of getting the amount of sleep you need, it's absolutely essential that you increase the quality of your sleep through good sleep hygiene. There are many hidden killers of quality sleep. The 10 habits that follow will help you identify these killers and clean up your sleep hygiene. Follow them, and you'll reap the performance and health benefits that come with getting the right quantity and quality of sleep.

It all starts with caffeine. The first tip for cleaning up your sleep hygiene is perhaps the most straightforward method. It's also the most important. For most people, this tip has the potential to have a bigger impact than any other action. The catch? You have to cut down on caffeine, and as any caffeine drinker can attest, this is easier said than done. You can sleep longer and vastly improve the quality of the sleep you get by reducing your caffeine intake and adjusting the timing of your consumption.

Eighty percent of Americans drink caffeine daily, and many give little thought to how it impacts their sleep. It's essential that you understand how caffeine works so that you can use this understanding to clean up your sleep hygiene. Caffeine is a powerful stimulant that interferes with sleep by increasing adrenaline production and blocking sleep-inducing chemicals in your brain. Caffeine has a six-hour half-life, which means it takes a full 24 hours to work its way out of your system. Have a cup of joe at 8 a.m., and you'll still have 25% of the caffeine in your body at 8 p.m. Anything you drink after noon will still be near 50% strength at bedtime.

Any caffeine in your bloodstream—the negative effects increasing with the dose—makes it harder to fall asleep and sleep deeply. When you finally fall asleep, caffeine disrupts the quality of your sleep by reducing rapid eye movement (REM) sleep—the deep sleep when your brain recuperates most. When caffeine disturbs your sleep, you wake up the next day with a cognitive and emotional handicap. You'll be naturally inclined to grab a cup of coffee or an energy drink to try to make yourself feel more alert. Caffeine withdrawal and lack of sleep leave you feeling tired in the afternoon, so you drink more caffeine, which leaves even more of it in your bloodstream at bedtime. Caffeine very quickly creates a vicious cycle.

Most people start drinking caffeine because it makes them feel more alert and improves their mood. Many studies suggest that caffeine actually improves cognitive task performance (memory, attention span, etc.) in the short term. Unfortunately, these studies failed to consider the participants' caffeine habits. Researchers at Johns Hopkins Medical School showed that performance increases due to caffeine intake are the result of caffeine drinkers experiencing a short-term reversal of caffeine withdrawal. By controlling for caffeine use in study participants, the Johns Hopkins researchers found that caffeine-related performance improvement is nonexistent without caffeine withdrawal. In essence, coming off caffeine reduces your cognitive performance and has a negative impact on your mood. The only way to get back to normal is to drink caffeine, and when you drink it, you feel like it's taking you to new heights. In reality, the caffeine is just taking your performance back to normal for a short period. As discussed in the chapter on beating stress, drinking too much caffeine can also alter your emotional intelligence because caffeine triggers the release of adrenaline, the source of the "fight or flight" response.

SIDE EFFECTS OF CAFFEINE

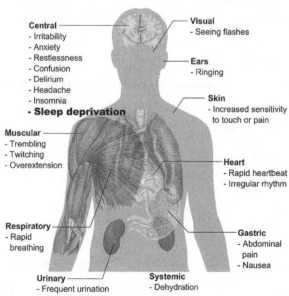

Central
- Irritability
- Anxiety
- Restlessness
- Confusion
- Delirium
- Headache
- Insomnia
- **Sleep deprivation**

Muscular
- Trembling
- Twitching
- Overextension

Respiratory
- Rapid breathing

Urinary
- Frequent urination

Systemic
- Dehydration

Visual
- Seeing flashes

Ears
- Ringing

Skin
- Increased sensitivity to touch or pain

Heart
- Rapid heartbeat
- Irregular rhythm

Gastric
- Abdominal pain
- Nausea

Like any stimulant, caffeine is physiologically and psychologically addictive. If you choose to lower your caffeine intake, you should do so slowly under the guidance of a qualified medical professional. The researchers at Johns Hopkins found that caffeine withdrawal causes headaches, fatigue, sleepiness, and difficulty concentrating. Some people reported feeling flu-like symptoms, depression, and anxiety after reducing their intake by as little as one cup a day. Slowly tapering your caffeine dosage each day can greatly reduce these withdrawal symptoms.

Stay away from sleeping pills. Sleeping pills are anything you take that sedates you so that you can sleep. Whether it's alcohol, Nyquil, Benadryl, Valium, Ambien, or what have you, these substances greatly disrupt your brain's natural sleep process. As you sleep and your brain removes harmful toxins, it cycles through an elaborate series of stages. Sedation interferes with these stages, which has dire consequences for the quality of your sleep. Therefore, many of the habits in this chapter eliminate factors that disrupt your sleep quality. If reducing your use of sleeping pills is difficult, try some of the other habits (such as cutting down on caffeine and reducing blue light in the evening) that will make it easier for you to fall asleep naturally and reduce your dependence on sedatives.

Avoid blue light at night. This is a big one—most people don't even realize it impacts their sleep. Short-wavelength blue light plays an important role in your mood, energy level, and sleep quality. In the morning, sunlight contains high concentrations of this "blue" light. When your eyes are exposed to it directly (not through a window or while wearing sunglasses), blue light halts production of the sleep-inducing hormone melatonin and makes you feel more alert. This is great, and exposure to morning sunlight can improve your mood and energy levels. If the sun isn't an option for you, try a blue-light therapy lamp.

In the afternoon, the sun's rays lose their blue wavelength light, which allows your body to produce melatonin and start making you sleepy. By the evening, your brain does not expect any blue-light exposure and is very sensitive to it. The problem this creates for sleep is that most of our favorite evening devices—laptops, tablets, televisions, and mobile phones—emit short-wavelength blue light. And in the case of your laptop, tablet, and phone, they do so brightly and right in your face. This exposure impairs melatonin production and interferes with your ability to fall asleep, as well as the quality of your sleep once you do nod off. Remember, the sleep cycle is a day-long process for your brain. When you confuse your brain by exposing it in the evening to what it thinks is morning sunlight, this derails the entire process with effects that linger long after you power down. The best thing you can do is avoid these devices after dinner (television is okay for most people, as long as they sit far enough away from the set). If you must use one of these devices in the evening, you can limit your exposure with blue light–blocking eyewear and filters.

Eliminate interruptions. Unfortunately for those with small children, the quality of your sleep suffers when it's interrupted. The key is to eliminate all interruptions that are under your control. If you have loud neighbors, wear earplugs to bed. If your mother likes to call at all hours of the night, silence your phone's ringer before you go to bed. If you have to wake up early one morning, make sure your alarm clock is back on its regular time when you go to bed. Don't drink too much water in the evening to avoid a bathroom trip in the middle of the night. If you think hard enough, there are lots of little things you can do to eliminate unnecessary sleep interruptions. You just have to prepare for them.

Learn how much sleep you really need. The amount of sleep you need is something that you can't control, and scientists are beginning to discover the genes that dictate it. The problem is that most people sleep much less than they really need and are underperforming because they think they're getting enough. Some discover this the hard way. Ariana Huffington was one of those frantic types who under slept and overworked until she collapsed unexpectedly from exhaustion one afternoon. She credited her success and well-being since then to the changes she made in her sleep habits. "I began getting 30 minutes more sleep a night, until gradually I got to 7 to 8 hours. The result has been transformational," Huffington said, adding that "all the science now demonstrates unequivocally that when we get enough sleep, everything is better: our health; our mental capacity and clarity; our joy at life; and our ability to live life without reacting to every bad thing that happens."

Huffington isn't the only one. Jeff Bezos, Warren Buffet, and Sheryl Sandberg have all touted the virtues of getting enough sleep. Even Bill Gates, an infamous night owl, has affirmed the benefits of figuring out how much sleep you really need: "I like to get 7 hours of sleep a night because that's what I need to stay sharp and creative and upbeat." It's time to bite the bullet and start going to bed earlier until you find the magic number that enables you to perform at your best.

Learn to meditate. Many people who learn to meditate report that it improves the quality of their sleep and that they can get the rest they need even if they aren't able to significantly increase the number of hours they sleep. At the Stanford Medical Center, insomniacs participated in a six-week mindfulness meditation and cognitive–behavioral therapy course. At the end of the study, participants' average time to fall asleep was cut in half (from 40 to 20 minutes), and 60% of the subjects no longer qualified as insomniacs. The subjects retained these gains upon follow-up a full year later. A similar study at the University of Massachusetts Medical School found that 91% of participants either reduced the amount of medication they needed to sleep or stopped taking medication entirely after a mindfulness and sleep therapy course. Give mindfulness a try. At the minimum, you'll fall asleep faster, as it will teach you how to relax and quiet your mind once you hit the pillow. The chapter on mindfulness will show you how.

Stop working. When you work in the evening, it puts you in a stimulated, alert state when you should be winding down and relaxing in preparation for sleep. Recent surveys showed that roughly 60% of people monitor their smartphones for work emails until they go to sleep. Staying off blue light–emitting devices (discussed above) after a certain time each evening is also a great way to avoid working so you can relax and prepare for sleep, but any type of work before bed should be avoided if you want quality sleep.

Wake up at the same time every day. Consistency is key to a good night's sleep, especially when it comes to waking up. Waking up at the same time every day improves your mood and sleep quality by regulating your circadian rhythm. When you have a consistent wake-up time, your brain acclimates to it and moves through the sleep cycle in preparation for you to feel rested and alert at your wake-up time. Roughly an hour before you wake, hormone levels increase gradually (along with your body temperature and blood pressure), causing you to become more alert. This is why you'll often find yourself waking up right before your alarm goes off.

When you don't wake up at the same time every day, your brain doesn't know when to complete the sleep process and when it should prepare you to be awake. Long ago, sunlight ensured a consistent wake-up time. These days, an alarm is the only way most people can pull this off. Doing this successfully requires resisting the temptation to sleep in, because you know you'll actually feel better by keeping your wake-up time intact. If you don't, you'll often end up feeling groggy and tired, because your brain hasn't prepared your body to be awake. This isn't a big deal on your day off, but it makes you less productive on Monday, because it throws your cycle off and makes it hard to get going again on your regular schedule.

When all else fails, take naps. One of the biggest peaks in melatonin production occurs during the 1:00 to 3:00 p.m. timeframe, which explains why most people feel sleepy in the afternoon. Companies like Google and Zappos are capitalizing on this need by giving employees the opportunity to take short afternoon naps. If you aren't getting enough sleep at night, you're likely going to feel an overwhelming desire to sleep in the afternoon. When this happens, you're better off taking a short nap (even as short as 15 minutes) than resorting to caffeine to keep you awake. A short nap will give you the rest you need to get through the rest of the afternoon, and you'll sleep much better in the evening than if you drink caffeine or take a long afternoon nap.

Sleep naked. What if I told you that in just 10 seconds a day you could sleep better and lose weight? All you have to do is take off your clothes. None of the other nine strategies for improving your sleep is as simple—and some are less effective—as stripping down before you go to sleep. As only 8% of people sleep naked, most people can discover the benefits of sleeping in the buff. This may sound far-fetched, but hear me out before you throw those cozy flannel pajamas on. Researchers at the University of Amsterdam found that lowering your skin temperature increases the depth of your sleep and reduces the number of times you wake up at night. Stripping down to your birthday suit is a great way to lower your skin temperature without changing the temperature of the room. A study conducted by the U.S. National Institutes of Health found that keeping yourself cool while you sleep speeds the body's metabolism because your body creates more brown fat to keep you warm. Brown fat produces heat by burning calories (300 times more heat than any organ in the body), and this boosts your metabolism all day to help you lose weight. In addition to the metabolic effects of sleeping in the buff, removing your clothes improves your blood circulation, which is good for your heart and muscles. The quality sleep you'll enjoy also increases the release of growth hormone and melatonin, both of which have anti-aging benefits.

BRINGING IT ALL TOGETHER

I know many of you reading this chapter are thinking something along the lines of "but I know someone who is always up at all hours of the night working or socializing, and they are the number one performer at our branch." My answer for you is simple: This person is underperforming. We all have innate abilities that we must maximize to reach our full potential. My job is to help people do that—to help the good become great by removing unseen performance barriers. Being number one in your branch is an accomplishment, but I guarantee that this individual has their sights set on bigger things that they aren't achieving because sleep deprivation has them performing at a fraction of their full potential. You should send them this book. It just might shake something loose. Because, after all, the only thing worth catching up on at night is your sleep.

12

Read Body Language Like a Pro

——

S ocial psychologist Amy Cuddy knows first-hand how attitude can out-weigh IQ. Cuddy was injured in a car accident at the age of 19, which resulted in brain damage that took 30 points from her IQ. Before the crash, Cuddy had an IQ near genius levels; her post-crash IQ was just average. As someone who had always built her identity around her intelligence, the significant dip in her IQ left her feeling powerless and unconfident. Despite her brain damage, she slowly made her way through college and was accepted into the graduate program at Princeton.

Once at Princeton, Cuddy struggled until she discovered that her lack of confidence was holding her back, not her lack of brainpower. This was especially true during difficult conversations, presentations, and other high-pressure, highly important moments. This discovery led Cuddy, now a Harvard psychologist, to devote her studies to the impact that body language has on your confidence, influence, and ultimately, success. Her biggest findings center on the powerful effects of positive body language. Positive body language includes things like appropriate eye contact, active engagement/listening, and targeted gestures that accentuate the message you're trying to convey. Studies have shown that people who use positive body language are more likeable, competent, persuasive, and emotionally intelligent.

Here's how positive body language works:

Positive body language changes your attitude. Cuddy found that consciously adjusting your body language to make it more positive creates a feedback loop that improves your attitude. When you choose to alter your body language, you choose to improve your attitude.

It increases testosterone. When you think of testosterone, it's easy to focus on sports and competition, but testosterone is much more important than its effect in athletics. Whether you're a man or a woman, testosterone improves your confidence and causes other people to see you as more trustworthy and positive. Researchers have shown that positive body language actually increases your testosterone levels.

It decreases cortisol. Cortisol is a stress hormone that impedes performance and creates negative long-term health effects. Decreasing cortisol levels minimizes stress and enables you to think more clearly, particularly in difficult and challenging situations. Researchers have found that positive body language decreases cortisol levels by 25%.

It creates a powerful combination. Although a decrease in cortisol or an increase in testosterone is great on its own, the two together are a powerful combination that is typically seen among people in positions of power. This combination creates the confidence and clarity of mind that are ideal for dealing with tight deadlines, tough decisions, and massive volumes of work. People who are naturally high in testosterone and low in cortisol are known to thrive under pressure. Of course, you can use positive body language to make this happen for you.

It makes you more likeable. In a Tufts University study, participants watched soundless clips of physicians interacting with their patients. Just by observing the physicians' body language, the study participants were able to guess which physicians ended up being sued by their patients. Body language is a huge factor in how you're perceived and can be more important than your tone of voice or even what you say. Using positive body language will make people like you and trust you more.

It conveys competence. In a study conducted at Princeton, researchers found that a one-second clip of candidates for senator or governor was enough for people to accurately predict which candidate was elected. This may not increase your faith in the voting process, but it shows that the perception of competence has a strong foundation in body language.

It's a powerful tool in negotiation (even virtually). There's no question that body language plays a huge role in your ability to persuade others to your way of thinking. Researchers studying the phenomenon in virtual communication have found that body language in video conferencing plays an important role in negotiation outcomes.

BODY LANGUAGE CUES INCREASE YOUR EMOTIONAL INTELLIGENCE

Your ability to effectively communicate your emotions and ideas is central to your emotional intelligence. Working to understand and improve your body language has a profound effect on your emotional intelligence. Furthermore, body language provides an amazing amount of information on what other people are thinking if you know what to look for. And who hasn't wanted to read people's minds at some point? Emotionally intelligent people know the power that unspoken signals have in communication, and they monitor body language accordingly.

You already pick up on more body language cues than you're consciously aware of. UCLA researchers have shown that only 7% of communication is based on the actual words we say. As for the rest, 38% comes from tone of voice, and the remaining 55% comes from body language. Learning how to become acutely aware of that 55% can give you a leg up with other people. Next time you're in a meeting, on a date, or even playing with your kids, watch for the following cues.

Crossed arms and legs signal resistance to your ideas. Crossed arms and legs are physical barriers that suggest the other person is not open to what you're saying. Even if they're smiling and engaged in a pleasant conversation, their body language tells the story. Gerard I. Nierenberg and Henry H. Calero videotaped more than 2,000 negotiations for a book they wrote on reading body language. Not one ended in an agreement when one of the parties had their legs crossed while negotiating. Psychologically, crossed legs or arms signal that a person is mentally, emotionally, and physically blocked off from what's in front of them. It's not intentional, which is why it's so revealing.

Real smiles crinkle the eyes. When it comes to smiling, the mouth can lie, but the eyes can't. Genuine smiles reach the eyes, crinkling the skin to create crow's feet around them. People often smile to hide what they're really thinking and feeling, so the next time you want to know if someone's smile is genuine, look for crinkles at the corners of their eyes. If they aren't there, that smile is hiding something.

Copying your body language is a good thing. Have you ever been in a meeting with someone and noticed that every time you cross or uncross your legs, they do the same? Or perhaps they lean their head the same way as yours when you're talking? That's actually a good sign. Mirroring body language is something we do unconsciously when we feel a bond with the other person. It's a sign that the conversation is going well and that the other party is receptive to your message. This knowledge can be especially useful when you're negotiating something because it shows you what the other person is really thinking.

Posture tells the story. Have you ever seen a person walk into a room, and immediately, you knew they were in charge? That effect is largely about body language, and often includes an erect posture, gestures made with the palms facing down, and open and expansive gestures in general. The brain is hardwired to equate power with the amount of space that people take up. Standing up straight with your shoulders back is a power position; it appears to maximize the amount of space you fill. Slouching, on the other hand, is the result of collapsing your form; you appear to take up less space and project less power. Slouching can also be seen as a sign of disrespect. It communicates that you're bored and have no desire to be where you are. You would usually never tell someone, "I don't understand why I have to listen to you," but if you slouch, you don't have to. Your body says it for you, loud and clear. Maintaining good posture commands respect and promotes engagement, whether you're a leader or not.

Eyes that lie. Most of us probably grew up hearing, "Look me in the eye when you talk to me!" Our parents were operating under the assumption that it's tough to hold someone's gaze when you're lying to them, and they were right to an extent. However, it's such common knowledge that people often deliberately hold eye contact in an attempt to cover up that they're lying. The problem is that most overcompensate and hold eye contact to the point that it feels uncomfortable. On average, Americans hold eye contact for seven to 10 seconds, longer when we're listening than when we're talking. If you're talking with someone whose stare is making you squirm (especially if they're very still and unblinking), something is up, and they might be lying to you. See the chapter, *Know When You're Being Lied To*, for more tips on detecting when someone is lying to you.

Raised eyebrows signal discomfort. Three main emotions make your eyebrows go up: surprise, worry, and fear. Try raising your eyebrows when you're having a relaxed, casual conversation with a friend. It's hard to do, isn't it? If somebody talking to you raises their eyebrows, and the topic isn't one that would logically cause surprise, worry, or fear, something else is going on.

Exaggerated nodding signals anxiety about approval. When you're telling someone something, and they nod excessively, this means that they are worried about what you think of them or that they think you doubt their ability to follow your instructions.

A clenched jaw signals stress. A clenched jaw, a tightened neck, or a furrowed brow are all signs of stress. Regardless of what the person is saying, these are signs of considerable discomfort. The conversation might be delving into something they're anxious about, or their mind might be elsewhere, and they're focusing on the thing that's stressing them out. The key is to watch for that mismatch between what the person says and what their tense body language is telling you.

The bottom line with these body language cues is that even if you can't read a person's thoughts, you can learn a lot from their body language, and that's especially true when their words and body language don't match.

BODY LANGUAGE BLUNDERS

The human brain is hardwired to judge. This survival mechanism makes it very hard to meet someone without evaluating and interpreting their behavior. Although we tend to think that our judgments are based on the content of conversations and other obvious behaviors, the research says otherwise. In fact, the majority of our judgments are focused on smaller, subtler things, such as handshakes and body language. We often form complete opinions about people based solely on these behaviors. We are so good at judging other people based on small things that in a University of Kansas study, the participants accurately predicted people's personality traits, such as extroversion/introversion, agreeableness, conscientiousness, and openness, simply by looking at pictures of the shoes they wore.

Our unconscious behaviors have a language of their own, and their words aren't always kind. These unconscious habits have likely become an integral part of who you are, and if you don't spend much time thinking about them, now is a good time to start, because they could be sabotaging you. The following subtle habits often catch people by surprise because in using them they're conveying important information to others, and they don't even realize it.

How you treat waiters and receptionists. How you treat support staff is so indicative of your makeup that it has become a common interview tactic. By gauging how you interact with support staff on your way in and out of the building, interviewers get a sense of how you treat people in general. Most people act the part when they're speaking to the hiring manager or other "important" people, but some pull a Jekyll and Hyde act the moment they walk out the door, treating others with disdain or indifference.

Business lunches and dates are other places this comes to light. No matter how nice you are to the people you have lunch with, it's all for naught if those people witness you behaving badly toward others.

How often you check your phone. There's nothing more frustrating than someone pulling out their phone mid-conversation. Doing so conveys a lack of respect, attention, listening skills, and willpower. Unless it's an emergency, it's wise to keep your phone holstered. A study from Elon University confirmed that pulling out your phone during a conversation lowers the quality and quantity of face-to-face interactions.

How long you take to ask questions. Have you ever had a conversation with someone during which they talked about themselves the entire time? The amount of time someone allows to pass before they take an interest in you is a strong personality indicator. People who talk only about themselves tend to be loud, self-absorbed "takers." People who only ask questions and share little about themselves are usually quiet, humble "givers." Those who strike a nice balance of give-and-take are reciprocators and good conversationalists.

Repetitive, nervous habits. Touching your nails or face or picking at your skin typically indicates that you're nervous, overwhelmed, and not in control. Research from the University of Michigan suggested that these nervous habits indicate perfectionism, and that perfectionists are more likely to engage in these habits when they're frustrated or bored.

Watching the clock while talking to someone is a clear sign of disrespect, impatience, and an inflated ego. It sends the message that you have better things to do than talk to the person you're with, and that you're anxious to leave them.

Scowling or having a generally unhappy expression sends the message that you're upset by those around you, even if they have nothing to do with your mood. Scowls turn people away, as they feel judged. Smiling, however, suggests that you're open, trustworthy, confident, and friendly. MRI studies have shown that the human brain responds favorably to a person who's smiling, and this leaves a lasting positive impression.

Turning away from others, or not leaning into your conversation, shows that you're unengaged, uninterested, uncomfortable, and perhaps even distrustful of the person speaking. Try leaning in toward the person speaking and tilting your head slightly as you listen to them. This shows the person speaking that they have your complete focus and attention.

Exaggerated gestures can imply that you're stretching the truth. Aim for small, controlled gestures to indicate confidence and open gestures—like spreading your arms apart or showing the palms of your hands—to communicate that you have nothing to hide.

Your handshake. It's common for people to associate a weak handshake with a lack of confidence and an overall lackadaisical attitude. A study at the University of Alabama showed that although it isn't safe to draw assumptions about someone's competence based on their handshake, you *can* accurately identify personality traits. Specifically, the study found that a firm handshake is equated with being less shy, less neurotic, and more extroverted. However, a handshake that is too strong could be perceived as an aggressive attempt at domination, which is just as bad. Adapt your handshake to each person and situation, but make sure it's always firm.

Showing up late. Being late leads people to think that you lack respect and tend to procrastinate, and that you're lazy and disinterested. Contrary to these perceptions, a San Diego State University study by Jeff Conte revealed that being late is typically seen in people who multitask or are high in relaxed Type B personality traits. Conte's study found that Type B individuals are often late because they experience time more slowly than the rest of us. The bottom line is not to read too much into people showing up late. It's better to ask why they're late than to make assumptions.

Too much or too little eye contact. As I mentioned previously, avoiding eye contact makes it look like you have something to hide, and that arouses suspicion. A lack of eye contact can also indicate a lack of confidence and interest, which you never want to communicate. Sustained eye contact, however, communicates confidence, leadership, strength, and intelligence. Eye contact that's too intense may be perceived as aggressive, or an attempt to dominate. The way we break contact sends a message, too. Glancing down communicates submission, while looking to the side projects confidence. The key to eye contact is balance. Although it's important to maintain eye contact, doing so 100% of the time is perceived as combative and creepy. At the same time, if you maintain eye contact for only a small portion of the conversation, you'll come across as disinterested, shy, or embarrassed. Studies show that maintaining eye contact for roughly 60% of a conversation strikes the right balance and makes you come across as interested, friendly, and trustworthy.

Inconsistency between your words and your facial expression causes people to sense that something isn't right, and they begin to suspect that you're trying to deceive them, even if they don't know exactly why or how. For example, a nervous smile while rejecting an offer during a negotiation won't help you get what you want. It will just make the other person feel uneasy about dealing with you, because they'll assume that you're up to something.

Handwriting. There are all manner of false stereotypes attempting to relate your handwriting to your behavior. For example, people believe that how hard you press down on the paper relates to how uptight you are, the slant of your writing indicates introversion or extroversion, and the neatness or sloppiness of your writing reveals organizational tendencies. When it comes to handwriting and understanding people, the research is inconclusive, at best. Because people mistakenly read so much into handwriting, if you have an important letter to write, stick to the keyboard to keep things neutral.

BRINGING IT ALL TOGETHER

We often think of body language as the result of our attitude or how we feel. This is true, but psychologists have also shown that the reverse is true:

Changing your body language changes your attitude. It's good to be knowledgeable about the subtleties of body language. Understanding body language increases your emotional intelligence because it helps you read people better and know how you are coming across to others. Sometimes, the little things in life make a huge difference.

13

Maintain a Positive Attitude

—

We've all received the well-meaning advice to "stay positive." The greater the challenge, the more this glass-half-full wisdom can come across as Pollyannaish and unrealistic. It's hard to find the motivation to focus on the positive when positivity seems like nothing more than wishful thinking. The real obstacle to positivity is that our brains are hardwired to look for and focus on threats. This survival mechanism served humankind well back when we were hunters and gatherers, living each day with the very real threat of being killed by someone or something in our immediate surroundings. That was eons ago. Today, this mechanism breeds pessimism and negativity through your mind's tendency to wander until it finds a threat. These "threats" magnify the perceived likelihood that things are going—or are going to go—poorly. When the threat is real and lurks in the bushes down the path, this mechanism serves you well. When the threat is imagined, and you spend two months convinced that the project you're working on is going to flop, this mechanism leaves you with a soured view of reality that wreaks havoc in your life.

Pessimism is trouble because it's bad for your health. Numerous studies have shown that optimists are physically and psychologically healthier than pessimists. Martin Seligman at the University of Pennsylvania has conducted extensive research on the topic. Seligman worked with researchers from Dartmouth and the University of Michigan on a study that followed people from age 25 to 65 to see how their levels of pessimism or optimism influenced their overall health. The researchers found that pessimists' health deteriorated far more rapidly as they aged. Seligman also found much higher rates of depression in people who pessimistically attribute their failures to personal deficits. Optimists, on the other hand, treat failure as a learning experience and believe that they can do better in the future.

Seligman's findings are similar to research conducted by the Mayo Clinic that found optimists have lower levels of cardiovascular disease and longer lifespans. Although the exact mechanism through which pessimism affects health has not been identified, researchers at Yale and the University of Colorado found that pessimism is associated with a weakened immune response to tumors and infection. Researchers at the University of Kentucky went so far as to inject optimists and pessimists with a virus to measure their immune response. The researchers found that optimists had a much stronger immune response than pessimists.

Keeping a positive attitude isn't just good for your health. Martin Seligman has also studied the connection between positivity and performance. In one study, he measured the degree to which insurance salespeople were optimistic or pessimistic about their work. Optimistic salespeople sold 37% more policies than pessimists, who were twice as likely to leave the company during their first year of employment. Seligman has studied positivity more than anyone, and he believes in the ability to turn pessimistic thoughts and tendencies around with simple effort and know-how. But Seligman doesn't just believe this. His research has shown that people can transform their tendency toward pessimistic thinking into positive thinking through simple techniques that create lasting changes in behavior.

Maintaining positivity is a daily challenge that requires focus, attention, and most of all, emotional intelligence. You must be intentional about staying positive if you're going to overcome your brain's tendency to focus on threats. It won't happen by accident. Your brain just needs a little help to defeat its negative inner voice. Three habits (in steps) will help you do just that. They will train your brain to focus on the positive, and with practice, can create lasting changes in the positivity of your mindset and your emotional intelligence.

Step 1. Separate Fact from Fiction.

The first step in learning to focus on the positive requires knowing how to stop negative self-talk. Most of our negative thoughts are just that—thoughts, not facts. When you find yourself believing the negative and pessimistic things your inner voice says, it's time to stop and write them down. Literally stop what you're doing and write down what you're thinking. Once you've taken a moment to slow down the negative momentum of your thoughts, you'll be more rational and clear-headed in evaluating their veracity. Evaluate these statements to see if they're factual. You can bet the statements aren't true any time you see words like *never, always, worst, ever,* etc.

Do you really *always* lose your keys? Of course not. Perhaps you forget them frequently, but most days, you remember them. Are you *never* going to find a solution to your problem? If you really are that stuck, maybe you've been resisting asking for help. Or if it really is an intractable problem, then why are you wasting your time beating your head against the wall? If your statements still look like facts once they're on paper, take them to a friend you can trust, and see if they agree with you. Then, the truth will surely come out.

When it feels like something *always* or *never* happens, this is just your brain's natural threat tendency inflating the perceived frequency or severity of an event. Identifying and labeling your thoughts as *thoughts* by separating them from facts will help you escape the cycle of negativity and move toward a positive new outlook.

Step 2. Identify a Positive.

Once you snap yourself out of self-defeating, negative thoughts, it's time to help your brain learn what you want it to focus on—the positive. This will come naturally after some practice, but first you have to consciously select something positive to think about. If you search hard enough, you can always find something positive to focus on. Step 1 stripped the power from negative thoughts by separating fact from fiction. Step 2 replaces the negative with a positive. Once you've identified a positive thought, draw your attention to that thought each time you find yourself dwelling on the negative. If that's difficult, you can repeat the process of writing down your negative thoughts to discredit their validity, and then allow yourself to freely enjoy positive thoughts.

Step 3. Cultivate an Attitude of Gratitude

As we learned in the chapter on stress, taking time to contemplate what you're grateful for isn't merely the "right" thing to do; it reduces the stress hormone cortisol by 23%. Pausing to appreciate what you're grateful for improves your mood, improves your energy levels, and results in substantially less anxiety due to lower cortisol levels. You just need to take time every day to focus on gratitude. If you don't do this naturally, put an alert on your phone's calendar. When it goes off, pause briefly to think of something you are grateful for or feel good about. You'll be shocked by how much this simple act alters the positivity of your mindset. Any time you experience negative or pessimistic thoughts, use this as a cue to shift gears and think about something positive. You cultivate an attitude of gratitude by taking time out every day to focus on the positive. You simply need to ensure that your day is peppered with positive thoughts. In time, a positive attitude will become a way of life.

STOP COMPLAINING

Complaining is most people's biggest obstacle to maintaining a positive attitude. Researchers have shown that people average a complaint a minute during a typical conversation. Complaining is tempting because it feels good, but like many other things that are enjoyable, such as drinking too much alcohol or eating bacon every day for breakfast, complaining isn't good for you. Complaining becomes habitual because your brain loves efficiency and doesn't like to work any harder than it has to. When you repeat a behavior, such as complaining, your neurons branch out to each other to ease the flow of information. This makes it much easier to repeat that behavior in the future—so easy, in fact, that you might not even realize that you're doing it.

You can't blame your brain. Who'd want to build a temporary bridge every time you need to cross a river? It makes a lot more sense to construct a permanent bridge. So, your neurons grow closer together, and the connections between them become more permanent. Scientists like to describe this process as "neurons that fire together wire together." Repeated complaining rewires your brain to make future complaining more likely. Over time, you find it's easier to be negative than to be positive, regardless of what's happening around you. Complaining becomes your default behavior, which changes how people perceive you. Here's the kicker: Complaining damages part of your brain. Researchers at Stanford University have shown that complaining shrinks the hippocampus—an area of the brain that's critical to problem solving and intelligent thought. Damage to the hippocampus is scary, especially when you consider that it's one of the primary brain areas destroyed by Alzheimer's.

Although saying that complaining has links to brain damage isn't an exaggeration, it doesn't stop there. When you complain, your body releases the stress hormone cortisol. Cortisol shifts you into fight-or-flight mode, directing oxygen, blood, and energy away from everything but the systems that are essential for immediate survival. One effect of cortisol, for example, is to raise your blood pressure and blood sugar so that you'll be prepared to escape or defend yourself. All the extra cortisol released by frequent complaining impairs your immune system and makes you more susceptible to high cholesterol, diabetes, heart disease, and obesity. It even makes your brain more vulnerable to strokes.

Because we human beings are inherently social, our brains naturally and unconsciously mimic the moods of those around us, particularly the people we spend a great deal of time with. This process is called *neuronal mirroring*, and it's the basis for our ability to feel empathy. The flip side, however, is that it makes complaining transmissible—you don't have to do it yourself to suffer the ill effects. You should be cautious about spending time with people who complain about everything. They suck you in and make it hard to maintain a positive attitude.

THE SOLUTION TO COMPLAINING

When you feel the need to complain, you can do two things. One is to culti-vate an attitude of gratitude, as discussed at the beginning of this chapter. Let the impulse to complain be your cue that it's time to shift your attention to something you're grateful for. Heck, you may want to complain so fre-quently that you won't even need to set up a gratitude calendar reminder. The second thing you can do—and only when you have something that's truly worth complaining about—is to engage in solution-oriented complain-ing. Think of it as complaining with a purpose. Solution-oriented complain-ing should do the following:

- **Have a clear purpose.** Before complaining, know what outcome you're looking for. If you can't identify a purpose, there's a good chance you just want to complain for its own sake, and that's the kind of complaining you should nip in the bud.

- **Start with something positive.** It may seem counterintuitive to start a complaint with a compliment, but starting with a positive helps keep the other person from getting defensive. For example, before launching into a complaint about poor customer service, you could say something like, "I've been a customer for a very long time and have always been thrilled with your service ...." If the complaint is about your own life or circumstances, it's even more critical that you identify something positive about the situation.

- **Be specific.** When you're complaining, it's not a good time to dredge up every minor annoyance from the past 20 years or every little aspect of what you're disappointed in. Be concise and focus on the heart of the matter. This way, you don't expand your complaint unnecessarily.

- **End on a positive.** If you end your complaint with "I'm never shopping here again," the person who's listening is not motivated to act on your complaint. If you end your complaint with "I'm never going to try for another promotion," the person who's losing future motivation is you. In either case, you're just venting, or complaining with no purpose other than to complain. Instead, restate your purpose, as well as your hope that the desired result can be achieved, for example, "I'd like to work this out because I like shopping here," or "This one hurts, but once I'm ready, I'm going to rework my resume and give it another go."

BRINGING IT ALL TOGETHER

Like many things in life that are tempting, complaining is bad for you. Given the mind's natural tendency to wander toward negative thoughts, we can all use a little help with staying positive. Developing and maintaining a positive attitude requires a great deal of emotional intelligence. These tips may sound incredibly basic, but they have tremendous power because they train your brain to have a positive focus. You can break old habits if you force yourself to use them. You'll reap the physical, mental, and performance benefits that come with a positive frame of mind.

14

Be Utterly Authentic

Oscar Wilde said, "Be yourself. Everyone else is already taken." Wilde made it sound so simple, but living with authenticity is a real challenge. To live authentically, you must own your actions and ensure that they align with your beliefs and needs. This can be difficult to maintain when external forces pressure you to do something you're not comfortable with or to be someone you're not. Most people have experienced the discomfort that comes with failing to behave authentically. Researchers at Harvard, Columbia, and Northwestern joined forces to measure this phenomenon scientifically. They found that when people failed to behave authentically, they experienced a heightened state of discomfort that's usually associated with immorality. People who weren't true to themselves were so distraught that they felt a strong desire to cleanse themselves physically.

It's clear that our brains know when we're living a lie, and like all lies, being inauthentic causes nothing but harm. How do you start living authentically? It can be tough, especially if you've been playing a role for most of your adult life. The key to living authentically lies in clearly understanding what makes you tick and using this to guide your path without fail. It's self-awareness and self-management in action on a very high level. Several habits will help you tap into this. Try them out so that you can be your most authentic self.

Don't hide your quirks. Authentic people often have unusual preferences that don't fit the norm. They're open and unabashed about who they are, which gives everyone a good look at these interesting tendencies. Billionaire Warren Buffett, for example, has never been suited to the high-rolling lifestyle. Instead, he still lives in the same modest house he bought in 1958 for $31,500. It might seem quirky—or even strange—for such an incredibly wealthy man to live so frugally, but Buffett doesn't sacrifice his preferences to what's expected of him.

Express your true feelings and opinions even when they're not popular. Authentic people don't live a go-along-to-get-along lifestyle. They're simply not capable of acting in a way that's contrary to what their principles dictate, even if there are repercussions. They prefer not to lie to other people, and they especially can't lie to themselves. This means that they're willing to live with the repercussions of staying true to themselves.

Give others room to breathe. Authentic people don't expect others to play a role, either. They don't make people feel as though they have to fit into a certain mold or project a certain image to be a part of their lives. Their commitment to being authentic gives other people the freedom to live authentically, too.

Check your ego at the door. An egomaniac is never authentic. Egomaniacs are always posturing and worrying about how they're perceived. It's exhausting, and it's also dishonest. Take Oprah Winfrey—an interesting and authentic person. In a speech to the Stanford University graduating class of 2008, she said, "The trick is to learn to check your ego at the door and start checking your gut instead. Every right decision I've made—every right decision I've ever made—has come from my gut. And every wrong decision I've ever made was a result of me not listening to the greater voice of myself." Oprah's advice is so important: Listen to your values, goals, and ambitions, rather than worrying about what will make you look good.

Avoid the bandwagon. Nothing is more boring than following the bandwagon, and authentic people are intent on forging their own paths. There's often nothing wrong with what everyone else is doing. It's just that authentic people are innovators who break with conformity to pursue new, exciting, and interesting ideas.

Don't worry about what others think of you. It's never fun accepting that someone doesn't like you, but a lot of times, that discomfort comes from trying to figure out what you did wrong or how you can fix it. Authentic people don't have that anxiety because they would never try to change themselves to influence someone else's opinion. They accept that other people have the right to be authentic about their own feelings, even if those feelings are negative toward them. Nothing is more unauthentic than hiding your true self because you're afraid that other people might not like it. Instead, authentic people are true to themselves wherever they are, whoever they're with, and whatever they're doing.

Don't take anyone's advice without evaluating it carefully. It's not that authentic people aren't willing to take advice; they are. But they don't put that advice into action just because other people have. First, they'll run it through the wringer from a critical perspective so that they can be sure it makes sense for them.

Try new things. Authentic people do what interests them. They know what they want, and they're brave enough to take the steps to get there. This often means trying new things—things at which they're often terrible at first.

Never stop learning. To authentic people, the world has infinite possibilities. This curiosity leads to constant learning, fueled by an ever-burning desire to discover the unknown. For example, despite Albert Einstein's intelligence and accomplishments, he retained a sense of wonder throughout his life that made him continue to ask questions about the world. Like Einstein, authentic people are in a constant state of wonder.

PASSION DRIVES AUTHENTICITY

Do you have enough passion in your life? Passion is the difference between playing the piano and being a pianist; it's who you are, not just what you do. Passion makes you leap out of bed in the morning, eager to start your day. Dr. Robert Vallerand at the University of Quebec has studied passion more than anyone, and he asserts that passion is self-defining. According to Vallerand, "Passion is a strong inclination towards a self-defining activity that people love, that they consider important, and in which they devote significant amounts of time and energy." It's important to note that passion doesn't require expertise—although there is a correlation, it's not a given. Vallerand and two other researchers studied 187 musicians and found that those who focused on perfecting their performance—what Vallerand calls "mastery"—developed a higher level of expertise than those who focused on merely being better than other musicians. If passion defines you, it makes sense that your personal best will be about you and no one else.

So, what does passion look and feel like? A great way to understand passion is to consider what makes passionate people different from everybody else. Try their habits out and see if they help you to magnify the passion and authenticity in your own life.

Passionate people are obsessed. Put simply, passionate people are obsessed with their muse, and I don't mean that in an unhealthy sort of way. I'm talking about a positive, healthy obsession, the kind that inspired the quote, "Do what you love, and you'll never work a day in your life." No matter what else is going on, their thoughts keep returning to their passion. Not because they feel burdened and pressured by it, but because they're just so dang excited about it. They're obsessed with their muse because it inspires them and makes them happy.

They don't waste time. You won't find passionate people wasting time. They don't have time to be bothered with things that don't matter or things that just kill time. They devote every minute available to their passion, and it's not a sacrifice, because there's nothing else they'd rather be doing.

They're optimistic. Passionate people are always focused on what can be, rather than what is. They're always chasing their next goal with the unwavering belief that they'll achieve it. You know how it feels when you're looking forward to a really special event? Passionate people feel like that every day.

They're early risers. Passionate people are far too eager to dive into their days to sleep in. It's not that they don't like to sleep; they'd just much rather be pursuing their passion. When the rooster crows, their minds are flooded with ideas and excitement for the day ahead.

They're willing to take big risks. How much you want something is reflected in how much you're willing to risk. Nobody is going to lay it all on the line for something they're only mildly interested in. Passionate people, on the other hand, are willing to risk it all.

They have only one speed—full tilt. Passionate people don't do anything halfheartedly. If they're going, they're going full tilt until they cross the finish line or crash. If they're relaxed and still, they're relaxed and still. There's no in-between.

They talk about their passions all the time. Again, we're talking about people whose passions are inseparable from who they are, and you couldn't form much of a relationship with them if they couldn't be real about who they are, right? It's not that they don't understand that you don't share their obsession; they just can't help themselves. If they acted differently, they'd be playing a role rather than being authentic.

They're highly excitable. You know those people who probably wouldn't get excited if an alien spaceship landed in their front yard? Yeah, that's not how passionate people operate. It's not that they're never calm, or even bored. It's just that it takes less to get them excited, so they get excited more frequently and stay excited longer. One theory is that they devote their energy to just one or two things, so they make more progress, and that momentum fuels their excitement.

BRINGING IT ALL TOGETHER

Never forget to keep exploring the world and staying true to yourself. Living authentically is a perpetual challenge that yields great rewards. It's a noble path you won't regret following. It just requires careful use of your self-awareness and self-management skills. It might not always be easy to incorporate these habits into your daily life, but that's what makes the people who do so authentic—they go against the grain. Much social anxiety stems from the fear we have of being "found out." We're afraid that somebody is going to discover that we're not as smart, experienced, or well connected as we pretend to be. Authentic people don't have that fear. Who they appear to be is who they really are. Their confidence comes from the fact that they have nothing to hide.

15

Increase Your Self-Control

What is it about self-control that makes it so difficult to rely on? It's a skill we all possess (honest), yet we tend to give ourselves little credit for it. Self-control is so fleeting for most that when Martin Seligman and his colleagues at the University of Pennsylvania surveyed two million people and asked them to rank their strengths in 24 different skills, self-control ended up in the very bottom slot. When it comes to self-control, it's so easy to focus on our failures that our successes tend to pale in comparison. And why shouldn't they? Self-control is an effort that's intended to help achieve a goal. Failing to control yourself sends you veering off course. If you shave 500 calories off your total daily intake on Monday and Tuesday, only to binge eat several thousand extra calories on Wednesday, your failure outweighs your success. You've taken two steps forward and four steps back.

With this success/failure dichotomy in mind, there are five great habits for exercising self-control that come straight from research conducted at Florida State University. Some are obvious, others counterintuitive, but all will help you eliminate those pesky failures and ensure your efforts to boost your willpower are successful enough to keep you headed in the right direction. The important thing to remember is that you have to give these habits the opportunity to work. This means recognizing the moments when you're struggling with self-control and rather than giving in to an impulse, taking another look at these habits and giving them a go first. This will slow you down and prevent your emotions from taking over, which is important because it's hard to exercise self-control when your emotional intelligence is lacking. The two go hand in hand.

Meditate. Meditation trains your brain to become a self-control machine. Even simple techniques like mindfulness, which involves taking as little as five minutes a day to focus on nothing more than your breathing and your senses, improve your self-awareness and your brain's ability to resist destructive impulses. Buddhist monks appear calm and in control for a reason. The chapter on meditation in the next section will show you how.

Eat. File this one in the counterintuitive category, especially if you're having trouble controlling your eating. Your brain burns heavily into your stores of glucose when attempting to exert self-control. If your blood sugar is low, you are far more likely to succumb to destructive impulses. Sugary foods spike your sugar levels quickly and then leave you drained and vulnerable. Eating something that provides a slow burn for your body, such as whole grain rice or meat, will give you a longer window of self-control. So, if you're having trouble keeping yourself out of the company candy bin when you're hungry, make sure you eat something else if you want to have a fighting chance.

Sleep. When you're tired, your brain cells' ability to absorb glucose is highly diminished. Without glucose, your brain cannot control your impulses. What's worse, without enough sleep, you're more likely to crave sugary snacks to compensate for your low glucose levels. So, if you're trying to exert self-control over your eating, getting a good night's sleep—every night—is one of the best habits you can make.

Ride the wave. Desire tends to ebb and flow like the tide. When the impulse you need to control is strong, waiting out this wave of desire is usually enough to keep yourself in control. The rule of thumb is to wait at least 10 minutes before succumbing to temptation. You'll often find that the great wave of desire is now little more than a ripple that you have the power to step right over.

Expect results. People who exercise self-control know that they're going to fail from time to time, but they never let that keep them from expecting results. Expecting results keeps you motivated and feeds the cycle of empowerment. If you don't think you're going to succeed, why bother?

Forgive yourself. A vicious cycle of failing to control yourself followed by feeling intense self-hatred and disgust is common in attempts at self-control. These emotions typically lead to over-indulging in the offending behavior. When you slip up, it's critical that you forgive yourself and move on. Don't ignore how the mistake makes you feel; just don't wallow in it. Instead, shift your attention to what you're going to do to improve yourself in the future. Emotionally intelligent people know that success lies in their ability to rise in the face of failure, and they can't do this when they're living in the past. When you live in the past, your past becomes your present, preventing you from moving forward.

KNOWING WHEN TO QUIT

Most of us grew up hearing the mantra "Don't be a quitter," and we've internalized it to the point where we feel guilty if we don't finish a book, even if it's boring us to death. Our parents weren't entirely wrong in saying that persistence is necessary for success, but sometimes quitting is the most effective course of action. Whether it's a failed project, a thankless job, or a doomed relationship, quitting can be a virtue. Knowing when to quit and actually doing it are absolutely essential for self-control. When you have self-control, you can recognize when the time is right to move on and actually do it.

As it turns out, some of us are really good at knowing when to quit, while others have a hard time getting "unstuck." Researchers at the University of Rochester found that people are motivated by either "approach goals" or "avoidance goals." Those who fall into the approach camp are motivated by challenges and don't waste time trying to solve problems that simply don't have a feasible solution. In other words, they know when to quit. People in the avoidance camp, however, worry a lot more about failing. They want to avoid failure at all costs, so they keep plugging away at things, long after logic suggests it's time to move on.

Knowing when to quit is a skill that can be learned to improve your self-control. If you tend to get stuck on things long after it's obvious that what you're doing isn't working, you can train yourself to do better. You just need to practice quitting. Thankfully, life provides plenty of opportunities to do this. Here are some things we should all use our emotional intelligence to quit doing.

Quit putting things off. Change is hard. Self-improvement is hard. Scrounging up the guts to go for what you want is hard, and so is the work to make it happen. When things are hard, it's always easier to decide to tackle them tomorrow. The problem is that tomorrow never comes. Saying you'll do it tomorrow is just an excuse, and it means that either you don't really want to do it or that you want the results without the hard work that comes along with them.

Quit thinking you have no choice. There's always a choice. Sure, sometimes it's a choice between two things that seem equally bad, but there's still a choice. Pretending that there isn't one makes you a victim who is voluntarily taking on a mantle of helplessness. When you play the victim, you relinquish your power. To demonstrate self-control, you have to quit giving your power away.

Quit feeling sorry for yourself. The worst thing about feeling sorry for yourself, other than it being annoying, of course, is that it shifts your locus of control outside yourself. Feeling sorry for yourself is, in essence, declaring that you're a helpless victim of circumstances. Emotionally intelligent people never feel sorry for themselves because that would mean giving up their power.

Quit doing the same thing over and over again and expecting a different result. Albert Einstein said that insanity is doing the same thing and expecting a different result. Despite his astute insight, many people seem determined that two plus two will eventually equal five. The fact is simple: If you keep using the same approach, you'll keep getting the same results, no matter how much you hope for the opposite. If you want different results, you need to change your approach, even when it's painful to do so.

Quit feeling entitled. Emotionally intelligent people believe that the world is a meritocracy, and that the only things they deserve are those they earn. People who aren't emotionally intelligent often feel entitled. They think that the world owes them something. Again, it's about locus of control. Emotionally intelligent people know that they alone are responsible for their successes or failures, and that is the essence of self-control.

Quit doubting yourself. Confidence plays a huge role in success. Hewlett-Packard conducted an interesting study in which they analyzed the process through which people applied for promotions at the company. Women, it turned out, applied only when they met 100% of the criteria for the job they wanted, while men applied when they met 60% of the criteria. The researchers postulated that one of the (many) reasons men dominated the upper echelons of the company is that they were willing to try for more positions than women. Sometimes, confidence is all it takes to reach the next level. The trick is, you have to believe in yourself. If you doubt yourself, it won't work. Faking confidence just doesn't produce the same results.

Quit thinking everything is going to work out on its own. It's tempting to think that it's all going to work out in the end, but the truth is you have to make it work. This has many implications. Don't expect your boss to notice when you're ready for a promotion, and don't think that anyone is going to stop walking all over you as long as you allow it. Everything will not magically work out on its own. You have to be proactive and take full responsibility for yourself. This requires considerable self-control.

BRINGING IT ALL TOGETHER

There are dozens of ways we get in the way of achieving our full potential. We doubt ourselves, we decide that something is just too hard, or we tell ourselves that we'll worry about it tomorrow. If you really want to succeed (and I mean really succeed), make the decision to improve your self-control. The important thing to remember is that you have to give the habits in this chapter the opportunity to work. Developing self-control takes practice and perseverance, which increases your emotional intelligence in the process.

16

Control Your Anger

If you enjoy Mark Twain quotes as much as I do, you appreciate their profound ability to simplify things that are easy to overcomplicate. Twain said, "Anger is an acid that can do more harm to the vessel in which it is stored than to anything on which it is poured." It's hard to argue with the fact that anger does great damage to the "vessel" in which it's stored. However, this knowledge isn't enough for most people to keep their anger in check. Just because most of us aren't running around keying cars and chucking our smartphones into the ocean doesn't mean we're immune to the ill effects of anger. But if anger is such a destructive emotion for the person in whom it burns, then why do we feel it so often? The answer is the anger funnel.

Anger is experienced so frequently that it is considered one of the five core emotions, but emotional intelligence black belts know that 99% of the time, anger is not really a unique emotional state. Unless you are experiencing anger that enables you to ward off immediate physical harm, your anger is simply a replacement for another, less palatable emotion. We live in a society where emotional expression is generally feared and avoided. We're taught to bottle up our emotions or avoid them altogether. Anger is considered more socially acceptable than other (presumably "weaker") emotions like fear or shame. This makes the experience of anger far more tolerable for most people than what they are really feeling. So, they funnel their fear, shame, regret, apprehension, guilt, embarrassment, sorrow, or what have you into anger.

If you think about it, it's much easier—and far more tolerable—to get angry and point the finger at someone or something else than it is to sit with a powerful, negative emotion. So, instead of sitting in fear or shame, we throw these tough feelings into the anger funnel, and they come out red hot on the other side. Although what comes out of the funnel is more bearable, it's usually far more destructive than what goes into it. The anger funnel gives you someone or something to blame for your situation. This becomes your preoccupation, instead of learning why you're feeling what you're feeling and, in turn, discovering what you should do about it to make things better for you.

PUTTING AWAY THE FUNNEL

The question we all need to ask ourselves is not, "Do I funnel my emotions into anger?" Rather, it's, "When, where, and how do I funnel my emotions into anger?" Turning off the anger funnel is really a matter of educating yourself on the sources of your anger. Only by breaking down and understanding the real emotions you funnel into anger can you understand yourself well enough to catch yourself the next time you're about to get angry.

Emotions are often funneled into anger in an instant. It's unrealistic to assume that you'll stop yourself every time you're about to pour your emotions into the funnel. Instead, you can turn off your anger as soon as it's aroused by asking yourself three simple questions. To help illustrate, I've put my own answers to these questions from an incident in which I was abruptly cut off by another car on the freeway.

Question 1: Why am I angry?

The answer to this question usually involves finger-pointing. That's OK, as it's part of the process. Usually, something or someone around you helped you begin moving toward anger. In my case, my answer was, "I'm angry because that car almost ran me off the road."

Question 2: How did this incident really make me feel?

You might also call this question, "What was the feeling that I funneled into anger?" As long as you're willing to feel vulnerable, the answer to this question should come pretty easily. In my case, the answer was obvious: fear. Getting cut off like that made me feel intense fear. The fear was so intense that a fuming, smoke-out-my-ears anger came out the other side of the funnel. I knew it was time to ask myself these three questions, as opposed to giving in to the thought of teaching the guy a lesson. My anger was like a big red balloon that was going to pop, but as soon as I realized this anger was a substitute for fear, it sent all of the air rushing out of the balloon. I went from shocked that I couldn't get the car in front of me out of my mind to shocked that anger that intense could simply evaporate.

Question 3: Why was this feeling so intolerable?

By the time you get to question 3, your anger will have largely subsided. In my case, the whole thing felt silly by this point. I felt silly for being so angry and silly for being so vulnerable to fear. So, I asked myself, why was I afraid? I've been driving for decades here in Southern California, where getting cut off is a regular occurrence. So, why did this time get me going? The answer is that when this happened I was a new father. My drive to remain safe and be there for my son magnified my fear. What was really intolerable was the thought of not being there for him. Learning why the feeling is so intolerable improves your self-awareness, so that you're less likely to use that funnel the next time someone inevitably cuts you off.

PERFECTIONISM FEEDS ANGER

We live in a world that idolizes perfectionism. From a very young age, parents, coaches, and teachers push us to be high achievers, but they fail to teach us balance. We live our lives with an ingrained desire to give our all in pursuit of lofty goals, but we don't know when to pull back. We don't know when enough actually is enough.

Most people lean hard into their perfectionism—they extol it as a virtue, to the point that it becomes a vice. Perfectionism creates a constant feeling that things are not as they should be. This nagging feeling that nothing is working out right increases your tendency to experience anger. Anger isn't the only issue with perfectionism. As I've mentioned previously, separate studies from the University of British Columbia and the University of Tehran showed that perfectionism is also linked to depression, anxiety, and a slew of mental health issues.

To defeat perfectionism, you have to learn to spot when it's holding you back. This task is difficult because perfectionistic tendencies like to hide under the guise of hard work and zeal. Tal Ben-Shahar suggested that you shift your mentality from that of a perfectionist to that of an optimalist. Optimalists strive just as hard for success, but they're more flexible, resilient, and adaptive in the pursuit of their goals. They try their best and are satisfied with the outcome, whatever that is. Unlike perfectionists, optimalists aren't paralyzed by the fear of failure. Shifting your approach from perfectionism to optimalism won't just quiet your anger; it will also make you happier and more productive. To make this happen, you need to recognize the signs that perfectionism is holding you back. The following are the nine habits that are signs that your perfectionism has gotten out of control.

You get defensive when receiving feedback. Perfectionists care deeply about what other people think of them, and this can make feedback hard to take. Even well-presented, useful feedback feels like a needle to the eye. You likely catch yourself acting defensively before you realize that you're taking issue with the feedback. It's a knee-jerk reaction. As a perfectionist, you naturally have an intense desire to succeed. Take comfort in the fact that feedback (even brutal feedback) ultimately helps you improve. Take it in stride, and feedback will actually help you get closer to perfection.

However, you're critical of others. Considering their inability to receive criticism, perfectionists can certainly dish it out. Perfectionists can't help but measure themselves against other people, so taking someone down a notch, especially if that person is a threat, feels good. However, this isn't always the reason. Perfectionists are also critical of others because they compare them to the same unobtainable standard to which they compare themselves.

You recognize that your perfectionism is a problem, but you think that's what it takes to be successful. Sometimes, you really need to push yourself hard to be successful. When your perfectionism gets out of control, using hard work as a justification for the unnecessary pain and suffering you endure is easy. Make no mistake about it—perfectionism creates unnecessary struggle and strife. When you get your perfectionism under control, you can work less and get more done.

You procrastinate all the time. Perfectionism and fear of failure go hand in hand. This combination leads to procrastination, because even mundane tasks are intimidating when they must be completed perfectly. Most writers spend countless hours brainstorming characters and plot, and they even write page after page that they know they'll never include in their book. They do this because they know that ideas need time to develop. We tend to freeze up when it's time to get started because we know that our ideas aren't perfect and that what we produce might not be any good. However, how can you ever produce something great if you don't get started and give your ideas time to evolve? Author Jodi Picoult summarized the importance of avoiding perfectionism perfectly: "You can edit a bad page, but you can't edit a blank page."

You have a guilty conscience. Perfectionists have a steady stream of guilty thoughts running through their minds because they're always feeling like they're coming up short. This guilt elevates stress and frustration and can easily spiral into depression and anxiety.

You take mistakes personally. Perfectionists take things so seriously that they tend to overestimate the impact of their mistakes. Minor events can cause them to experience bitter disappointment. This issue is significant because it makes you less resilient, and the ability to bounce back from failure is critical to success. Perfectionists must learn that failure is not a confirmation that they aren't good enough.

You take pleasure in other people's failures. This little-known secret of perfectionists is not as evil as it sounds. Misery loves company, and perfectionists can't help but find satisfaction in knowing that other people experience the same frustrations they do. These moments of relief are short-lived, and they make perfectionists feel bad for being so competitive.

You're afraid to take risks. With the fear of failure comes the fear of taking risks. Perfectionists' hard work, research, and attention to detail produce novel ideas. Unfortunately, their great ideas are often placed on the back burner because of their fear of risk. The only way to get comfortable with taking risks is to take them. Starting the process is never easy, but by actively leaning into the very things that make you uncomfortable, you build up your confidence and realize that it's never as bad as you build it up in your mind to be.

You live in fear of rejection. Perfectionists need the approval of others to feel successful. This mentality leads to a crippling fear of rejection. Perfectionists dread certain things, such as asking for a raise or pursuing their passions in lieu of something that will win approval from others. Living in fear of rejection feels terrible, stifles creativity, and slows down your progression as a person. Whenever you find yourself overly concerned with what other people think of you, remember this famous take on authenticity (commonly misattributed to Dr. Seuss): "Be who you are and say what you feel, because those who mind don't matter, and those who matter don't mind."

BRINGING IT ALL TOGETHER

To increase your emotional intelligence and tame your anger, you need to learn to spot and avoid the anger funnel. This can be tricky in the moment, as emotions tend to quickly get placed in the funnel. The questions in this chapter will help you analyze different situations and understand when and why you let this happen. This way, you can keep yourself from repeating the same mistakes. Before long, you'll catch yourself using the funnel in the moment and will have better control over your anger as it happens. To minimize anger, you also need to minimize perfectionism as much as you can. Avoiding the funnel and getting your perfectionism under control will reduce your anger in short order.

17

Unlock the Power of
Your Personality

—

As explained in the first chapter, emotional intelligence (EQ) is distinct from intelligence (IQ). There is no known connection between EQ and IQ. Personality is the final piece of the puzzle. It's the stable "style" that defines each of us. Your personality is the result of your ingrained preferences, such as whether you tend to be introverted or extroverted. However, like IQ, personality can't be used to predict emotional intelligence. Personality is stable over a lifetime. Personality traits appear early in life, and they don't go away. People often assume that certain traits (e.g., extroversion) are associated with higher EQ, but those who prefer to be with other people are no more emotionally intelligent than people who prefer to be alone. You can use your personality to assist in developing your EQ, but the latter doesn't depend on the former. EQ is flexible, while personality does not change. Think of your personality as the vessel that holds your emotional intelligence. When you understand your personality, it is easier to increase your EQ. Personality, EQ, and IQ assessed together is the best way to get a picture of the whole person. When you understand all three in a single individual, they don't overlap much. Instead, each covers unique ground that helps to explain what makes a person tick.

*Emotional intelligence is an
essential part of the whole person.*

The remainder of this chapter will take a close look at important aspects of personality in people. What you discover will help improve your understanding of how personality shapes behavior. You'll glean insight into how personality operates both within yourself and the people you encounter every day. This knowledge will increase your self-awareness, as well as your ability to read and respond to other people.

WHAT EVERY TYPE A PERSONALITY WISHES YOU KNEW

Robert Frost once said, "The brain is a wonderful organ; it starts working the moment you get up in the morning and does not stop until you get into the office." He certainly wasn't thinking about Type A people when he said that. They barrel into the office like they're racing for a pot of gold, and they never seem to lose momentum. It's as if they're driven by a motor that never shuts off.

We each have our own understanding of what it means to have a Type A personality, but what does this term *really* mean, and where did it come from? It actually started in a waiting room shared by a pair of cardiologists. The doctors noticed that their chairs didn't have wear on the backs as expected—wear was visible only on the front edge of the seats and the armrests, suggesting that patients were literally waiting on the edge of their seats, ready to jump up the second their names were called. So, the cardiologists—Doctors Friedman and Rosenman—wanted to find out if the strange wear pattern on their chairs was because impatient people are more prone to heart disease. They discovered that their hunch was correct. They also found that people's personalities tend to lean in one of two directions, which they labeled Type A and Type B.

Most think of Type A people as driven and highly strung, and Type B people as carefree and even keeled, but there's so much more to it. Type As, in particular, are often misunderstood, as we just don't understand the motivation behind their behavior. To fully grasp what it means to be Type A, you need to hear it from the horse's mouth. Don't take my word for it—let's see what they have to say:

We believe that winning is the only option. We're really hard on ourselves. Our desire to do our best often morphs into a desire to be the best. After all, if someone else does something better than us, then we mustn't have been trying hard enough, right? This ensures that even the most mundane activities become a competition.

We live and die by our goals. We don't do anything "just because." There's an end aim for everything. That morning cup of coffee? The goal is to wake up. Half an hour of Pokémon Go at lunch? It's about squeezing in some exercise and capturing more Pokémon than our friend down the hall. Heaven help anyone who slows us down or gets in our way. We're nothing if we don't achieve our goals.

We're always stressed. Achieving our goals is so important to us that we often get stressed about our progress. That specter of wasted time or missed opportunities hanging over our heads gets us all riled up.

We squeeze something into every possible moment. It may seem hypocritical that we're sometimes late, although the rest of the time we're impatiently drumming our fingers, waiting for meetings to start on time. The problem is that we try to squeeze a task into every possible minute, and sometimes we overdo it. In our determination to avoid downtime, we sometimes inadvertently create downtime for other people.

We want you to get to the point. Skip the long preamble. If we have questions, we'll ask. There's no need to waste time on the setup when you have something important to tell us—just tell us. The theme here is efficiency; we're interested in hearing the main points so that we can begin taking action.

We hate to wait. We don't hate being stuck at a red light or cooling our heels in a doctor's waiting room because we think we're too good to wait. We just like to be efficient with our time and don't like things getting in our way. Every minute spent waiting is a minute we could have spent doing something productive. It's a minute that we'll never get back.

We're conscientious. Like "later," "good enough" isn't part of our vocabulary. Things are either right or they're wrong. And they always, *always* have to be right. No matter what we're doing, we care too much to settle for mediocrity.

We multitask. We're not being rude, and we're not bored. We just have a sense that the value of our day is measured by how much we get done, and we accomplish more when we do two (or more!) things at once.

We have a tough time relaxing. Relaxation isn't a measurable goal, and it feels like a waste of time when we're not getting anything done. It's very difficult for us to sit around and "just be." Instead, we prefer to be actively "becoming" whatever is our current ambition. Anything else is lost time.

We have an unrealistic sense of urgency. From our perspective, "now" is the only time that exists. There's no sense in putting something off until another time. Although that's often a good thing, we tend to give trivial issues a greater sense of urgency than they deserve.

We follow a schedule. Our time is carefully orchestrated so that each day we accomplish what we intended. Again, like "later," "whenever" isn't part of our vocabulary. Everything gets scheduled and added to lists, and we take great satisfaction in ticking all the boxes.

We're restless. Our motors are always running, so when we have to idle, that excess energy manifests in various nervous habits, such as fidgeting or biting our nails. Don't worry, we're not freaking out. This behavior is normal for us.

Type A people know they can be awfully hard on everybody, but that's because they're even harder on themselves. This may be difficult to see because no one else is privy to the perfectionist inside their heads who's goading or berating every move. Just know this: They care (they care a lot), and they really are sorry if their personality makes them hard to get along with sometimes.

WHAT EVERY TYPE B PERSONALITY WISHES YOU KNEW

Nobel Prize winner Edith Wharton once said, "There are two ways of spreading light: to be the candle or the mirror that reflects it." This is an amazingly accurate description of the difference between Type A and Type B personalities. Type A personalities are the candles—and they're usually burning at both ends. Type B personalities, however, put out just as much light. They just don't get as much recognition for it.

Type Bs don't have all of that sparkle and sizzle that attract everyone's attention. Because Type Bs aren't as in your face about their contributions, they tend to get mislabeled as lazy or indifferent. That bias goes all the way back to the origin of the Type A/Type B personality paradigm in the waiting room of cardiologists Friedman and Rosenman. Once the doctors discovered that their hunch was correct, they labeled the impatient individuals "Type A." "Type B" was simply a label they assigned to anyone who wasn't Type A. It's as if Type Bs lack the distinguishing characteristics that drive them to be successful. Type Bs, however, know that this couldn't be further from the truth. The very traits that people assume are the products of laziness or indifference are distinct personality characteristics that help Type Bs achieve and prosper. Unlike Type As, Type Bs don't feel like they have to be perfect, which means they are OK with recognizing and admitting their weaknesses. This acknowledgment equips them to shore up those weaknesses. Type Bs are also easier to get along with, as they tend to be supportive rather than rushing, pushing, and criticizing others.

Type Bs don't jump to conclusions. Because they're not in a constant rush, they take the time to analyze all the facts, instead of hurrying their analysis just to reach a decision. Type Bs also won't keep beating a dead horse. Whereas Type As can become obsessed with making their chosen strategy work, Type Bs easily switch gears when it becomes obvious something isn't working. In a nutshell, Type B personalities deserve a lot more credit than they get. To fully grasp what it means to be Type B, you need to hear them describe themselves. Let's see what they have to say:

We're not lazy; we're just laid-back. Just because our goals aren't pulsating like strobe lights on our foreheads doesn't mean we don't have any. We have goals, and we care about them just as much as you care about yours. But we see achieving those goals as a journey, not a sprint. We may stop and smell the proverbial roses along the way, but we stay focused on where we're going and what we need to do to get there.

We have a plan. Just because we're not barreling from step one to step two at breakneck speed doesn't mean we don't have a plan. We do. We just keep it to ourselves and follow it quietly, rather than assigning timekeepers and judges to monitor our progress and help us stay on track.

We care. Being laid-back is different from being disengaged or indifferent. The truth is that we care enough to work at the pace we're most effective. If we didn't care, we'd let you rush us, even if that compromised quality.

We're content. We think it's great that you're so focused on your goals, but we simply don't think as much about "What's next?" because we're pretty happy right where we are. In fact, we Type B people report a higher level of satisfaction with our lives, and that lets us enjoy today without worrying so much about what we're going to achieve tomorrow.

We're healthier than you are. Overall, we suffer less stress, which can lead to everything from heart disease and insomnia to relationship problems and substance abuse. Our ability to relax not only paves the way for better decision-making but also helps us maintain a healthy weight, avoid cancer, and fight off infections.

We make great friends. We see the best in everyone—including you. Because we don't view life as a competition, we're the first to cheer you on and support you along the way. And we cheer and support *you*, not just your achievements. We think that Robert Louis Stevenson knew what he was talking about when he said, "Don't judge each day by the harvest you reap but by the seeds that you plant."

We work best when we're allowed to color outside the lines. Don't give us a paint-by-numbers kit; we'd much rather have a blank canvas and a shiny new palette of colors. While you're squinting at those small spaces and trying to make sure you stay within the lines, we're backing up all the way across the room to get a new perspective.

We like group projects. We know you don't like group projects, and we know why. There are always a few group members who don't feel that every second has to be accounted for or who don't share your sense of urgency to do everything NOW! We focus on the process as well as the outcome. We're happy to share the successes, the failures, and the credit, and we enjoy the give-and-take and collaboration that are part of working with a group, even if it slows things down a bit.

We admire and respect you—but we wouldn't trade places. We're awed by your drive and by your breathtaking pace. We recognize the rewards that come your way, and we're impressed. But we're wise enough to know that we're not wired that way. We'd be miserable, and so would everyone around us. So, we're content to hang out in the slow lane and see you at the finish line. We'll be the ones who are smiling calmly, rather than gasping for breath.

Type Bs really don't mind ceding the limelight to Type A personalities; just don't count them out. They have a lot to offer, and they want to contribute. They want to succeed at a high level. However, they'd rather enjoy the game and leave the scorekeeping to somebody else. After all, it doesn't matter until the game is over.

ARE YOU AN AMBIVERT?

I'm sure you've been asked many times whether you're an introvert or an extrovert. For some people, it's an easy choice, but for most of us, it's difficult to choose one way or the other. It's hard to choose because the introvert/extrovert dichotomy reflects a tired and outdated view of personality. Personality traits exist along a continuum, and the vast majority of us aren't introverts or extroverts—we fall somewhere in the middle.

As mentioned at the start of the chapter, personality consists of a stable set of preferences and tendencies through which you approach the world. Many important things about you change over the course of your lifetime, but your personality isn't one of them. The continuum from introversion to extroversion captures one of the most important personality traits. It's troubling that we're encouraged to categorize ourselves one way or the other, because critical strengths and weaknesses are commonly associated with each type.

Adam Grant at Wharton studied this phenomenon, and his findings are fascinating. First, he found that two-thirds of people don't strongly identify as introverts or extroverts. These people (a.k.a., the vast majority of us) are called ambiverts, who have both introverted and extroverted tendencies. The direction ambiverts lean toward varies greatly depending on the situation. Think of introversion and extroversion as a spectrum, with ambiversion lying somewhere in the middle:

Ambiverts have a distinct advantage over true introverts and extroverts. Because ambiverts' personalities don't lean too heavily in either direction, they have a much easier time adjusting their approach to people based on the situation. This enables ambiverts to connect more easily and more deeply with a wider variety of people. Grant's research disproved the powerful and widely held notion that the best-performing salespeople are extroverts. He found that ambiverts' greater social flexibility enabled them to outsell all other groups, moving 51% more product per hour than the average salesperson. Grant explained the finding this way: "Because they naturally engage in a flexible pattern of talking and listening, ambiverts are likely to express sufficient assertiveness and enthusiasm to persuade and close a sale, but are more inclined to listen to customers' interests and less vulnerable to appearing too excited or overconfident."

How social you are is largely driven by dopamine, the brain's feel-good hormone. We all have different levels of dopamine-fueled stimulation in our neocortex (the area of our brain that's responsible for higher mental functions, such as language and conscious thought). Those who have high levels of stimulation naturally tend to be introverts—they try to avoid any extra social stimulation that might make them feel anxious or overwhelmed. Those with low levels of stimulation tend to be extroverts. Under-stimulation leaves extroverts feeling bored, so they seek social stimulation to feel good. Most people's levels of natural stimulation don't reach great extremes, although the levels do fluctuate. Sometimes you may feel the need to seek out stimulation, while other times you may avoid it.

It's important to pin down where you fall on the introversion/extroversion continuum. By increasing your awareness of your type, you can develop a better sense of your tendencies and play to your strengths. If you think that you might be an ambivert but aren't certain, see how many of the following statements apply to you. If most of them apply, you're most likely an ambivert.

- I can perform tasks alone or in a group. I don't have much preference either way.

- Social settings don't make me uncomfortable, but I tire of being around people too much.

- Being the center of attention is fun for me, but I don't like it to last.

- Some people think I'm quiet, while others think I'm highly social.

- I don't always need to be moving, but too much downtime leaves me feeling bored.

- I can get lost in my own thoughts just as easily as I can lose myself in a conversation.

- Small talk doesn't make me uncomfortable, but it gets boring.

- When it comes to trusting other people, sometimes I'm skeptical, and other times, I dive right in.

- If I spend too much time alone, I get bored, but too much time around other people leaves me feeling drained.

The trick with being an ambivert is knowing when to force yourself to lean toward one end of the spectrum when it isn't happening naturally. Ambiverts with low self-awareness struggle with this. For example, at a networking event, a self-aware ambivert will lean toward the extroverted side of the scale, even when it's been a long day, and they've had enough of people. This requires perspective on yourself and the situation, combined with intention. Not matching your approach to the situation can be frustrating, ineffective, and demoralizing for ambiverts.

SENSITIVE? IT MIGHT BE YOUR PERSONALITY

Sensitive people get a bad rap. Research suggests that genes are responsible for the 15–20% of people who qualify as "highly sensitive." Psychologist Elain Aron has studied this phenomenon extensively. Using MRI scans of highly sensitive people's brains, she found that they experience sounds, feelings, and even the presence of other people much more intensely than the average person.

The good news is that highly sensitive people aren't more or less emotionally intelligent than others. Highly sensitive people simply experience things more intensely. Their strong emotions are easier to identify (and potentially use to their benefit) than the average person. This also helps them communicate effectively because they don't just hear the words coming out of other people's mouths; they also catch on to subtleties in gesture and tone. There are trade-offs, however, as strong emotions that are left unchecked can have disastrous consequences. Highly sensitive people can use emotional intelligence to their benefit only once they understand that they're highly sensitive. This awareness ensures that they reap the benefits of their heightened emotional awareness while spotting and defeating their negative tendencies.

You're likely wondering if you or someone you know is highly sensitive. The following are the most common qualities that highly sensitive people possess. See how many apply.

You think deeply. When life throws you a curveball, you retreat deep into your shell, thinking through every aspect of what transpired before taking any action. Small things (in your own life and other people's lives) can have a big impact on you.

You're emotionally reactive. When left to your own devices, you have a knee-jerk reaction to your feelings. You also have strong reactions to what other people are going through. When your emotions come on strong, it's easy to let them hijack your behavior. The hard part is channeling your feelings into producing the behavior that you want.

You're detail oriented. You're as sensitive to details as you are to feelings. You see details that others miss, and you aren't content until you've dotted all the i's and crossed the t's. This strength is highly valuable in the right profession.

You take longer to reach decisions. Because you're prone to digging deep beneath the surface, you tend to drag out decisions. You can't help but try to run every possible outcome through your head, and this is often at the expense of the ticking clock.

You're crushed by bad decisions. When you finally make a decision, and it turns out to be a poor choice, you take it much harder than most. This can create a vicious cycle that slows down your decision-making process even more, as the fear of making a bad decision is part of what slows you down in the first place.

You take criticism hard. Your strong feelings and intense emotional reactions can make criticism hard to take. Although you may initially over-react to criticism, you also tend to think hard about things and explore them deeply. This exploration of criticism can play out well for you in the long run, as your inability to "shrug it off" helps you make the appropriate changes.

You work well in teams. Your unique ability to take other people's feelings into account, weigh different aspects of multifaceted decisions, and pay attention to the smaller details makes you extremely valuable in a team environment. Of course, this can backfire if you're the one who is responsible for making final decisions, as you're better suited to offering input and analysis than to deciding whether to push the red button.

You have great manners. Your heightened awareness of the emotions of other people makes you highly conscientious. You pay close attention to how your behavior affects other people and have the good manners to show for it. You also get particularly irked when other people are rude.

Open offices drive you crazy. Your sensitivity to other people, loud noises, and other stimuli makes it practically impossible for you to work effectively in an open-office environment. You're better off in a cube or working from home.

Like many things in life, being a highly sensitive person is both a blessing and a curse. It all comes down to what you make of it.

BRINGING IT ALL TOGETHER

The upper echelons of top performance are filled with people who are highly self-aware. By gaining a better sense of your personality, you can build real insight into your tendencies and preferences. The personality characteristics introduced in this chapter cover important aspects of your personality. It makes a big difference when you know how sensitive you are, whether you're Type A or B, and where you fall on the introversion/extroversion continuum. Understanding how these personality characteristics apply to you will give you a better understanding of yourself. This will increase your self-awareness and emotional intelligence, and ultimately, improve your performance in life.

18

Increase Your Intelligence

———

Intelligence, or IQ, isn't what you know but the pace at which you acquire new information. Longitudinal studies have shown that IQ doesn't really change all that much for adults, so you're basically stuck with what you've got. Although IQ is far from being the only thing that determines success in life (research shows that it isn't even the most important factor), a high IQ isn't a bad thing to have. In fact, I don't know anyone who wouldn't mind having one. Most of us move through life never knowing exactly how smart we are. IQ is difficult to measure, and unless you're willing to fork over several hundred dollars to a trained professional, you'll never know for certain what your IQ is. But there are some hints that can give you a pretty good idea. Research has provided some interesting clues linking early life experiences to, among other things, high intelligence. If any of the following apply to you, you just might have a high IQ to go along with your high EQ.

You're anxious. It's hard to think of anxiety as a good thing, but evidence suggests that it might not be all bad. Psychiatrist Jeremy Coplan studied patients with anxiety disorders and found that the people with the worst symptoms had higher IQ scores than those with milder symptoms. Other studies have found higher verbal IQ scores in people with higher levels of anxiety. A more complex experiment was conducted at the Interdisciplinary Center Herzliya in Israel. Researchers asked participants to evaluate artwork presented by a software program and then triggered a fake computer virus, making it look as if it was the result of something the participant did. The researchers then sent the participants on an urgent mission to get tech support, only to throw yet another series of obstacles in their way. The researchers found that the most anxious participants were also the most focused and effective at executing tasks. The next time somebody tells you to stop worrying so much, just tell them it's your oversized intellect getting in the way of your EQ.

You were an early reader. A British study of 2,000 pairs of identical twins found that despite their identical genes, the children who started reading earlier had higher IQ scores (both verbal and nonverbal) than their siblings. On the surface, this seems easy to explain away: The kids who learned to read early did so because they were smarter. But that wasn't the case. The researchers concluded that learning to read early actually had a developmental impact—it made the kids smarter. So, if you were an early reader, it might not be because you're smart. It may be that you're smart because you were an early reader.

You're left-handed. It turns out that all those teachers who tried to force lefties to write with their right hands may have had it backward. Although there is a small and, as of today, unexplained correlation between being left-handed and being a criminal, being a southpaw has some intellectual benefits. One large study demonstrated that left-handedness is associated with divergent thinking. This unique ability to combine two unrelated objects in a meaningful way is a sign of intelligence.

You took music lessons as a kid. A number of studies have shown that musical training enhances verbal intelligence and executive function, a skill that's critical for focus and self-control. In a study conducted by psychologist Sylvain Moreno, 48 children between the ages of four and six participated in a computerized training program led by a teacher. For one hour a day, five days a week for four weeks, half the students completed a musical program, and the other half completed a visual arts program. At the end of the experiment, 90% of the children who received the musical training showed improvements in their verbal IQ. So, if you took music lessons when you were a kid, that's a good sign.

You're funny. Class clowns, rejoice! Research has shown there's a strong connection between being funny and scoring high in verbal intelligence and abstract reasoning. It appears that your witty banter is the product of a sharp mind. Now, you just need to come up with a joke about *that*.

The previous list is far from exhaustive, so if none of the items apply to you, it doesn't mean you don't have a high IQ. But if a lot of the items do apply to you, you just might be smarter than the average bear. It's great to be smart, but intelligence is a hard thing to pin down. In many cases, how smart people *think* you are is just as important as how smart you actually are. When you consider that you can't improve your IQ much in adulthood anyway, improving how intelligent others perceive you to be is the next best thing. This is where emotional intelligence comes in. Intelligence explains only about 20% of how you do in life anyway. Much of the other 80% is due to your emotional intelligence (EQ). The hallmark of emotional intelligence is self-awareness, which involves not just knowing how you are but also how other people perceive you to be. People with high emotional intelligence are masters of influence—they're skilled at altering their behavior to make the most of a given situation.

You might not be able to alter your genetics or experiences, but several proven habits can help you appear to be even smarter than you are. Some of these habits may seem arbitrary, but researchers have shown that they make a massive difference. That makes this good information to have, especially when you need to sway someone to your way of thinking. Try these habits out. You'll be surprised by the difference they make.

Make graphs. Research conducted at Cornell suggested that people are more likely to trust a source if it contains graphs. In one of the Cornell studies, participants read a document on the effectiveness of a new cold medication. One report contained a graph; the other didn't. Other than that, the reports were exactly the same. Still, 96% of the participants who read the report with a graph believed the claims, while only 67% of those who read the document without a graph thought the same. So, next time you create a document, stick in a graph. It doesn't have to be complex; it just has to be accurate.

Skip that drink. And that's not just because people tend to do stupid things when they've been drinking. A joint study conducted by the University of Michigan and the University of Pennsylvania revealed that merely seeing someone hold a drink is enough to make them seem less intelligent. It's not that we assume less intelligent people are more likely to drink; it's that the perceived correlation between drinking and cognitive impairment is so strong that we assume someone's impaired even if they aren't. For example, although job candidates frequently think that ordering a glass of wine at a dinner interview will make them appear intelligent and worldly, it actually makes them appear less intelligent and less hirable. There's even a name for it: the "imbibing idiot bias."

Use a middle initial. John F. Kennedy. Franklin D. Roosevelt. It turns out that there might be a reason why so many people who hold a prominent place in history used a middle initial. Using a middle initial not only enhances your perceived social status but also boosts others' expectations of your intelligence capacity and performance. In one study, participants were asked to read and rate Einstein's essay on the theory of relativity, with authorship attributed to David Clark, David F. Clark, David F. P. Clark, or David F. P. R. Clark. Not only did David F. Clark get higher ratings than David Clark, but David F. P. R. Clark outdid them all. In another study, participants were asked to choose team members for academic competitions. People who used middle initials were selected more frequently than those who didn't. (It was quite a different story for athletic competitions.) So, if you want a quick perceived IQ boost, start using that middle initial.

Believe in yourself. Nothing projects intelligence quite like confidence. When you believe in yourself, it shows, and research has shown that believing in yourself improves your performance on cognitive tasks. Self-doubt, however, impairs your performance. What's worse is that other people pick up on this doubt, which makes you appear less intelligent to them. If you want people to believe in you, you have to believe in yourself.

Write simply. If you're really smart, you shouldn't have to use big words to broadcast it. True intelligence speaks for itself, so you don't have to show off your impressive vocabulary. In addition, you always run the chance of being wrong. Using a big word incorrectly makes you look, well, not so smart. So, if you want to appear more intelligent, stop studying the dictionary and just focus on communicating effectively.

Speak expressively. Communication expert Leonard Mlodinow has made the case that even if two people say exactly the same thing, the one who says it most expressively will be perceived as smarter. "If two speakers utter exactly the same words, but one speaks a little faster and louder and with fewer pauses and greater variation in volume, that speaker will be judged to be more energetic, knowledgeable, and intelligent," Mlodinow said. If you want to come across as more intelligent, modulate your speech by varying your pitch, volume, speed, and energy level.

Look 'em in the eye. We know we're supposed to do this anyway—it's good manners, right? That's true, but it also makes you look smarter. In a study conducted at Loyola University, participants who intentionally managed their eye contact scored significantly higher on perceived intelligence.

Wear nerd glasses. Did your mom ever tell you to be nice to the nerds because you'll probably be working for them someday? As usual, Mom was onto something. Research has shown that people wearing glasses—especially thick, full-framed ones—are perceived as being more intelligent. So, if you want to seem smarter (when you're giving a presentation, perhaps?), leave the contacts at home and wear your glasses.

Dress for success. This should not be surprising. Extensive research shows that how you dress affects how people see you. Dressing well makes you seem more intelligent, and showing skin makes you seem less intelligent as it directs people's attention to your body rather than to your mind. But did you know that how you dress also affects your performance? A study by Northwestern University found that making people wear lab coats improved their performance on tasks that required intelligence and concentration.

WHEN SMART MEANS SOCIALLY AWARE

We've all said things that people interpreted very differently than we thought they would. These seemingly benign comments lead to the awful feeling that comes only when you've planted your foot firmly in your mouth. When this happens, we sure don't look or feel smart. Verbal slip-ups often occur because we say things without knowing the subtle implications they carry. Understanding these implications requires acute *social awareness*—the ability to pick up on the emotions and experiences of other people. TalentSmartEQ research has shown that social awareness is a skill that many of us lack. We lack social awareness because we're so focused on what we're going to say next—and how what other people are saying affects us—that we completely lose sight of other people. The end result is that we end up saying something that makes us look stupid.

This is a problem because people are complicated. You can't understand someone until you focus *all* your attention on them. The beauty of social awareness is that a few simple adjustments to what you say can vastly improve your relationships with other people. It can also keep you from looking dumb. To that end, there are some phrases that emotionally intelligent people are careful to avoid in casual conversation. The following are the worst offenders. You should avoid them at all costs.

"You look tired." Tired people are incredibly unappealing—they have droopy eyes and messy hair, they have trouble concentrating, and they're grouchy. Telling someone they look tired implies all of the above and then some.

Instead, say, "How are you doing?" Most people ask if someone is tired because they mean to be helpful (they want to know if the other person is okay). Instead of assuming someone's disposition, just ask. This way, they can open up and share. More importantly, they will see you as concerned instead of rude.

"As I said before..." We all forget things from time to time. This phrase makes it sound as if you're insulted at having to repeat yourself, which is hard on the recipient (someone who is genuinely interested in hearing your perspective). Getting insulted over having to repeat yourself suggests that either you're insecure or you think you're better than everyone else (or both!). Few people who use this phrase actually feel this way.

Instead: When you say it again, see what you can do to convey the message in a clearer and more interesting manner. This way, they'll remember what you said.

"You always..." or **"You never..."** No one always or never does anything. People don't see themselves as one-dimensional, so you shouldn't attempt to define them as such. These phrases make people defensive and closed off to your message, which is a really bad thing because you likely use these phrases when you have something important to discuss.

Instead: Simply point out what the other person did that's a problem for you. Stick to the facts. If the frequency of the behavior is an issue, you can always say, *"It seems like you do this often."* or *"You do this often enough for me to notice."*

"It's up to you" or **"Whatever you want."** Although you may be indifferent to the question, your opinion is important to the person asking (or else they wouldn't have asked you).

Instead, say, "I don't have a strong opinion either way, but a couple of things to consider are..." When you offer an opinion (even without choosing a side), it shows that you care about what the person is asking.

"Wow, you've lost a ton of weight!" Once again, a well-meaning comment—in this case, a compliment—creates the impression that you're being critical. Telling someone they've lost a lot of weight suggests that they used to look fat.

Instead, say, "You look fantastic." This is an easy fix. Instead of comparing how they look now to how they used to look, just compliment them for looking great. It takes the past right out of the picture.

"You look great for your age." Using "for your" as a qualifier always comes across as condescending and rude. No one wants to be smart for an athlete or in good shape relative to other people who are also knocking on death's door. People simply want to be smart and fit.

Instead, say, "You look great." This is another easy fix. Genuine compliments don't need qualifiers.

"Well, at least I've never ___." This phrase is an aggressive way to shift attention away from your mistake by pointing out an old, likely irrelevant mistake that the other person made (and one you should have forgiven them for by now).

Instead, say, "I'm sorry." Owning up to your mistake is the best way to bring the discussion to a more rational, calm place so that you can work things out. Admitting guilt is an amazing way to prevent escalation.

"You were too good for her anyway." When someone severs ties of any type, personal or professional, this comment implies that they had bad taste and made a poor choice in the first place.

Instead, say, "Her loss!" This provides the same enthusiastic support and optimism without any implied criticism.

"Good luck." This one is subtle. It certainly isn't the end of the world if you wish someone good luck, but you can do better, because this phrase implies that they need luck to succeed.

Instead, say, "You've got this. I know you have what it takes." This is better than wishing them luck because suggesting that they have the skills needed to succeed provides a huge boost of confidence. You'll stand out from everyone else who simply wishes them luck.

In everyday conversation, it's the little things that make all the difference. Try these new habits out, and you'll be amazed at the positive response you get.

WHEN SMART PEOPLE ACT STUPID

It's good to be smart. After all, intelligent people earn more money, accumulate more wealth, and even live longer. On the surface, being smart looks like easy living. But there's another side to the story. Intelligent people have a reputation for making dumb mistakes, especially in situations that require common sense. The simplicity of these situations and the abundant intelligence of those who tend to muck them up can be downright comical. Indeed, common sense is not so common. After decades of research, scientists are finally beginning to understand why this happens. Shane Frederick at Yale University was among the first to conduct research that explained why rational thinking and intelligence don't tend to go hand in hand. In his studies, Frederick gave people simple problems to solve, like this one:

A bat and ball cost a dollar and ten cents. The bat costs a dollar more than the ball. How much does the ball cost?

Frederick found that some people tend to confidently blurt out the wrong answer, stating that the ball costs ten cents. You, of course, knew that the correct answer is that the ball costs five cents, and you're completely justified if you're wondering if the, well, less-than-smart people were the ones blurting out the wrong answer.

Psychologists at James Madison University and the University of Toronto wondered the same thing. They gave similar tests of logic to hundreds of people and compared the accuracy of their answers to their levels of intelligence. The researchers found that smart people are more likely to blurt out the wrong answer because they actually make more mental mistakes when problem-solving. Smart people are more likely to make silly mistakes because of blind spots in how they use logic. These blind spots exist because smart people tend to be overconfident in their reasoning abilities. That is, they're so used to being right and having quick answers that they don't even realize when they're blowing it by answering without thinking things through.

The dummies getting the bat-and-ball question wrong aren't so dumb, either. When Frederick gave the question to students at Harvard, Princeton, and MIT, more than half of them got it wrong. Even students at some of the most prestigious universities in the world make stupid mistakes. Perhaps the scariest thing about the errors that highly intelligent people make is how unaware they are of them. People with all levels of intelligence succumb to what's called the "bias blind spot." That is, we're great at spotting other people's mistakes and terrible at recognizing our own. The sillier the mistake, the harder it is for an intelligent person to accept that they've made it.

Although it might seem like we don't spend our days solving logic problems like the bat-and-ball question, the brain functions involved in solving these problems are the same ones we use in everyday thinking. Thus, the tendency to do stupid things that they aren't aware of follows smart people around. Here are some of the most common ways smart people manage to shoot themselves in the foot. Avoiding these bad habits is good for your emotional intelligence.

Smart people are overconfident. A lifetime of praise and pats on the back leads smart people to develop unflappable faith in their intelligence and abilities. When you rack up accomplishments while people stroke your ego, it's easy to expect that things will always go your way. But this is a dangerous expectation. Smart people often fail to recognize when they need help, and when they do recognize it, they tend to believe that no one else is capable of providing it.

They push people too hard. Smart people develop overachieving personalities because things come so easily to them. They simply don't understand how hard some people have to work to accomplish the same things, and because of that, they push people too hard. Smart people set the bar too high, and when people take too long or don't get things quite right, they assume it's due to a lack of effort. So, they push even harder and miss the opportunity to help others achieve the goals they're so anxious for them to reach.

They always need to be right. It's hard for anyone to graciously accept that they're wrong. It's even harder for smart people because they grow so used to being right all the time that it becomes a part of their identity. For smart people, being wrong can feel like a personal attack, and being right a necessity.

They lack emotional intelligence. Although intelligence (IQ) and emotional intelligence (EQ) don't occur together in any meaningful way (smart people, on average, have just as much emotional intelligence as everyone else), when a smart person lacks emotional intelligence, it's painfully obvious. These high-IQ, low-EQ individuals see the world as a contest. Achievements are all that matter, and people and emotions just get in the way. This is a shame because even among the upper echelons of IQ, the top performers are those with high emotional intelligence.

They give up when they fail. Have you ever watched a sporting event and seen the stunned look on the face of an athlete everyone expected to win but didn't? Smart people can easily fall into the trap of seeing failure as the end of the world, because frequent success creates expectations that make failure hard to tolerate. People who have to work hard for what they achieve have plenty of practice learning how to deal with failure. They learn to embrace it because they know that failure is just a stepping-stone to success.

They fail to develop grit. When things come really easily to you, it's easy to see hard work as a negative (a sign that you don't have what it takes). When smart people can't complete something without a tremendous amount of effort, they tend to feel frustrated and embarrassed. This leads them to make the false assumption that if they can't do something easily, there's something wrong with them. As a result, smart people tend to move on to something else that affirms their sense of worth before they've put in the time to develop the grit they need to succeed at the highest possible level.

They multitask. Smart people think very quickly, which can make them impatient. They like to get several things going at once so that there isn't any downtime. They think so quickly that, when they multitask, it feels like it's working, and they're getting more done. However, as I've said before,

Stanford researchers have shown that this isn't the case. Not only does multitasking make you less productive, but people who multitask often because they think they're good at it are actually worse than people who prefer to do one thing at a time.

They have a hard time accepting feedback. Smart people tend to undervalue the opinions of others, which means that they have trouble believing that anyone is qualified to give them useful feedback. This tendency not only hinders their growth and performance but can also lead to toxic relationships, both personally and professionally.

BRINGING IT ALL TOGETHER

You might not be able to change your IQ much, but you can definitely alter the way people perceive you. When it comes to succeeding in the real world, perception is half the battle. Emotionally intelligent people know this, and they do everything they can to paint themselves in the best light possible. To some, parts of this chapter will read like I'm trashing smart people, but I'm not. Some of life's greatest gifts, including high intelligence, can also come with challenges. If you aren't willing to take an honest look at the whole picture, you're selling yourself short. And that isn't smart.

19

Make Smart Decisions

—

Your days are filled with a constant stream of decisions. A study from Columbia University found that we're bogged down by a good 70 decisions a day. Some decisions are minor, like what to eat, which route to drive to work, or in what order to tackle tasks. Others are more difficult, like deciding between two job offers, whether to move to a new city for someone you love, or whether to cut a toxic person out of your life. With so many decisions taking up each day, learning to prioritize them and make them effectively is essential to your success and happiness. This requires emotional intelligence. There are many strategies for effective decision-making. The following habits are the cream of the crop.

Turn small decisions into routines. Decision-making works like a muscle: As you use it over the course of the day, it gets too exhausted to function effectively. One of the best strategies successful people use to work around their decision fatigue is to eliminate smaller decisions by turning them into routines. Doing so frees up mental resources for more complex decisions. Steve Jobs famously wore a black turtleneck to work every day. Mark Zuckerberg still wears a hoodie. Both men have stated that these iconic images are the simple result of daily routines intended to cut down on decision fatigue. They were both aware of our finite daily ability to make good decisions, as is Barack Obama, who said, "You'll see I wear only gray or blue suits. I'm trying to pare down decisions. I don't want to make decisions about what I'm eating or wearing, because I have too many other decisions to make."

Make big decisions in the morning. Another great way to beat decision fatigue is to save small decisions for after work (when decision fatigue is greatest) and tackle complex decisions in the morning, when your mind is fresh. When you're facing a stream of important decisions, a great trick is to wake up early and work on your most complicated tasks before you get hit with a bunch of distracting minor decisions (phones ringing, emails coming in). A similar strategy is to do some of the smaller things the night before to get a head start on the next day. For instance, lay out your outfit at night, so you don't even have to think about it when you wake up.

Pay close attention to your emotions. There's an old saying: "Don't make permanent decisions based on temporary emotions." Emotionally intelligent people recognize and understand their emotions (including their intensity and their impact on behavior) so that they are able to look at decisions as objectively and rationally as possible. Unfortunately, most people aren't good at recognizing their emotions. Strong decision makers, however, know that a bad mood can make them lash out or stray from their moral compass just as easily as a good mood can make them overconfident and impulsive.

Evaluate your options objectively. When really wrapped up in a decision, emotionally intelligent people weigh their options against a pre-determined set of criteria because they know that this makes decision-making easier and more effective. Here are some helpful criteria to consider: How does this decision benefit me? How does it hurt me? How does this benefit ___? How does it hurt ___? Does the decision reflect my values? Would I regret making this decision? Would I regret not making this decision?

Sleep on it. Sleeping on your decision ensures that you have clarity of thought when you approach it the next day. It also allows time for your emotions to run their course. When you act too quickly, you tend to *react*, but when you give more focus and time to your decision, you expose important facets of it that you didn't see before.

Don't sleep on it for too long. Emotionally intelligent people know the importance of gathering as much information as they can, but at the same time, they make certain not to fall prey to analysis paralysis. Instead of waiting for the moons to align, emotionally intelligent people know that they need to have a timetable for making their decision. Once they set that date, they are motivated to do their homework and some soul searching to meet the deadline.

Use exercise to recharge. This isn't the first time I've touted the benefits of exercise for emotional intelligence, and it won't be the last. The stress of a major decision naturally produces cortisol, the chemical that triggers the fight-or-flight response. Cortisol clouds your ability to think clearly and rationally. When you find yourself stressing about a decision, try exercising. As little as 30 minutes is all it takes to get a good endorphin-fueled buzz and return to mental clarity. Exercise also helps you get past that fight-or-flight state by putting the cortisol to practical use. Researchers have shown that long-term exercise improves the overall functioning of the brain regions responsible for decision-making.

Seek outside counsel. When approaching a decision, we naturally tend to pick an alternative and then gather information to support that decision, instead of gathering information and then choosing a side (this is called *confirmation bias*). A great way to beat confirmation bias is to seek outside opinions and advice from people who bring different perspectives to your situation. Their perspectives help you weigh your options more objectively and spot your subjective or irrational tendencies.

Reflect on previous decisions. Mark Twain described the complicated nature of decision-making as follows: "Good decisions come from experience, but experience comes from making bad decisions." This isn't to say that the only way to become a great decision maker is to make a ton of mistakes. It just means that it's important to keep past decisions front of mind.

Emotionally intelligent people are aware enough of their past decisions and use them to their benefit when something similar comes up.

TRUSTING YOUR INTUITION

Steve Jobs once said that intuition is more powerful than intellect. As it turns out, Jobs was onto something, and the scientific community backs him up. It seems that we've been giving intuition far too little respect. In a Salk Institute study, participants were asked to play a card game in which they pulled cards from two different decks. The decks were rigged so that one would "win" more often than the other, but the participants didn't know that—at least not overtly. It took about 50 cards for participants to consciously realize that the decks were different and about 80 to figure out the difference. However, what was really interesting was that it took only about 10 cards for the participants' palms to start sweating slightly every time they reached for a card from the "losing" deck. This was about the same time they started subconsciously favoring the "winning" deck.

Although that's all very interesting in a clinical setting, does it hold true in real life? Apparently, it does. When you make major decisions, your intuition can matter as much as your intellect. For example, in a study, car buyers who carefully analyzed all the available information were happy with their purchases about 25% of the time, while buyers who made quicker, more intuitive purchases were happy with their purchases about 60% of the time.

Intuition comes from the primitive brain; it's an artifact of the early days of humans, when our brain's ability to detect hidden dangers ensured our survival. Today, we use this capability so little that we don't know how to listen to it properly. Whether you listen to it or not, your intuition is healthy and functioning. If you want to make better decisions in life, it's a good idea to brush up on your use of intuition. You can start by emulating some of the habits of highly intuitive people.

Slow down enough to hear your inner voice. Before you can pay attention to your intuition, you first have to be able to hear it amid the cacophony of your busy life. You have to slow down and listen, which often requires solitude. Taking some time away from the everyday, even something as brief as going for a walk, is a great way to turn up the volume of your intuition.

Follow your inner voice. One of the primary reasons that some people are more intuitive than others is that they actually listen to their gut feeling instead of dismissing or doubting it. That doesn't mean that they ignore their analytical mind and their critical thinking skills. There's a difference between using reason as a system of checks and balances and using it to talk yourself out of what your intuition knows to be true.

Practice empathic accuracy. I'd probably lose you if I said that highly intuitive people read minds, so I'll use the scientific term: empathic accuracy. It's not magic; it's an intuitive awareness of what other people are thinking and feeling, using cues such as body language and tone of voice. It's an extremely powerful form of empathy that helps foster deep connections with other people.

Practice mindfulness. "Mindfulness" sounds even more New-Agey than trusting your intuition, but it's really just a fancy term for focusing on being in the moment. Mindfulness is a great technique for filtering out all of the distractions in your environment—and your brain. When you do that, you can hear your intuition loud and clear. The chapter on mindfulness in the next section will show you how to do it.

Nurture your creativity. Did you have a paint-by-number kit when you were a kid? Talk about turning art into a science—all you have to do is put the right color in the right little space. You may end up with a pretty painting, but the only intuition involved is guessing what colors you're supposed to use in those really tiny spaces. No paint-by-numbers kit in the world can make a skilled artist create something as novel and monumental as the Sistine Chapel or the *Mona Lisa*. The missing ingredient is intuition.

Just as intuition is the secret ingredient in creativity, being intentionally creative strengthens your use of intuition.

Listen to your body. Have you ever made a decision and immediately felt sick—maybe even kind of clammy? That affective experience is your body's way of informing you that the decision your analytic mind came to is at odds with your instinct.

Analyze your dreams. If you accept the science that demonstrates the power of intuition, it's not much of a leap to accept that your dreams are often manifestations of intuition. Sure, sometimes dreams are nonsense, but they often try to tell us something. Intuitive people don't just think, "Wow, that was a weird dream!" They ask themselves, "Where did that come from, and what can I take away from it?"

DEALING WITH UNCERTAINTY

Our brains are hardwired to make much of modern life difficult. This is especially true when dealing with uncertainty. Our brains give us fits when we're facing uncertainty because they're wired to react to it with fear. A Caltech neuroeconomist imaged subjects' brains as they were forced to make increasingly uncertain bets—the same kind of bets we're forced to make on a regular basis. The less information the subjects had, the more irrational and erratic their decisions became. You might think the opposite would be true—the less information we have, the more carefully and rationally we evaluate the validity of that information. Not so. As the uncertainty of the scenarios increased, the subjects' brains shifted control over to the limbic system, the place where emotions, such as anxiety and fear, are generated.

When you face uncertainty, your brain pushes you to overreact. Emotionally intelligent people are able to override this mechanism and shift their thinking in a rational direction. They make sound decisions in the face of uncertainty, even when their brains fight against this. If you know the right

tricks, you can override your brain's irrational tendencies and handle uncertainty effectively. There are proven habits that you can use to improve
the quality of your decisions when your emotions cloud your judgment. The
following are the best habits that emotionally intelligent people use to make
sound decisions in these moments.

Quiet your limbic system. Your limbic system responds to uncertainty with a knee-jerk fear reaction, and fear inhibits good decision-making.
People who are good at dealing with uncertainty are wary of this fear and
spot it as soon as it surfaces. This way, they can contain it before it gets
out of control. Once they are aware of the fear, they label all the irrational
thoughts that try to intensify it as irrational fears—not reality—and the
fear subsides. Then they can focus more accurately and rationally on the information they have. Throughout the process, they remind themselves that
a primitive part of their brain is trying to take over and that the logical part
needs to be the one in charge. In other words, they tell their limbic system
to settle down and be quiet unless a hungry tiger shows up.

Don't seek perfection. Emotionally intelligent people don't set perfection as their target because they know there's no such thing as a perfect decision in an uncertain situation. Think about it: Human beings, by our very
nature, are fallible. When perfection is your goal, you're always left with a
nagging sense of failure, and you end up spending your time lamenting what
you failed to accomplish and what you should have done differently instead
of enjoying what you achieved.

Know what you know—and what you don't. When uncertainty makes
a decision difficult, it's easy to feel as if *everything* is uncertain, but that's
hardly ever the case. People who excel at managing uncertainty start by taking stock of what they know and what they don't know and assigning a factor of importance to each. They gather all the facts they have, and they take
their best shot at compiling a list of things they don't know, for example,
what a country's currency is going to do or what strategy a competitor will
employ. They actually try to identify as many of these things as possible,

because this takes away their power. Then they can make the best decision possible with the facts they have.

Embrace that which you can't control. We all like to be in control. After all, people who feel like they're at the mercy of their surroundings never get anywhere in life. But this desire for control can backfire when you see everything that you can't control or don't know as a personal failure. People who excel at managing uncertainty aren't afraid to acknowledge what's causing it. In other words, they live in the real world. They don't paint any situation as better or worse than it actually is, and they analyze the facts for what they are. They know that the only thing they really control is the process through which they reach their decisions. That's the only rational way to handle the unknown, and the best way to keep your head on level ground. Don't be afraid to step up and say, "Here's what we don't know, but we're going forward based on what we do know. We may make mistakes, but that's a lot better than standing still."

Focus on what matters. Some decisions can make or break you. Most just aren't that important. The people who are the best at making decisions in the face of uncertainty don't waste their time getting stuck on decisions where the biggest risk is looking foolish. When it comes down to it, almost every decision contains at least a small factor of uncertainty—it's an inevitable part of life. Learning to properly balance the many decisions on your plate, however, allows you to focus your energy on the things that matter and to make more informed choices. It also removes the unnecessary pressure and distraction caused by a flurry of small worries.

Know when to trust your gut. Our ancestors relied on their intuition—their gut instinct—for survival. Since most of us don't face life-or-death decisions every day, we have to learn how to use this instinct to our benefit. I explained the importance of trusting your intuition earlier in this chapter, but the importance of your intuition in making good decisions is magnified the more you're facing uncertainty. People who successfully deal with uncertainty recognize and embrace the power of their gut instincts, and they rely on some tried-and-true strategies to do so successfully:

They recognize their own filters. They're able to identify when they're overly influenced by their assumptions and emotions or by another person's opinion, for example. Their ability to filter out the feelings that aren't coming from their intuition helps them focus on what is.

They give their intuition some space. Gut instincts can't be forced. Our intuition works best when we're not pressuring it to come up with a solution. Albert Einstein said he got his best ideas while sailing, and when Steve Jobs was faced with a tough problem, he'd head out for a walk.

They build a track record. People who deal well with uncertainty take the time to practice their intuition. They start by listening to their gut on small things and seeing how it goes so that they'll know whether they can trust it when something big comes around.

Have contingency plans. Staying on top of uncertainty is as much about planning for failure as it is about hoping for the best. Experts at handling uncertainty aren't afraid to admit that they could be wrong, and that frees them up to make detailed, rational, and transparent contingency plans before taking action. Emotionally intelligent people know they aren't always going to make the right decision. They know how to absorb and understand mistakes so that they can make better decisions in the future. And they never let mistakes get them down for too long.

BRINGING IT ALL TOGETHER

The science is clear: Intuition is a powerful force of the mind that can help us make better decisions. With repercussions that can last days, weeks, and even years, making great decisions is an effort that's worth every bit of your time and energy. The ability to strategically manage ambiguity is one of the most important skills you can cultivate in an increasingly uncertain world. You can't make great decisions without emotional intelligence. By putting good habits in place, you will harness the power of your intuition and greatly improve the quality of your decision-making.

20

Crush Cognitive Biases

The human brain is a natural wonder. It produces more than 50,000 thoughts each day and 100,000 chemical reactions each second. With this amount of processing power, you might think your judgment would be highly accurate, but that's far from the case. Our judgments are often inaccurate because our brains rely on cognitive biases instead of hard evidence. Cognitive bias is the tendency to make irrational judgments in consistent patterns. Researchers have found that cognitive bias wreaks havoc by forcing people to make poor choices:

- A Queensland University study found that blonde women earned, on average, 7% higher salaries than redheads and brunettes.

- A Duke study found that people with "mature" faces experienced more career success than those with "baby" faces. "Baby" faces were defined as those with small chins, wider cheeks, and bigger eyes. "Mature" faces were those with bigger chins, narrower facial features, and smaller eyes.

- A Yale study found that female scientists were not only more likely to hire male scientists but also paid them $4,000 more than female scientists.

It's highly unlikely that the people in these studies actually wanted to pay blondes more money, enable people with mature faces to succeed at the expense of those with baby faces, or hire male scientists disproportionally and pay them more money. Our unconscious biases are often so strong that they lead us to act in ways that are inconsistent with reason as well as our values and beliefs. This can be a major detriment to emotional intelligence.

Let's explore some of the most common types of cognitive biases that entrench themselves in our lives. Awareness is the best way to beat these biases, so pay careful attention to how they influence you. Don't allow them to hinder your emotional intelligence.

Confirmation bias. Confirmation bias is the tendency to seek out information that supports our pre-existing beliefs. In other words, we form an opinion first and then seek out evidence to back it up, rather than basing our opinions on facts. Social media apps have been accused of using this bias to keep us engaged by loading our feeds with what we already believe, rather than challenging us with new information.

Fundamental attribution error. This is the tendency to attribute situational behavior to a person's fixed personality. For example, people often attribute another person's poor work performance to laziness when there are so many other possible explanations. It could be that the individual in question is receiving projects they aren't passionate about, their rocky home life is carrying over to their work life, or they're burned out. When you're the one being lazy, you don't assume it's a character flaw. You attribute this to the situation you're in. That's how the fundamental attribution error works.

The decoy effect. This occurs when someone believes they have two options, but you present a third option to make the second one feel more palatable. For example, you visit a car lot to consider two cars, one listed for $30,000 and one for $40,000. At first, the $40,000 car seems expensive, so the salesman shows you a $65,000 car. Suddenly, the $40,000 car seems reasonable by comparison. This salesman is preying on your decoy bias—the decoy being the $65,000 car that he knows you won't buy.

The ideometer effect. This refers to the fact that our thoughts can make us feel real emotions. This is why actors envision terrible scenarios, such as the death of a loved one, in order to make themselves cry on cue. It's also why activities such as cataloging what you're grateful for can have such a profound, positive impact on your well-being.

The halo effect. The halo effect occurs when someone creates a strong first impression and that impression sticks. This is extremely noticeable in grading. For example, often a teacher grades a student's first paper, and if it's good, the teacher is prone to continue giving the student high marks for future papers even if their performance doesn't warrant it. The same thing happens at work and in personal relationships.

The horn effect. This effect is the exact opposite of the halo effect. When you perform poorly at first, you can easily get pegged as a low performer, even if you work hard enough to disprove that notion.

Conservatism bias. This bias leads people to believe that pre-existing information takes precedence over new information. Don't be quick to reject something just because it's radical or different. Great ideas usually are.

Affect heuristic. Affect heuristic is the human tendency to base our decisions on our emotions. For example, consider a study conducted at Shukutoku University, Japan. Participants judged a disease that killed 1,286 people out of every 10,000 as being more dangerous than one that was 24.14% fatal (despite this representing twice as many deaths). People reacted emotionally to the image of 1,286 people dying, whereas the percentage didn't arouse the same mental imagery and emotions.

The ostrich effect. The ostrich effect is aptly named after the mistaken belief that ostriches, when scared, literally bury their heads in the ground. This effect describes our tendency to hide from impending problems. We may not physically bury our heads in the ground, but we might as well. For example, if your company is experiencing layoffs or you're having relationship issues, it's common to attempt to push all these problems away, rather than face them head on. This never works.

Reactance. Reactance is our tendency to react to rules and regulations by exercising our freedom. A prevalent example of this is children with overbearing parents. Tell a teenager to do what you say because you told them so, and they're very likely to start breaking your rules. Similarly, employees who feel mistreated or "Big Brothered" by their employers are more likely to take longer breaks, use extra sick days, or even steal from their company.

Planning fallacy. Planning fallacy is the tendency to think that we can do things more quickly than we actually can. For procrastinators, this leads to incomplete work, and this makes Type As overpromise and underdeliver.

The bandwagon effect. The bandwagon effect is the tendency to do what everyone else is doing. This creates a kind of groupthink, where people run with the first idea that's put onto the table instead of exploring a variety of options. The bandwagon effect illustrates how we like to make decisions based on what feels good (doing what everyone else is doing), even when it's a poor alternative.

Bias blind spot. If you begin to feel that you've mastered your biases, keep in mind that you're most likely experiencing the bias blind spot. This is the tendency to see biases in other people but not in yourself.

PSYCHOLOGICAL FORCES THAT MAKE GOOD PEOPLE DO BAD THINGS

Given the right circumstances, good people can get caught up in some very bad things. More often than not, psychology is to blame. When it comes to unethical behavior, good people don't tend to go right off the deep end like Bernie Madoff, Sam Bankman-Fried, or Elizabeth Holmes. Rather, the mind plays tricks on them, pushing them down the slippery slope of questionable behavior. Dr. Muel Kaptein, Professor of Business Ethics and Integrity Management at the Rotterdam School of Management, has studied bad behavior for decades. A study he published sheds considerable light on what motivates good people to do bad things. The following are eight of Dr. Kaptein's most compelling findings. They provide great insight into how the mind tricks good people, through cognitive biases, into losing their moral compass and going astray.

The compensation effect. The compensation effect refers to people's tendency to assume that they accumulate moral capital. We use good deeds to balance out bad deeds, or alternately, we give ourselves breaks from goodness, like a piece of chocolate cake after a week of salads. This makes people more inclined to do bad things under the guise of "I'm a good person" or "It's just this one thing." A great example of this is a study in which people were observed lying and cheating more after they made the decision to purchase products that were good for the environment.

Cognitive dissonance. Cognitive dissonance is the discomfort humans feel when they hold two contradictory opinions or when their behavior is inconsistent with their beliefs. It's one of the strongest psychological forces driving human behavior. When people who feel they are good do bad things, cognitive dissonance makes them ignore this behavior because they can't tolerate the inconsistency between their behavior and their beliefs. This only leads to more bad behavior.

The power of names. What you name something is important, because it can skew people's sense of reality. If companies assign unethical practices simple and humorous euphemisms (like "financial engineering" for accounting fraud), employees are less likely to take their unethical behavior seriously. Thomas Watson, the founder of IBM, was famous for saying, "Doing business is a game, the greatest game in the world if you know how to play it." Something as simple as calling business a game can make people less likely to see that their actions have serious real-world consequences.

Obedience to authority. It's quite difficult for most people to ignore the wishes of those in positions of authority. People also feel that they're less responsible for wrongdoings if they act under the direction of someone else. Both reasons explain why employees are likely to act out the unethical wishes of their supervisors—and feel far less guilt than if they had decided to do it themselves.

The Pygmalion effect. The Pygmalion effect refers to people's tendency to act the way that other people treat them. For example, if employees are treated like they're upright members of a team, they're more likely to act accordingly. Alternately, if they're treated with suspicion, they're more likely to act in a way that justifies that perception.

The pressure to conform. The pressure to conform is powerful. When a group engages in unethical behavior, individuals are far more likely to participate in or condone that behavior rather than risk standing out.

Conspicuous consumption. When companies splash money around, they contribute to unethical behavior. Flashy displays of wealth lead to increased selfishness. Employees either aim hard for these carrots or develop jealousy of their high-rolling colleagues who achieve them. This leads to people who are more likely to put their own needs ahead of doing the right thing.

The blinding effect of power. People in power typically see themselves as inherently different from their employees. This can lead them to set ethical boundaries for their employees that are more stringent than the ones they set for themselves. What happens next is the stuff of newspaper headlines.

BRINGING IT ALL TOGETHER

Recognizing and understanding bias is invaluable because it enables you to think more objectively and interact more effectively with other people. Incorporating your knowledge of biases into your approach to people can help you be more introspective and greatly increase your emotional intelligence. Some biases can lead to really bad behavior, and we ignore them at our peril. Perhaps the most shocking thing about these mistakes is the simple, almost mundane conditions that can contribute to them. Thankfully, a little bit of knowledge goes a long way in removing yourself from environments that contribute to this behavior.

21

Make Your Relationships Last

—

A new relationship—whether personal, romantic, or professional—is a lot like buying a new car. Driving it off the lot is pure bliss. As you look around, you can scarcely take it all in. Everything smells, sounds, and looks terrific. You coast through weeks or months—maybe even years—of happy driving before you're aware of anything that needs fixing. And like a car, when a relationship breaks down, it's overwhelming. You're left stuck on the side of the road, wondering what went wrong.

A trained eye knows when a car is in trouble. From the sound of the idle to the color of the exhaust exiting the tailpipe, there are telltale signs of distress. The same is true of relationships, and you can use your emotional intelligence to be your own mechanic. Researchers at the University of Washington discovered four clear indicators of relationship failure (dubbed "The Four Horsemen of the Apocalypse") so profound that they predict the future success of a relationship with 93% accuracy. The researchers conducted their studies with married couples, and their accuracy rate for predicting divorce has held up for more than 14 years after watching the couples interact.

THE FOUR HORSEMEN OF THE APOCALYPSE

The Four Horsemen reveal problems for relationships of all types, not just romantic ones. They represent the counterproductive acts we can easily fall victim to when our emotions get the better of us. As you read each of the Horsemen and consider its relevance in your relationships, remember that conflict itself is not a problem. Conflict is actually a normal and (ideally) productive part of two people with different needs and interests coming together. The researchers found that the amount of conflict between two people had no bearing on the success of the relationship. How conflict is handled determines a relationship's success, and the Four Horsemen's presence means that conflict is not being dealt with constructively or productively.

The First Horseman: Criticism

Criticism is not to be confused with delivering feedback or otherwise seeking improvement or change in another person. Criticism becomes, well, criticism when it isn't constructive ("Your driving is terrible."). Criticism, in its most troubling form, focuses on the individual's personality, character, or interests rather than the specific action or behavior you'd like to see changed ("You are terrible at driving. You are too timid for it."). It's one thing to criticize without being constructive; it's another to go after someone for something they are unable to change.

If you find yourself criticizing when you planned on being constructive, it's best if you don't deliver your feedback and commentary unless you've planned ahead. You'll need to think through what you're going to say and stick to your script to remain constructive and avoid criticism. It's also best if you focus your feedback on a single specific behavior, as your reactions to multiple behaviors at once can easily be perceived as criticism. Try to deliver feedback in a bite-sized, actionable strategy that the receiver can work to implement. If you find that you cannot deliver feedback without generalizing it to the other person's personality, you're better off saying nothing at all.

The Second Horseman: Contempt

Contempt is any open sign of disrespect toward another person. Contempt often involves comments that aim to take the other person down a notch, as well as direct insults. Contempt is also seen in indirect and veiled forms, such as rolling your eyes and couching insults within "humor." Contempt makes people feel disliked or even hated. It's often hard for those on the receiving end of contempt to understand where it's coming from.

Contempt stems from a lack of interest in another person. When you find that you don't enjoy or admire someone (perhaps there are things about them that used to be interesting or charming, and now they've lost their luster), contempt can surface unexpectedly. If your disinterest is unavoidable, and the relationship isn't going anywhere (such as a family member or coworker), then you need to focus on finding common ground. Common ground, no matter how small, is a commodity to be sought and cherished. In the immortal words of Abraham Lincoln, "I do not like that man. I must get to know him better."

The Third Horseman: Defensiveness

Denying responsibility, making excuses, meeting one complaint with another, and other forms of defensiveness are problematic in any relationship. They prevent conflict from reaching any sort of resolution. Defensiveness accelerates the anxiety and tension experienced by both parties, which makes it difficult to focus on the larger issues at hand that need to be resolved.

To overcome defensiveness, you first need to be aware of when you're the one being defensive. This sounds easy but can be quite difficult, as most of us feel our defensive behavior is justified. When you catch yourself being defensive, you must be willing to stop and listen carefully to the other party's complaint, even if you don't see things the same way. This doesn't mean you have to agree with them. Instead, focus on fully understanding the other person's perspective so that you can work together to resolve the conflict. It's critical that you work to remain calm. Once you understand why the other person is upset, it's much easier to find common ground than if you dismiss their opinions defensively.

The Fourth Horseman: Stonewalling

Stonewalling is what happens when a person shuts the discussion down by refusing to respond. Examples of stonewalling include the silent treatment, being emotionally distant or devoid of emotion, and ignoring the other person completely. Stonewalling is problematic because it aggravates the person being stonewalled and prevents the two from working on resolving the conflict together.

The key to overcoming stonewalling is to participate in the discussion. If you're stonewalling because the circumstances are leaving you feeling overwhelmed, let the other person know how you feel and ask for some time to think before continuing the discussion. If you stonewall as a matter of practice, you need to realize that participating in discussions and working together to resolve conflict are the only ways to keep your relationships from crumbling.

REPAIRING A DAMAGED RELATIONSHIP

My grandfather was blind most of my life. After several decades of farming the sandy soil in eastern South Dakota, he contracted a disease that destroyed his vision. When I was in my early 20s and he in his 90s, he was a wonderfully captive audience for questions about relationships. He was a worthy target for my barrage of questions—he had been married to the same person for more than 70 years. He and my grandmother compared their relationship to their many years spent farming: Proper focus plus hard work pulled them through difficult times. More than just sticking with it, they actively worked together and reaped the benefits of seven decades of love and companionship.

When they reminisced about the bond that held them together, they spoke of an allegiance to compromise. Whether raising young children during the height of the Great Depression or being trapped indoors for days during the great blizzard of '62, they invested energy in repairing arguments, as opposed to intensifying them. Even during conflict, they shared a commitment to finding and understanding the other person's perspective. They were able to tend to each other as they did their fields of corn—they avoided the slash-and-burn technique at all costs. Their enduring search for common ground kept them together all those years.

Relationships are tough, especially when they're damaged. If you want to know how to repair a damaged relationship, you first need to remember that the frequency of conflict has no bearing on the quality of a relationship. Conflict is a normal part of two people with different needs, interests, and motivations coming together. How conflict is handled determines the quality and ultimate success of a relationship. Researchers at the University of Washington (the same researchers who predicted the future success of a relationship with 93% accuracy) discovered that successful relationships address conflict using a single technique—a technique that's so effective at addressing conflict that it's called a repair.

A repair is a gesture that shows respect and concern for each other despite the disagreement. Repairs take many forms, but all are aimed at resolving the conflict together—as opposed to winning the conflict on your own. A repair can be anything from suggesting a compromise to owning your half of the situation to voicing respect for the other party, or even using humor to break the tension. In the heat of an argument, a repair sends an instant signal that you think the other person is important, you respect them, and you're willing to put the good of the relationship ahead of your self-interest. Repairs don't just improve the outcome of the conflicts you weave them into; they inject health into relationships that have been damaged by discord.

Repairs are critical because many disagreements between partners are based on permanent differences of opinion. If you think it's best to shut off the air conditioner at 6 p.m. on hot summer days to save money, and your spouse thinks the best time is 8 p.m., neither one of you will ever be right. But that won't stop you from arguing about it all summer. Disagreements are a given. It's what you do about them that matters. A repair can be anything from suggesting a compromise ("This summer, let's turn the air conditioner off at 7 p.m.") to owning your half of the situation ("I realize that turning it off at 6 p.m. makes the house hot during dinner") to using humor to break the tension ("You know we wouldn't have this problem if we lived in Alaska"). A repair attempt sends the powerful signal that you care, you respect your partner, and your love is more important than proving you are right.

It's safe to assume that we've all had conversations that could use repairs. Simple discussions can break into disagreements or get stuck going around in circles. In these broken conversations, past mistakes are brought to the surface, regretful comments are made, and blame is prevalent. No matter who said what, or who "started it," it's time to refocus and fix it. It's time for you to step back, quickly assess the situation, and begin repairing the conversation. Repairs happen in a four-step process. If you're new to repairs, you'll likely be conscious of each step. Once you get some practice under your belt, the steps will blend together, and the entire process will feel smooth and seamless.

Step 1: Take Your Emotions Out of the Driver's Seat

A repair is an act of moving beyond the expression of anger, resentment, and hostility toward the other party. Your first hope for a successful repair lies in your self-awareness. You cannot improve an argument if you are being thrown over a barrel by your emotions. Disagreements bring your emotions rushing to the surface, and you cannot perform a repair unless you understand them. Do not waste time feeling guilty about your feelings. Just focus your energy on understanding them for what they are. If you find your emotions are so strong that it's hard to think clearly, it is probably best to save the discussion for later. If you're so emotional that you are getting tunnel vision, feeling sick, or just in a haze, the most successful repair is explaining to the other party that you feel overwhelmed and need some time to cool off and get your thoughts together before continuing. Your argument isn't going anywhere, so don't pressure yourself into a discussion when you can't think clearly.

Step 2: Take a Look at the Field from the Other Sideline

If you are composed enough to have some perspective on the situation, you can initiate the next step in a repair. Focus your thoughts on what things must be like standing in the other person's shoes. Not what you think they are like; rather, imagine what the other person is thinking and feeling. What's important to them, and how is that driving their behavior? You can't launch a successful repair until you fully understand why the other person is doing whatever it is they're doing. To make a repair, you have to show the other person that you care about how things look from their point of view, even if you do not agree with their perspective. This can't happen until you actually see their perspective. To do this, you need to let go of the blame and focus on the repair. Do you want to be right, or do you want a resolution? Move beyond thinking of ways you can convince the other party of your opinions, and ask yourself what you can do to honor their feelings. Respecting another's opinions, right or wrong, is the key to compromise.

Step 3: Make a Repair and Evaluate Its Effectiveness

At this stage, all you can do is craft your repair and give it a whirl. Keep in mind that an effective repair will:

- Show respect for the other party.
- Show concern for the other party's perspective.
- Find common ground.
- Be neutral in tone.

The look of a successful repair is as varied as the problems it can solve. A repair that works in one situation, with one person, may just make things worse in another. Saying, "What exactly do you mean by that?" can sound like you're minimizing the issues in the middle of one argument and be received as a sign of wanting to make things better in another. To repair successfully, arm yourself with the knowledge that many attempts will crash and burn. Even an empathetic comment like "I understand what you're saying" can be perceived as belittling if the other party is defensive or not accustomed to you saying this. Be ready to try multiple repairs in a single argument and expect that they will not all go off without a hitch. People with the best skills in repairing disagreements are the ones who try the most often. The more you attempt repairs, the more the other party will be receptive and do the same. Your persistence will pay off because it is a demonstration of your desire to meet in the middle and understand each other.

Step 4: Discuss Repairs Together

Discussing repairs together will also help your relationship. If you can talk about improving your arguments, you are both more likely to initiate repairs the next time you have one. When repair attempts are always one-sided, the relationship usually fails. Both parties need to work toward resolving challenges together. When you talk about repairs, you develop an understanding that they're important. Even if the other party has trouble making repairs the next time the two of you argue, they will likely recognize your effort and realize it is an attempt to make things better.

TEACHING CHILDREN SELF-LEADERSHIP

Perhaps the only relationship that's as important as the one you have with your significant other is your relationship with your children. Although we have many roles as parents, much of what we do is driven by a desire to ensure that our children are equipped to live a fulfilling life. We want our children to grow to be courageous, passionate, and authentic. We want them to get more out of life than they ever thought possible. We want them to be emotionally intelligent. As parents and caretakers of children, we hold their path to self-leadership in our hands. We can model and teach the skills that will equip them to be inspired and lead themselves in this hyper-competitive world, or we can allow them to fall victim to the status quo. It's a big responsibility—but when isn't being a parent a massive responsibility?

One of the best things you can do to improve the quality of your relationship with your children is to teach them emotional intelligence through self-leadership. The beauty of teaching children self-leadership is that it's the little things we do every day that mold them into the people they'll become. Focus on the seven habits that follow, and you'll build emotional intelligence in your children and improve your relationship in the process.

Allow them to experience risk and failure. Success in life is often driven by risk. When parents go overboard protecting their children, they don't allow them to take risks and reap the consequences. When you aren't allowed to fail, you don't understand risk. A person can't take appropriate risks until they know the bitter taste of failure that comes with risking it all and coming up short. The road to success is paved with failure. When you try to shield your children from failure to boost their self-esteem, they have trouble tolerating the failure required to succeed. Don't rub their faces in it, either. Children need your support when they fail. They need to know you care. They need to know *that you know* how much failure stings. Your support allows them to embrace the intensity of the experience *and* to know that they'll make it through it all right. That, right there, is solid character building.

Don't overpraise. Children need praise to build a healthy sense of self-esteem. Unfortunately, piling on the praise doesn't give them *extra* self-esteem. Children need to believe in themselves and develop the self-confidence required to become successful, but gushing every time they put pen to paper or kick a ball (the "everyone gets a trophy" mentality) creates confusion and false confidence. *Always* show your children how proud you are of their passion and effort. Just don't paint them as superstars when you know it isn't true.

Say no. Overindulging children is a surefire way to limit their development. To succeed, one must be able to delay gratification and work hard for things that are really important. Children need to develop this patience. They need to set goals and experience the joy that comes with working diligently toward them. Saying no to your children will disappoint them momentarily, but they'll get over that. They'll never get over being spoiled.

Let children solve their own problems. There's a certain self-sufficiency that comes with being a self-leader. When you're the one making the calls, you should also be the one who needs to stay behind and clean up the mess these create. When parents constantly solve their children's problems for them, they never develop the critical ability to stand on their own two feet. Children who always have someone swooping in to rescue them and clean up their mess spend their whole lives waiting for this to happen. Leaders take action. They take charge. They're responsible and accountable. Make certain your children are, as well.

Don't obsess about achievement. Parents get sucked into obsessing about achievement because they believe that this will make their children into high achievers. Instead, fixating on achievement creates all sorts of problems for kids. This is especially true when it comes to self-leadership, where focusing on individual achievement gives kids the wrong idea about how things get done. Simply put, the best leaders surround themselves with great people because they know they can't do it alone. Achievement-obsessed children are so focused on awards and outcomes that they never fully understand this. All they can see is the player who's handed the MVP trophy and the celebrity CEO who makes the news—they assume it's all about the individual. It's a rude awakening once they discover how real life works.

Walk your talk. Emotionally intelligent self-leaders are transparent and forthcoming. They aren't perfect, but they earn people's respect by walking their talk. Your children can develop this quality naturally, but only if it's something they see you demonstrate. To be authentic, you must be honest in all things, not just in what you say and do but also in who you are. When you walk your talk, your words and actions will align with who you claim to be. Your children will see this and aspire to do the same.

Show you're human. No matter how indignant and defiant your children are at any moment, you're still their hero and their model for the future. This can make you want to hide your past mistakes for fear that they'll be enticed to repeat them. The opposite is true. When you don't show any vulnerability, your children develop intense guilt about every failure because they believe that they're the only ones to make such terrible mistakes. To develop self-leadership, children need to know that the people they look up to aren't infallible. Leaders must be able to process their mistakes, learn from them, and move forward to be better people. Children can't do this when they're overcome by guilt. They need someone—a real, vulnerable person—to teach them how to process mistakes and learn from them. When you show them how you've done this in the past, you're doing just that.

BRINGING IT ALL TOGETHER

Recognizing the Four Horsemen is the first step to improving your relationships. The presence of a Horseman is a sign that your relationship is struggling and you need to take action. Repairs are the actions you take to make things better. Great relationships are driven by this recognition of challenges, followed by a willingness to take constructive steps to make things better. When both parties can spot the Horsemen and initiate repairs in response to them, the relationship builds an unshakable strength.

Perhaps no relationship you have in life is more important than the one you have with your children. We can mold our children to be capable and lead themselves, but only if we work at it. We must model emotionally intelligent behavior that enables them to be resilient, authentic, and good problem solvers. Few things in life are as worth your time and effort as this.

- Become a Great Leader
- Increase Your Productivity
- Practice Mindfulness
- Get Motivated
- Make Your Workplace a Better Place
- Survive a Bad Boss
- Learn Your Lesson
- Break the Bad Habits That Are Holding You Back
- Build Powerful New Success Habits
- Master Conflict
- Master Communication
- Beat Procrastination
- Accelerate Your Climb Up the Corporate Ladder
- Be Persuasive and Get Your Point Across
- Avoid Integrity Traps
- Create True Work-Life Balance

PART TWO

EMOTIONAL INTELLIGENCE AT WORK

—

22

Become a Great Leader

eadership is the art of persuasion—the act of motivating people to do more than they ever thought possible in pursuit of a greater good. It has nothing to do with your title. It has nothing to do with authority or seniority. You're not a leader just because you have people reporting to you. And you don't suddenly become a leader once you reach a certain pay grade. A true leader influences others to be their best. Leadership is about social influence, not positional power. You don't even need to have people reporting to you to be a leader. A janitor can influence people and lead just like a CEO can. In the words of John Quincy Adams, "If your actions inspire others to dream more, learn more, do more and become more, you are a leader."

Likewise, anyone can become a follower, even while holding a leadership position. If you're a slave to the status quo, lack vision, or don't motivate everyone around you to be their absolute best, then you're a follower. Even if you happen to have a leadership title, people won't follow you when they see those behaviors present. A senior executive who creates unnecessary bureaucracy, locks himself in his office, and fails to interact with others in any meaningful way is no more a leader than an antisocial software engineer who refuses to do anything but write code.

Of course, the real question is—are *you* a leader or a follower? The habits that define great leaders are covered later in this chapter. You can compare yourself to them and see if you do them naturally. For now, ask yourself some very important questions. Think carefully as you respond to each one, and you'll soon know for certain whether you're a leader or a follower.

Do you go above and beyond?

Followers do their jobs, and that's it. No matter how good they may be at those jobs, it rarely occurs to them to go beyond their basic functions. Leaders, however, see their job descriptions as the bare minimum—the foundation on which they build greatness. Leaders see their real role as adding value, and they add it whenever and wherever they see an opportunity.

Are you confident?

Followers see the talents and accomplishments of other people as a threat. Leaders see those talents and accomplishments as an asset. Leaders want to make things better, and they'll take help anywhere they can find it. Leaders are true team players. They aren't afraid to admit that they need other people to be strong where they're weak.

Are you optimistic?

Followers see the limitations inherent in any situation; leaders see the possibilities. When things go wrong, leaders don't dwell on how bad things are. They're too busy trying to make things better.

Are you open to change?

Followers are content to stick with the safety of the status quo. They see change as frightening and troublesome. Leaders are maximizers who see opportunity in change. Because leaders want constant improvement, they're never afraid to ask, "What's next?"

Are you decisive?

Followers often hesitate to act, out of fear that they'll do the wrong thing. Leaders aren't afraid to make a call, even when they're not sure if it's the right one. They'd rather make a decision and be wrong than suffer from the paralysis of indecision.

Are you accountable?

When mistakes are made, followers are quick to blame their circumstances and other people. Leaders, however, are quick to accept accountability for their actions. They don't worry that admitting fault might make them look bad, because they know that shifting the blame would just make them look worse.

Are you unflappable?

Followers often let obstacles and mishaps throw them off course. When something goes wrong, they assume the whole project is doomed. Leaders expect obstacles and love to be challenged. They know that even the best-laid plans can run into unexpected problems, so they take problems in stride and stay the course.

Are you humble?

Followers are always chasing glory. Leaders are humble. They don't allow any authority they may have to make them feel that they are better than anyone else. Thus, they don't hesitate to jump in and do the dirty work when needed, and they won't ask anyone to do anything they wouldn't be willing to do themselves.

Are you passionate?

Followers are trapped in the daily grind. They go to work and complete their tasks so that they can go home at the end of the day and resume their real lives. Leaders love what they do and see their work as an important part of—not a weak substitute for—real life. Their job isn't just what they do; it's an important part of who they are.

Are you motivated from within?

Followers are motivated only by external factors: the next title, the next raise, the next gain in status. Leaders are internally motivated. They don't work for status or possessions. They are motivated to excel because it's who they are. True leaders keep pushing forward, even when there's no carrot dangling in front of them.

Do you focus on titles?

Followers care a lot about titles, both their own and those of the people they work with. They're very conscious of who outranks whom because they lack the skill and motivation to create leadership from within. Leaders, however, focus on what each individual brings to the table, regardless of what's printed on a business card.

Are you focused on people?

Followers focus on what they can achieve individually. Leaders are team players because they know that greatness is a collective feat. A leader is only as good as what they can achieve through other people.

Are you willing to learn?

Leaders, although confident, know that they're neither superhuman nor infallible. They're not afraid to admit when they don't know something, and they're willing to learn from anyone who can teach them, whether that person is a subordinate, a peer, or a superior. Followers are too busy trying to prove that they're competent to learn anything from anyone else.

THE DEFINING HABITS OF GREAT LEADERS

No one wants to work for leaders who aren't transparent and competent. After all, they play a big role in our future paths. Human beings crave certainty. Your brain is so geared up for certainty that your subconscious can monitor and store more than two million data points, which your brain uses to predict the future. That isn't just a neat little side trick—it's the primary purpose of your neocortex, which is 76% of your brain's total mass. Your brain rewards you for certainty. If our nomadic ancestors were anxious about where their next meal was coming from, finding it would result in increased dopamine levels in their brains, in addition to a full stomach. You get the same rush from listening to music that has a predictable repeating pattern or from completing a puzzle. Predictability satisfies our craving for certainty.

In business, things change so quickly that there's a great deal of uncertainty about what's going to happen next. Uncertainty takes up a lot of people's mental energy and makes them less effective at their jobs. Great leaders use emotional intelligence to demonstrate conviction and create an environment of certainty and stability for everyone. When a leader is absolutely convinced that they've chosen the best course of action, everyone who follows them unconsciously absorbs this belief and the accompanying emotional state. Mirror neurons are responsible for this involuntary response. They mirror the emotional states of other people—especially those we look to for guidance. This ensures that leaders with conviction put us at ease. Leaders with conviction show us that the future is certain and that we're all headed in the right direction. Their certainty is neurologically shared by everyone. When leaders have conviction, people's brains can relax, so to speak, letting them concentrate on what needs to be done. When people feel more secure about their future, they're happier and produce higher-quality work.

Conviction is critical, but it isn't an all-encompassing quality. Many other qualities contribute to conviction and help make a leader great. Nevertheless, great leadership can be difficult to pin down and understand. You know a great leader when you're working for one, but even they can have a hard time explaining the specifics of what they do that makes their leadership so effective. Great leaders change us for the better. They see more in us than we see in ourselves, and they help us learn to see it, too. They dream big and show us all the great things we can accomplish.

When I ask audiences to describe the best and worst leaders they've worked for, they inevitably ignore innate characteristics (intelligence, extraversion, attractiveness, etc.) and instead focus on qualities that are completely under the leader's control, such as passion, insight, and honesty. Most of the habits they describe are products of emotional intelligence. This means that all of us can study the unique habits of great leaders and learn and improve. Great leadership is founded on good habits. Through a leader's actions (what they do and say on a daily basis), the essence of their leadership becomes apparent. Behavior can change, and leaders who work to improve their habits get results. The following are the essential habits that exceptional leaders rely on every day. Give them a try and see where they take your leadership skills.

Great leaders are passionate. Few things are more demotivating than a leader who is bored with their life and job. If the boss doesn't care, why should anybody else? Great leaders are passionate about what they do. They believe in what they're trying to accomplish, and they have fun doing it. This makes everyone else want to join the ride. Passion and enthusiasm are contagious. So are boredom and apathy. No one wants to work for a boss who's unexcited about their job, or one who's just going through the motions.

Great leaders play chess, not checkers. Think about the difference. In checkers, all the pieces are basically the same. That's a poor model for leadership, because nobody wants to feel like a faceless cog in the proverbial wheel. In chess, however, each piece has a unique role, unique abilities, and unique limitations. Great leaders are like great chess masters. They recognize what's unique about each member of their team. They know their strengths, weaknesses, likes, and dislikes, and they use these insights to draw the very best from each individual.

They are a port in a storm. Great leaders don't get rattled, even when everything is going haywire. Under immense pressure, they act like Eugene Kranz, flight director for the Apollo 13 mission. In the moments after the explosion, when death looked certain, and panic seemed like the only option, Kranz kept his cool, saying, "Okay, now, let's everybody keep cool. Let's solve the problem, but let's not make it any worse by guessing." In those initial moments, he had no idea how they were going to get the astronauts home, but as he later explained, "You do not pass uncertainty down to your team members." People who've worked for a great leader often look back later and marvel at their coolness under pressure. That's why, more than 50 years after Apollo 13, people are still talking about Eugene Kranz and his leadership during that crisis.

They are who they are all the time. Great leaders don't lie to cover up their mistakes, and they don't make false promises. Their people don't have to exert energy trying to figure out their motives or predict what they're going to do next. Equally important, they don't hide things they have the freedom to disclose. Instead of hoarding information and being secretive to boost their own power, they share information and knowledge generously. Have you ever worked for an information hoarder? Some bosses seem to think that every piece of information they share reduces their authority. In fact, just the opposite is true: Great bosses know that sharing information empowers their employees, instead of diluting their own power.

They are empathetic. Bad leaders see their employees only from the perspective of how they reflect on them. If their employees are doing a great job, they look good; if their employees are performing poorly, they look bad. Great leaders, however, see their employees as more than just extensions of themselves. They're able to get inside their employees' skins and under-stand things from their perspective. That doesn't mean they're pushovers, or that they just say, "Oh, sorry you're having a bad day; don't worry about that deadline." But it does mean that they recognize that their employees are human and treat them as such.

They look for and celebrate wins. Bad leaders think the work their employees do is something the employees owe them. After all, they're get-ting paychecks, right? That's true—but great leaders look past work as a transactional relationship and realize that people are putting a huge part of themselves into the work they do. They say thank you, even if it is "just part of the job." Great leaders don't have a "Why should I praise you for doing your job?" attitude. They look for reasons to praise their employees, both privately and publicly, and they take the time to celebrate milestones, instead of just driving everybody on to the next project or deadline. They understand that getting a paycheck doesn't cancel out that inherent need to feel valued and appreciated.

They create a sense of purpose. Whereas vision is a clear idea of where you're going, a sense of purpose refers to an understanding of why you're going there. People like to feel like they're part of something bigger than themselves. Great leaders give people that feeling. I think Ken Kesey said it well: "You don't lead by pointing and telling people some place to go. You lead by going to that place and making a case."

They are accountable. Bad leaders are quick to point their fingers when something goes wrong. Great leaders understand that a large part of their job is being accountable for the team's performance. They know that this just goes along with accepting a leadership role. That doesn't mean that they don't offer the team feedback on what's going wrong, but it does mean that they take the blame publicly. Even privately, they see the team's failure as a failure of leadership on their part, and they act quickly to correct it.

They are approachable. You know those people who have time for you only if you can do something for them? Great leaders truly believe that everyone, regardless of rank or ability, is worth their time and attention. They make everyone feel valuable because they believe that everyone is valuable. Great leaders make it clear that they welcome challenges, criticism, and viewpoints other than their own. They know that an environment in which people are afraid to speak up, offer insight, and ask good questions is destined for failure. By ensuring that they're approachable, great leaders facilitate the flow of great ideas throughout the organization.

They're self-aware. Leaders' gaps in self-awareness are rarely because they're deceitful, have Machiavellian motives, or have severe character deficits. In most cases, leaders—like everyone else—view themselves in a more favorable light than other people do. Self-awareness is the foundation of emotional intelligence, a skill that 90% of top-performing leaders possess in abundance. Great leaders' high self-awareness means they have a clear and accurate image not only of their leadership style but also of their own strengths and weaknesses. They know where they shine and where they're weak, and they have effective strategies for leaning into their strengths and compensating for their weaknesses.

They respect your time. Great leaders don't give you the impression that their time is more valuable than yours. They don't keep you waiting for scheduled meetings. They show up prepared and get to the point, instead of trying to impress you. And they don't goof off on your time. It's not that they're unwilling to have fun at work, but they don't do it at your expense, causing you extra stress or making it necessary for you to stay late to catch up.

They don't forget that people have lives outside of work. Bad leaders tend to see people as one-dimensional: They show up and get the work done, and the boss doesn't have to worry about them again until the next day. Great leaders, however, never forget that work is just one facet of their employees' lives. They never forget that they have families, friends, hobbies, and other interests and obligations outside of work, and they don't infringe on their "real" lives—by asking someone to work late, for example—without a very good reason. And when they do have a good reason, they acknowledge that they're asking for a sacrifice and express their gratitude accordingly.

They create leaders. Have you ever noticed how sometimes all the promotions come from within one manager's team? That's no accident. Great leaders pull the very best out of their people. They inspire, coach, and lean into people's strengths, and when their employees are ready for new challenges, they gladly send them on their way.

GREAT LEADERS' HABITS ARE DRIVEN BY THEIR BELIEFS

John Wooden, considered by many to be the greatest collegiate basketball coach of all time, once said, "I am just a common man who is true to his beliefs." He was absolutely right—a leader's actions are driven by their beliefs.

A leader's beliefs become their habits, and those habits are the essence of how they lead people. A leader's beliefs are established through time and reflection. Once a belief becomes deep seeded, it's hard for a leader to shake. This creates problems when a leader holds a belief that, even if well-intentioned, is hard on morale. Still, there's always an opposing, positive belief that the same leader can adopt and incorporate into their belief system to make the workplace a better place.

Great leaders are emotionally intelligent, and they believe in their people, first and foremost. This belief drives them to create an environment in which people thrive. Let's explore some of the driving beliefs that set great leaders apart from the rest of the pack.

Growth should be encouraged, not feared. Average bosses fear their smartest, hardest-working employees, believing that these individuals will surpass them or make them look bad. They hesitate to share information or to enable authority. Exceptional bosses, however, love to see their employees grow. They're always grooming their replacements and doing whatever they can to create leaders. Research shows that the number one thing job seekers look for in a position is growth opportunity and that 80% of all job growth occurs informally, such as in conversations with managers. Great leaders want their best employees to maximize their potential, and they know that good feedback and guidance are invaluable.

Employees are equals, not subordinates. Ordinary bosses treat their employees like children; they believe that they need constant oversight. These bosses think that their role is to enforce rules, make sure things run their way, and watch over people's shoulders for mistakes. Great leaders see employees as peers who are perfectly capable of making decisions for themselves. Rather than constantly stepping in, great leaders make it clear that they value and trust their employees' work and intervene only when it's absolutely necessary.

Diversity, not like-mindedness, bears fruit. Average bosses want their employees' ideas to align with their own, and because of this, they try to hire like-minded individuals. They encourage their employees to think similarly and reward those who "just put their heads down and work." Exceptional leaders actively seek out a diverse range of individuals and ideas. They expose themselves and their companies to new ways of thinking.

Motivation comes from inspiration, not agony. Ordinary bosses think that strict rules and rule enforcement drive employees to work effectively. They believe that people need to fear layoffs, explosions of anger, and punishment in order to operate at 100%. People then find themselves in survival mode, where they don't care about the product, the company, or the customer experience; they care only about keeping their jobs and appeasing their boss. Great leaders motivate through inspiration—they know that people will respond to their infectious energy, vision, and passion more than anything else.

Knowledge should be constantly pursued. Great leaders know more than others do because they're constantly working to improve. They vow constant growth. Whenever they have a spare moment, they fill it with self-education. They don't do this because it's "the right thing to do"; they do it because it's their passion. They believe in it. They're always looking for opportunities to improve and new things to learn about themselves and the world around them.

Change is an opportunity, not a curse. Ordinary bosses operate by the motto, "This is the way we've always done it." They believe that change is unnecessary and that it causes more harm than good. Exceptional leaders see change as an opportunity for improvement. They constantly adapt their approach and embrace change to stay ahead of the curve.

GREAT LEADERS FOCUS ON RESULTS AND PEOPLE

People often debate what makes a better leader: the no-nonsense, results-focused type or the motivational, people-focused type. Research has provided the answer—neither. For *The Extraordinary Leader: Turning Good Managers into Great Leaders,* James Zenger surveyed more than 60,000 employees to see which leadership characteristics made leaders "great" in the eyes of their employees. Two of the characteristics that Zenger looked at were "results focus" and "people focus," and he found that neither characteristic consistently produced great leadership.

Leaders who primarily focused on results were seen as great just 14% of the time, and leaders who primarily focused on people were seen as great only 12% of the time. However, leaders who balanced their approach and focused equally on results and people (which, according to a study by David Rock, is less than 1% of all leaders), were seen as great a whopping 72% of the time. In other words, results focus and people focus are weak predictors of great leadership on their own. It's the potent combination of the two that consistently makes leaders great.

Leaders who can focus equally on results and people motivate people to be their best without losing sight of the bigger picture. This balance enables them to achieve extraordinary results because they do six things that few other leaders are able to accomplish.

They put the right team of people together to execute a plan. Putting together a good plan of attack can require a heavy-handed focus on results. You have to foresee obstacles, find the right approach, and then make certain you have the right people to make it happen. Many *good* leaders out there are capable of putting together a perfect plan. However, it takes a *great* leader to actually pull a motivated team of people together who can execute that plan and are interested in doing so. Leaders capable of blending a people focus into their results-oriented plans select the ideal people and know their strengths and weaknesses and how these can be made to work together.

They deliver feedback flawlessly. It takes a tactful leader to deliver feedback that is accurate and objective but also considerate and inspirational. Leaders who are balanced know how to take into account the feelings and perspectives of their employees while still delivering the message they need to hear in order to improve.

They solve problems as a team. Research shows that poorly structured meetings stifle creativity and hinder teams from reaching good solutions. Often, this is because people either yield to the most outspoken member of the team, are afraid to share their opinions, or don't know how to effectively critique others' ideas. When results-focused leaders bring a people-focused mentality to the table, they create the right environment for new ideas to thrive. These leaders are able to draw out as many good ideas from their team as possible while prudently steering a process that creates workable solutions. Their work is truly a team effort, and their people feel accomplished when group goals are met.

They sacrifice themselves for their people. Some leaders throw their people under the bus without a second thought. Great leaders pull their people from the bus's path before they're in danger. They coach, and they move obstacles out of the way, even if their people put those obstacles there in the first place. Sometimes they clean up messes their people never even knew they made. If they can't stop the bus, they'll jump out in front of it and take the hit themselves. The best leaders will do anything for their teams, and they have their people's backs, no matter what. They don't try to shift blame, and they don't avoid shame when they fail. They're never afraid to say, "The buck stops here," and they earn people's trust by backing them up.

They hire the best employees. The foundation of any good company is a great hiring system. Effective hiring leads to high levels of performance, a strong workplace culture, and a high retention rate. We've all seen new hires who are brilliant but a horrible fit socially. Bad leaders think nothing of hiring a jerk with great credentials because they're only interested in how that person will perform. Likewise, we've all experienced the new hire who fits in socially and makes friends but who doesn't produce quality work. Great leaders know how to find employees who do their jobs effectively and are good social and cultural fits. This kind of hire builds morale and improves your bottom line. Great leaders think of the entire team. They recognize that their current employees are going to have to work with the new hire every single day, and they look for someone who will complement the team holistically rather than just fill in a certain skills gap.

They balance work and fun. There are plenty of bosses out there who know how to have fun. Unfortunately, this is often at the expense of results. And for every boss out there who has a bit too much fun, there's one who doesn't know how to have any fun at all. It takes a balanced leader to know how to motivate and push employees to be their best but to also have the wherewithal to slow it down at the appropriate time in order to celebrate results and have fun. This balance prevents burnout, builds a great culture, and gets results. Great leaders love their jobs and believe that everyone else can, too. They give people assignments that align with their strengths, passions, and talents. They celebrate accomplishments and douse people with positive feedback when they do good work.

GREAT LEADERS ARE GREAT COMMUNICATORS

Communication is the sine qua non of leadership. Great leaders are always great communicators. However, many leaders struggle with communication. It seems that some leaders will do anything to avoid giving a straight answer. They don't want to say something they can be held accountable for later. Others just don't want to be bothered with clear explanations and solid answers. Great leaders say what they mean and mean what they say—and they say it clearly so that people don't have to read between the lines or try to guess their real meaning.

Communication is the real work of leadership. It's a fundamental element of how leaders accomplish their goals every day. You simply can't become a great leader until you are a great communicator. Great communicators inspire people. They create a connection with their followers that is real, emotional, and personal, regardless of any physical distance between them. Great communicators forge this connection through an understanding of people and the ability to speak directly to their needs. They use their emotional intelligence. Great communicators are intentional about it, and they rely on specific habits to deliver a powerful message. Put these habits to work in your communication and watch your leadership skills soar.

They know their audience. Great communicators don't worry about sounding important, showing off their expertise, or boosting their own egos. Instead, they think about what people need to hear, and how they can deliver this message so that people can hear it. This doesn't mean that leaders tell people what they *want* to hear. Quite the opposite—they tell people what's important for them to know, even if it's bad news.

Their vision is infectious. Great leaders know that having a clear vision isn't enough. You have to make that vision come alive so that your followers can see it as clearly as you do. Great leaders do that by telling stories and painting verbal pictures so that everyone can understand not just where they're going, but what it will look and feel like when they get there. This inspires others to internalize the vision and make it their own.

They are experts in body language. Great communicators are constantly tracking people's reactions to their message. They are quick to pick up on cues like facial expressions and body language because they know this is the only feedback many people will give them. Deference to authority is common, and many times, body language is the only way for a leader to know what people really think. Great communicators use this expertise to tailor their message on the fly and adjust their communication style as needed. The chapter on reading body language in the first section will help you with this.

They are honest. The best leaders know that for communication to be effective, it has to be real. They can't have people parsing every word, trying to separate fact from spin. When great communicators can't share certain information, they come right out and say it, because makeshift, half-truth answers breed distrust and anxiety. In good times and bad, honesty builds trust. Great leaders trust that honesty and integrity, although painful at times, always work out for the best in the long run. They know that honesty allows for genuine connections with people in a way that dishonesty can't, and that lying always comes back to bite you in the end.

They are human, and they aren't afraid to show it. Great leaders are personable and easy to relate to. They're warm. They realize that people have emotions, and they aren't afraid to express their own. They relate to their people as a person first and a boss second.

They speak to groups as individuals. Leaders rarely have the luxury of speaking to one person at a time. Whether it's a huddle around a conference table or an overflowing auditorium, great leaders know how to work the room and make every person feel as if they're being spoken to directly. They make people feel like they're having a one-on-one conversation, as if they're the only person in the room who matters. And for that moment, they are. Great leaders communicate on a very personal and emotional level. They never forget that there's a flesh-and-blood human being standing in front of them.

They are authentic. Great communicators don't try to be someone they're not just because they've stepped behind a podium. Great leaders know that when they stay true to who they are, people gravitate toward their message. They also know that the opposite happens when leaders put on an act. Authenticity refers to being honest in all things—not just what you say and do, but who you are. When you're authentic, your words and actions align with who you claim to be. Your followers shouldn't be compelled to spend time trying to figure out if you have ulterior motives. Any time they spend doing so erodes their confidence in you and their ability to execute. Leaders who are authentic are transparent and forthcoming. They aren't perfect, but they earn people's respect by walking their talk. The chapter on authenticity in the first section will help you to live as authentically as possible.

They speak with authority. Great communicators don't try to cover their backs by being ambiguous, wishy-washy, or unassertive. Instead, they stick their necks out and speak very directly about how things are and how they need to be.

They're proactive. Leaders with the best communication skills don't waste time playing catch-up. They're quick to head off the rumor mill by sharing bad news in a timely manner. They also give clear, concise goals and directions, so people don't waste their time heading in the wrong direction.

They have ears (and they use them). Great leaders know that communication is a two-way street, and what they hear is often more important than what they say. When someone else is speaking, great communicators aren't thinking ahead and planning what they'll say next. Instead, they're actively listening and fully focused on understanding the other person's perspective.

They use phrases like "It's my fault," "I was wrong," and "I'm sorry." When great leaders make a mistake, they admit it right away. They don't wait for someone else to find and point out their blunder. They model accountability through their words and actions, even when they could have easily "gotten away" with the mistake. And they do it matter-of-factly, without drama or false humility.

They solicit feedback. The best communicators never assume that the message people hear is the one they intended to deliver. They check in to verify that their message was understood, and if it wasn't, they don't blame the audience. Instead, they change things up and try again.

GREAT LEADERS ARE LIKEABLE

If you want to be a leader people follow with absolute conviction, you have to be a likeable leader. Tyrants and curmudgeons with brilliant vision can command a reluctant following for a time, but it never lasts. They burn people out before they ever get to see what anyone is truly capable of. Many bosses assume that a leader needs to be aloof and tough on employees in order to be effective. They fear that looking "soft" will erode their employees' motivation and respect. To prove their case, they cite examples of brilliant leaders who modeled a tough leadership style, such as Steve Jobs, who berated his employees. When it comes to success as a leader, radically tough leadership styles are exceptions to the rule, not the rule.

Researchers have shown that overly tough bosses create significant health and motivation problems in their employees because these bosses create stress, and lots of it. A University of London study found an especially strong link between heart disease and boss-inflicted stress, while a University of Concordia study found that employees who rated themselves as highly stressed added 46% to their employers' healthcare costs. Researchers at the Institute of Naval Medicine found that overly tough bosses cause people to seek jobs elsewhere, perform at a lower level, decline promotions, and even quit. Finally, a survey conducted by Randstad Consulting showed that most employees would trade in their bosses for better ones rather than receive a $5,000 pay raise. The thing is, nice, likeable bosses don't just prevent health and motivational problems among their employees; they create massive benefits that hard-nosed bosses can't.

So, what exactly does a likeable leader look like, and how do you pull this off without being a pushover? It's all in their habits. Let's find out.

They're kind without being weak. One of the toughest things for leaders to master is kindness. It's a balancing act, and the key to finding balance is to recognize that true kindness is inherently strong—it's direct and straightforward. Telling people the difficult truth they need to hear is much kinder than protecting them (or yourself) from a difficult conversation. This is weak. Moreover, true kindness doesn't come with expectations. Kindness is thin when you use it in a self-serving manner—people can see right through kindness when a kind leader has an agenda.

They're strong without being harsh. Strength is an important quality in a leader. People wait to see if a leader is strong before they decide to follow their lead or not. People need courage in their leaders. They need someone who can make difficult decisions and watch over the good of the group. They need a leader who will stay the course when things get tough. People are far more likely to show strength when their leader does the same. For the courageous leader, adversity is a welcome test. Like a blacksmith's molding of a red-hot iron, adversity is a trial by fire that refines leaders and sharpens their game. Adversity emboldens courageous leaders and leaves them more committed to their strategic direction. Leaders who lack courage simply toe the company line. They follow the safest path—the path of least resistance—because they'd rather cover their backside than lead.

Many leaders mistake domineering, controlling, and otherwise harsh behavior for strength. They think that taking control and pushing people around will somehow inspire a loyal following. Strength isn't something you can force on people; it's something you earn by demonstrating it time and again in the face of adversity. Only then will people trust that they should follow you.

They're confident without being cocky. We gravitate to confident leaders because confidence is contagious, and it helps us believe that there are great things in store. The trick, as a leader, is to make certain your confidence doesn't slip into arrogance and cockiness. Confidence is about passion and belief in your ability to make things happen, but when your confidence loses touch with reality, you begin to think that you can do things you can't and have done things you haven't. Suddenly, it's all about you. This arrogance makes you lose credibility.

Great, confident leaders are still humble. They don't allow their accomplishments and position of authority to make them feel that they're better than anyone else. Thus, they don't hesitate to jump in and do the dirty work when needed, and they don't ask their followers to do anything they aren't willing to do themselves. The chapter on confidence in the first section will help you with your confidence.

They stay positive but remain realistic. Another major challenge that leaders face is finding the balance between keeping things positive and being realistic. Think of a sailboat with three people aboard: a pessimist, an optimist, and a great leader. Everything is going smoothly until the wind suddenly sours. The pessimist throws their hands up and complains about the wind; the optimist sits back, saying that things will improve; but the great leader says, "We can do this!," and they adjust the sails and keep the ship moving forward. The right combination of positivity and realism is what keeps things moving forward.

Likeable leaders maintain a positive outlook, and this shows in how they describe things. They don't *have* to give a presentation to the board of directors; they *get* to share their vision and ideas with the board. They don't *have* to go on a plant tour; they *get* to meet and visit with the people who make their company's products. They don't even *have* to diet; they *get* to experience the benefits of eating healthfully. Even in undeniably negative situations, likeable leaders emanate an enthusiastic hope for the future, a confidence that they can help make tomorrow better than today. Likeable leaders see this brighter future with crystal clarity, and they have the energy and enthusiasm to ensure that everyone else can see it, too. Their belief in the good is contagious.

They have substance. Daniel Quinn said, "Charisma only wins people's attention. Once you have their attention, you have to have something to tell them." Likeable leaders understand that their knowledge and expertise are critical to the success of everyone who follows them. Therefore, they regularly connect with people to share their substance (as opposed to superficial small talk). Likeable leaders don't puff themselves up or pretend to be something they're not, because they don't have to. They have substance, and they share it with their people.

They're role models, not preachers. Likeable leaders inspire trust and admiration through their actions, not just through their words. Many leaders say that integrity is important to them, but great leaders walk their talk by demonstrating integrity every day. Harping on people all day long about the behavior you want to see has a tiny fraction of the impact you achieve by demonstrating that behavior yourself.

They're graceful. Graceful people are the perfect combination of strong and gentle. They don't resort to intimidation, anger, or manipulation to get a point across, because their gentle, self-assured nature gets the job done. The word gentle often carries a negative connotation (especially in the workplace), but in reality, it's the gentleness of being graceful that gives likeable leaders their power. They're accessible, affable, and easy to get along with—all qualities that make people highly amenable to their ideas.

They're generous. We've all worked for someone who constantly holds something back, whether it's knowledge or resources. They act as if they're afraid you'll outshine them if they give you access to everything you need to do your job. Likeable leaders are unfailingly generous with whom they know, what they know, and the resources they have access to. They share credit and offer enthusiastic praise. They want to inspire all of their employees to achieve their personal best—not just because it will make the team more successful, but because they care about each person as an individual. They want you to do well more than anything else because they understand that this is their job as a leader and because they're confident enough to never worry that your success might make them look bad. In fact, they believe that your success is their success.

They appreciate potential. Robert Brault said, "Charisma is not so much getting people to like you as getting people to like themselves when you're around." Likeable leaders not only see the best in their people but also make sure that everyone else sees it, too. They draw out people's talents so that everyone is bettering themselves and the work at hand.

BRINGING IT ALL TOGETHER

Remember the questions I asked you at the beginning of the chapter? Take another quick look at them. Not one is about title, position, or place on the org chart. That's because you can have the title and position without being a real leader, let alone a great one. You may have worked for someone who fits that description, and you probably have colleagues who are phenomenal leaders without a title. Leadership and followership are mindsets. They're completely different ways of looking at the world. One is reactive, and the other is proactive. One is pessimistic; the other is optimistic. Where a follower sees a to-do list, a leader sees possibilities. So don't wait for the title. Leadership isn't something that anyone can give you—you have to earn it and claim it for yourself.

Leadership, like most things in life, requires balance and emotional intelligence. You can't succeed without focusing on your people, and they won't succeed unless you're focused on results. Great leadership is dynamic; it melds a variety of unique skills into an integrated whole. Great leaders are great communicators. They're honest. They're authentic. They listen. They excel in communication because they value it, and that's a critical step toward becoming a great leader. Great leaders are also likeable. Likeability isn't a birthright; it results from acquirable skills that are crucial to your professional success. And just like any other professional skill, you can study the people who have them, copy what works, and adapt them to your own style.

If you're currently a leader with a title, do you embody the habits in this chapter? If not, you're leaving money, effort, and productivity lying on the table. You're also probably losing some good employees, if not to other jobs, then at least to disengagement and lack of interest. For many great leaders, things clicked once they stopped thinking about what their people could do for them and started thinking about what they could do to help their people succeed. Inspire. Teach. Protect. Remove obstacles. Be human. If you cultivate these habits, you'll become the unforgettable leader that your people will remember for the rest of their careers.

23

Increase Your Productivity

When it comes to productivity, we all face the same challenge—there are only 24 hours in a day. Yet some people seem to have twice the time; they have an uncanny ability to get things done. Even when juggling multiple projects, they achieve their goals without fail. We all want to get more out of life. There's arguably no better way to accomplish this than by finding ways to do more with the precious time you've been given. It feels incredible when you leave the office after an ultra-productive day. It's a workplace high that's hard to beat. With the right approach, you can make this happen every day. You don't need to work longer or push yourself harder—you just need to work smarter and use your emotional intelligence. In the words of Thomas Edison, "Time is really the only capital that any human being has, and the only thing he can't afford to lose."

Being busy has somehow become a badge of honor. The prevailing notion is that if you aren't super busy, you aren't important or hardworking. The truth is, busyness makes you less productive. When we think of a super busy person, we think of a ringing phone, a flood of emails, and a schedule that's bursting at the seams with major projects and side projects hitting simultaneously. Such a situation inevitably leads to multitasking and interruptions, which are deadly to productivity. David Meyer at the University of Michigan published a study that showed switching what you're doing mid-task increases the time it takes you to finish both tasks by 25%. "Multitasking is going to slow you down, increasing the chances of mistakes," Meyer said.

Microsoft studied this phenomenon in their employees and found that it took people an average of 15 minutes to return to their important projects (such as writing reports or computer code) every time they were interrupted by emails, phone calls, or other messages. They didn't spend the 15 minutes on the interrupting messages, either; the interruptions led them to stray to other activities, such as surfing the web for pleasure. "I was surprised by how easily people were distracted and how long it took them to get back to the task," said Eric Horvitz, the Microsoft research scientist who conducted the study. "If it's this bad at Microsoft, it has to be bad at other companies, too."

Beyond interruptions, busyness reduces productivity, because there's a bottleneck in your brain that prevents you from concentrating on two things at once. When you try to do two things at once, your brain lacks the capacity to perform both tasks successfully. In a breakthrough study, René Marois and his colleagues at Vanderbilt University used fMRIs to successfully pinpoint the physical source of this bottleneck. As it turns out, the bottleneck is threefold. Three areas of your brain have trouble processing more than a single task at once, and they happen to be the areas of your brain primarily responsible for cognitive control. "We are under the impression that we have this brain that can do more than it can," Marois explained. "Neural activity seemed to be delayed for the second task when the two tasks were presented nearly simultaneously. They showed 'queuing' of neural activity—the neural response to the second task was postponed until the response to the first was completed." We're so enamored with busyness that we think we're getting more done all at once, although our brains aren't physically capable of this. Regardless of what we might think, we are most productive when we manage our schedules enough to ensure that we can focus effectively on the task at hand.

I doubt these findings completely surprise you, as we've all felt the distracting pull of competing tasks when we're busy. So, why do we keep doing it? Researchers at the University of Chicago have the answer. They found that the belief that busyness is a sign of success and hard work is so prevalent that we actually fear inactivity. The researchers coined the term "idleness aversion" to describe how people are drawn to being busy, regardless of how busyness harms their productivity. The researchers found that we use busyness to hide from our laziness and fear of failure. We burn valuable time doing things that aren't necessary or important because this busyness makes us feel productive—for instance, responding to non-urgent emails when you know you have a big project that you need to finish. It's tough, but you need to recognize when you're using trivial activities to shield yourself from sloth or fear.

There's a reason why people who are the calmest and least stressed are the ones who get the most done—they understand the importance of staying organized and productive (not just busy), and they've adapted their habits accordingly. As they move through their days, they rely on productivity hacks that make them far more efficient. They squeeze every drop out of every hour without expending any extra effort. The good news is that you can become more organized and productive, too, just by emulating the habits they rely on.

They don't let their desks get cluttered. You may think you know exactly where, and in which stack of paper, you can find a particular document. But you're kidding yourself if you don't think you'd be more productive with a clean and organized desk. Just the act of organizing the stuff on your desk helps you organize it in your mind. In addition, research conducted at Princeton University revealed that the more your brain is bombarded by the competing stimuli on a cluttered desk, the less you're able to focus. This wasn't subjective evidence. The researchers were able to see the difference on MRIs of the subjects' brain activity.

They fight the tyranny of the urgent. The tyranny of the urgent refers to the tendency of little things that have to be done right now to get in the way of what really matters. This creates a huge problem, as urgent actions often have little impact. If you succumb to the tyranny of the urgent, you can find yourself going days, or even weeks, without touching the important stuff. Productive people are good at spotting when putting out fires is getting in the way of their performance, and they're willing to ignore or delegate the things that get in the way of real forward momentum.

They never touch things twice. Productive people never put anything in a holding pattern because touching things twice is a huge time-waster. Don't save an email or a phone call to deal with later. As soon as something gets your attention, you should act on it, delegate it, or delete it.

They eat frogs. "Eating a frog" is the best antidote for procrastination; ultra-productive people start each morning with this tasty "treat." In other words, they do the least appetizing, most dreaded item on their to-do list before they do anything else. After that, they're freed up to tackle the stuff that excites and inspires them.

They have a high level of self-awareness. Highly productive and organized people have a clear sense of who they are. They know their weaknesses, and they put organizational structures in place to overcome them. If they tend to let meetings run too long, they set a timer. If they have trouble keeping meetings productive, they make an agenda. If they forget to check their voicemail in the morning, they set a reminder. The details don't matter. What's important is that they think carefully and use specific aids and routines that work with their organizational weaknesses.

They work from a single to-do list. Are you old enough to remember the days when people used to buy those expensive leather-bound planners and fill them up with a to-do list color-coded by priority? They might seem a bit old school now, but no one can deny that it was effective. Why were those planners effective? They reminded us how important it is to keep a single to-do list. When you consolidate everything into one list, you always know where to look, and you can stop wasting time trying to remember which list has the information you need.

They make time for lunch. We've all been there—you're head-down busy, and by the time you look up, it's way past lunchtime. You end up either going without or grabbing a donut or a bag of chips from the snack machine. Both are really bad ideas. The donut will give you an energy boost for about 20 minutes, but after that, your energy will drop like a rock. Skipping meals affects not only your concentration, productivity, and problem-solving skills but also your waistline—and not in the way you might expect. Researchers at Ohio State University showed that the weight you lose by skipping meals is muscle weight that you regain later as fat.

They stick to the schedule during meetings. Meetings are the biggest time-waster there is. Ultra-productive people know that a meeting will drag on forever if they let it, so they inform everyone at the onset that they'll stick to the schedule. This sets a limit that motivates everyone to be more focused and efficient.

They tidy up at the end of each day. The best remedy for clutter is to set aside about 10 minutes at the end of each day to organize your desk. Although we know that it's best to touch things only once, we've all stopped halfway through a task because the phone rang or somebody stopped by to chat. You really can't prevent such things, but you can end the day by resolving all the things you left half-finished.

They plan their days the night before. Productive people go to bed each night secure in the knowledge of what they'll accomplish the following day. They get their priorities straight the night before, so that once the day starts, they're less likely to get distracted by the "tyranny of the urgent."

They make full use of technology. There's a lot in other chapters about how modern technology extends the workday, making it so that we're always on the clock. Although that's true, technology can also make you more productive and help you focus. Whether it's setting up an email filter to keep your inbox spam-free, or using apps that help you organize information you're going to need again, technology isn't always bad. Used properly, it can save a lot of time. Ultra-productive people put technology to work for them. Beyond setting up filters in their email accounts so that messages are sorted and prioritized as they come in, they set up contingencies on their smartphones that alert them when something important happens. This way, when your stock hits a certain price, or you have an email from your best customer, you'll know. There's no need to waste time constantly checking your phone for status updates.

HAVE A GREAT MORNING ROUTINE

Researchers at the University of Nottingham recently published findings from their exploration of 83 studies on energy and self-control. What they found will change the way you start your day. The researchers found that self-control and energy are not only intricately linked but also finite, daily resources that tire much like a muscle. Although you don't always realize it, as the day goes on, you have increased difficulty exerting self-control and focusing on your work. As your self-control wears out, you feel tired and find tasks to be more difficult, and your mood sours. This exhaustion of self-control kills your productivity, and it makes the morning hours, when your self-control is highest, the most important hours of the day. But the trick isn't just to spend your morning hours working; it's to do the right things in the morning that will make your energy and self-control last as long as possible.

The Nottingham research led me to uncover ways you can form good habits in the morning and maximize your energy and self-control throughout the day. Whether you naturally wake up feeling alert and productive, or rise with the brainpower of a zombie, these habits will help you use your emotional intelligence to transform your morning routine and set a positive tone that lasts the entire day.

Start with exercise. Starbuck's Howard Schultz, Richard Branson, Tim Cook, and Disney's Bob Iger all wake up well before 6:00 a.m. to get their bodies moving. Although their ungodly wake-up hours and exercise routines may seem difficult, research supports this extra effort. People who exercise regularly feel more competent, they have more energy, and it gives them a more positive outlook, all of which are critical for getting things done. Exercising first thing in the morning ensures that you'll have the time for it, and it improves your self-control and energy levels over the course of the entire day.

But drink some lemon water first. Drinking lemon water as soon as you wake up spikes your energy levels physically and mentally. Lemon water gives you steady, natural energy that lasts the length of the day by improving nutrient absorption in your stomach. You need to drink it first thing in the morning (on an empty stomach) to ensure full absorption. You should also wait 15–30 minutes after drinking it before eating (perfect time to squeeze in some exercise). Lemons are packed with nutrients; they're chock full of potassium, vitamin C, and antioxidants. If you're under 150 pounds, drink the juice of half a lemon (a full lemon if you're over 150 pounds). Don't drink the juice without water because it's hard on your teeth.

Practice mindfulness. Mindfulness has become increasingly popular in the business world, largely due to the huge dividends it pays in productivity and overall well-being. Researchers have shown that mindfulness fights off stress by reversing the fight-or-flight response, improves your ability to focus, boosts creativity, and increases your emotional intelligence. Mindfulness meditation in the morning, no matter how brief, is a great way to start your day. It helps you relax and focus, and you can use it to set your intentions for the day. The chapter on mindfulness will show you how.

No Internet until breakfast. When you dive straight into emails, texts, and Facebook, you lose focus, and your morning succumbs to the wants and needs of other people. It's much healthier to take those precious first moments of the day to do something relaxing that sets a calm, positive tone for your day. Jumping right into electronics has the opposite effect—it's a frantic way to start your day. Exercising, meditating, or even watching the birds out the window are all great ways to start the day. Of course, you can also work on something productive, just no browsing the web or checking apps.

Eat a healthy breakfast. Eating anything at all for breakfast puts you ahead of a lot of people. People who eat breakfast are less likely to be obese, they have more stable blood sugar levels, and they tend to be less hungry over the course of the day. And these are the statistics just for people who eat breakfast. When you eat a healthy breakfast, the doors to a productive day swing wide open. A healthy breakfast gives you energy, improves your short-term memory, and helps you concentrate more intensely and for longer periods.

Set goals for the day. Benjamin Franklin was obsessive about planning his days. Each morning, he woke up at 4:00 a.m. and meticulously pieced together a schedule. There's a clear message to take from Franklin's habit: Prudent goal setting pays dividends. When you plan out your day as carefully as possible, your chances of accomplishing your goals skyrocket. I like to set my daily goals after my mindfulness practice because the added calm and clarity help me set effective, specific goals.

Make certain your goals are realistic. There's no point in setting goals if they aren't realistic. Take the time to ensure that your schedule for the day is doable by assigning times to your to-do list. A good rule of thumb is to make your day as top heavy as possible. Think about the things that have the ability to advance your career, no matter how daunting the tasks, and schedule them first. When you complete difficult tasks first, you carry positive energy and a feeling of accomplishment into the rest of your day. Vague goals such as "I want to finish writing my article" are counterproductive, because they fail to include the "how" of things. This can be re-phrased in a more functional way: "I am going to finish my article by writing each of the three sections, spending no more than an hour on each section." Now you have more than simply something you want to achieve—you have a way to achieve it.

No checking email until you've eaten three frogs. In the previous section, "eating frogs" was introduced as an antidote to procrastination and low productivity. Frogs are tastiest first thing in the morning, and eating them before checking email ensures you are off to a productive start before you get sidetracked putting out fires. Email is a major distraction that enables procrastination and wastes precious mental energy. Spend your morning on something that requires a high level of concentration that you don't want to do, and you'll get it done in short order.

BRINGING IT ALL TOGETHER

We are naturally drawn to being busy, although this can hinder our productivity. As it turns out, you really do have to slow down to do your best. When you don't, the consequences can be severe. The good news is that there are many tools for staying organized and productive, so even the most disorganized among us can put a system in place to keep us in check. Developing a successful morning routine is an essential part of it. You won't be highly productive without one. In the end, we're all searching for ways to be more efficient and productive. I hope the habits from this chapter help you find that extra edge.

24

Practice Mindfulness

—

There's no shortage of advice out there claiming to make you better, but mindfulness meditation is the rare, research-proven technique that boosts your performance by physically altering your brain. Researchers at the University of British Columbia pooled data from more than 20 studies to understand how practicing mindfulness affects the brain. The researchers found significant changes in eight brain regions, and in two of those regions, the simple act of practicing mindfulness increased brain activity and the density of brain tissue:

1. *The anterior cingulate cortex (ACC)*, which is responsible for self-control. It enables you to resist distractions, focus, and avoid impulsivity in order to work efficiently and make great decisions. The ACC is also responsible for flexibility, and people who have problems in this brain area are known to stick to ineffective problem-solving strategies when they should be adjusting their approach.

2. *The hippocampus,* which, among other things, is responsible for resilience in the face of setbacks and challenges. The hippocampus is readily damaged by stress, making it a need area for most people.

Mindfulness is a simple yet effective form of meditation that enables you to gain control of unruly thoughts and behaviors. People who practice mindfulness are more focused, even when they are not meditating. Mindfulness is an excellent technique for reducing stress because it allows you to stop feeling out of control, to stop jumping from one thought to the next, and to stop ruminating on negative thoughts. Overall, it's a great way to make it through your busy day calmly and productively. Mindfulness is an increasingly popular notion in the workplace, with companies such as Apple, Yahoo, Starbucks, and Google using it to their benefit. Google, for example, offers employees a 19-hour course on the subject, which is so popular that thousands of Googlers take it each year.

Ellen Langer, a Harvard University psychologist who studies mindfulness, described it this way: "Mindfulness is the process of actively noticing new things. When you do that, it puts you in the present. It makes you more sensitive to context and perspective. It's the essence of engagement. And it's energy-begetting, not energy-consuming. The mistake most people make is to assume it's stressful and exhausting—all this thinking. But what's stressful is all the mindless negative evaluations we make and the worry that we'll find problems and not be able to solve them."

Although mindfulness has many benefits, perhaps the most important reason that companies such as Google are sold on it is its ability to directly improve performance. Langer has conducted a host of studies that show practicing mindfulness improves your performance on all types of tasks. However, the mindfulness movement isn't all about performance; there are many other important reasons why companies are making mindfulness a priority. Five of these reasons follow—all great illustrations of why you should practice mindfulness.

Mindfulness is the ultimate stress-reliever. Stress is more than a performance killer; it's a people killer. According to the Centers for Disease Control and Prevention, roughly two-thirds of all hospital visits are for stress-related problems, and 75% of healthcare expenses are stress related. Stress can cause high blood pressure, autoimmune diseases, cancer, heart disease, insomnia, depression, anxiety, and more. Mindfulness is a great stress reliever because it takes you out of fight-or-flight mode and brings you into a relaxed state of mental clarity and calm.

Mindfulness improves your ability to focus. Mindfulness improves your ability to focus on *one* thing at a time. This focus carries over into everything you do. Mindfulness teaches you to avoid distractions and to bring a heightened level of concentration to your work. While you may have fallen prey to multitasking in the past, mindfulness will help you kick this nasty, productivity-killing habit. A focused mind is a productive mind.

Mindfulness boosts your creativity. Creativity hinges on your mental state. Mindfulness helps you get into a creative frame of mind by defeating the negative thoughts that stifle creative thinking and self-expression. The fact that mindfulness focuses on "the now" helps you think freely and creatively.

Mindfulness improves your emotional intelligence. The heightened awareness that exists in a mindful state allows you to feel, label, and understand your emotions more clearly. This turbocharges your emotional intelligence because it greatly increases your self-awareness, which is the foundation of high emotional intelligence.

Mindfulness makes you a better person. A Harvard study found strong connections between mindfulness and prosocial behavior. Subjects who meditated showed compassion and kindness to others 50% more often than those who didn't. There's something about feeling present and calm that brings out the best in people.

HOW TO PRACTICE MINDFULNESS

Practicing mindfulness increases the density of your brain matter where it counts. It's perhaps the only technique that can change your brain in this way, which produces a ripple of other positive effects. Thankfully, you can reap the benefits of mindfulness in as little as a few minutes a day.

Gandhi was once with a group of followers who inquired about his schedule. He told them, "I need to set aside at least one hour each day to meditate." They were vexed by this and told him, "There's no way you have that much time!" He responded, "Well, if that's the case, then I need to set aside two hours a day to meditate." Like Gandhi, you'll soon find that mindfulness is one of very few things that are well worth your precious time, and the busier you are, the more important it is to have a clear mind if you want to be productive.

Mindfulness doesn't have to take place in the mountains of Nepal or a weekend retreat under a vow of silence. The beauty of the technique is that it's so simple that you can do it anywhere and just about any time. Mindfulness is the simple act of focusing all of your attention on the present. This requires you to observe your thoughts and feelings objectively, without judgment, which helps you awaken your experience and live in the moment. This way, life doesn't just pass you by. This might sound a bit abstract and complicated, but it isn't. Here's how you can do it, even with your busy schedule:

Focus on your breathing. Sit in a comfortable chair with your feet flat on the floor, and spend a few minutes doing nothing but breathing slowly in and out. Focus all your attention on your breath. Feel the air travel into your mouth, down your windpipe, and into your lungs. Then, feel your body shift as it pushes the air out of your lungs. When thoughts surface that distract you from your breathing, don't worry. Just let them pass, and shift your attention back to your breathing. After some practice, you should be able to spend several minutes doing nothing but immersing yourself in the act of breathing at the expense of all other thoughts.

Go for a walk. You can also meditate just by going for a walk. All you have to do is focus on each step. Feel your legs move, and your feet hit the ground. Focus solely on the act of walking and the sensations of your surroundings (the cool breeze, the hot sun, or the dog barking in the distance). When you feel other thoughts creeping into your mind, focus even harder on the sensation of walking. Focusing on something that's second nature is refreshing because it alters your frame of mind as you turn off the never-ending stream of thoughts that normally dominates your attention. You can do the same thing when you brush your teeth, comb your hair, or eat a meal.

Feel your body. You don't even have to stop doing what you're doing to practice mindfulness. All you have to do is focus all your attention on what you're doing without thinking about why you're doing it, what you should do next, or what you should be doing. Whether it's the gentle stroke of your fingers on the keyboard or your posture in your chair, you can direct your attention from your thoughts to your bodily sensations at the spur of the moment.

Try a body scan. If you're having trouble feeling your body, try lying on your back on the floor with your legs extended, arms out, and palms facing toward the ceiling. As you lay there, focus your attention on each part of your body, moving slowly from head to toe. As you focus on each part of your body, feel the weight of it against the floor. Feel the varying temperature and sensations that are unique to each part of your body. This process of focusing solely on your body will quiet your mind and keep you fully immersed in the moment.

Repeat one positive thing about yourself, over and over. One of the main goals of mindfulness is to stop the stream of thoughts that cycle through your mind over and over again each day. Funnily enough, a great way to do this is to choose a short, positive message about yourself and repeat it over and over with each breath to keep your mind on track. A great phrase of choice is "I am capable." The simplicity keeps you grounded in the exercise and keeps other thoughts from taking over. The right phrase also builds a little confidence, which never hurts.

Interrupt the stress cycle. Any moment when you feel stressed, overwhelmed, or stuck on something is the perfect moment to practice mindfulness. Just stop what you're doing, let your thoughts go for a moment, and practice your favorite mindfulness technique (breathing, walking, or focusing on body sensations). Even a few minutes of this can make a huge difference in quieting your mind and reducing stress. You'll be surprised at how reasonable things look once you've taken a few moments to clear your head.

BRINGING IT ALL TOGETHER

Mindfulness is the simple mental state of having active, open attention to the present. Few things can improve your brain and emotional intelligence the way mindfulness meditation can. It can improve your performance now as well as your capacity to perform in the future. The best thing about mindfulness is that you can do it anytime anywhere, and it takes only a few minutes. Give it a try. You might be surprised where it takes you.

25

Get Motivated

If you're ambitious, you're bound to feel like a failure from time to time. Lofty goals lead to inevitable moments when you aren't yet living up to your expectations. We live in a world that reinforces this feeling. Although most people won't admit it (other than the guy with the *"He who dies with the most toys wins"* bumper sticker), in the back of our minds, we equate material possessions with success. It's a shame we fall prey to materialistic thinking, because we certainly know better. A study by Strayer University found that 90% of Americans believe happiness is a bigger indicator of success than power, possessions, or prestige. Digging a little deeper, 67% defined success as "good relationships with friends and family," and 60% said it's loving what you do for a living. Only 20% stated that monetary wealth determines success. But saying and doing are two very different things.

When it comes to success, our eyes often lead us astray. It's hard not to feel like the most successful people are those with the biggest houses, the most expensive cars, and the most influential friends. Regardless of what you achieve, there's always someone with more, and this can make you feel like you're losing. The problem isn't your lack of toys; it's believing that toys indicate true success. Real success is about who you are and how far you've come. If you ever worry that you're not as successful as you should be, you may be evaluating yourself against the wrong criteria. Sometimes, you just need a reminder of what you've really accomplished in life. The following habits will help you do just that, and they'll increase your emotional intelligence in the process.

You keep things in perspective. Sometimes bad things happen. It's part of life. For most of us, however, our very worst day would seem like a vacation to somebody who has real problems—like not having enough to eat or trying to survive a civil war. Locking your keys in the car—or even getting passed over for a promotion—aren't that bad once you learn to develop perspective. If you've mastered the ability to keep your problems in perspective, mark it down as a huge success.

You're no longer the center of the universe. We all know "successful" people who act like they're the center of the universe. It's their world, and the rest of us just live in it, right? That's not success. True success requires the ability to feel empathy—to realize that other people's feelings and dreams are just as important as ours, and that we cannot succeed without them.

You stay positive. Hope and optimism are essential components of a happy life. If you dwell on things that go wrong, you become bitter and resentful. When that happens, you fail—no matter what you may have achieved. Real success means always seeing the bright side and believing that you have the power to make even the worst situations better.

You realize that life isn't a zero-sum game. It's not a seesaw, either. Just because somebody else achieves a big success doesn't mean you suffer a loss in equal proportion. You just didn't win that particular time. One sure sign of success is the ability to celebrate others' achievements with sincere enthusiasm.

You ask for help when you need it. Refusing to ask for help, no matter how much you're struggling, is a sign of emotional immaturity. Asking for help means that you no longer feel like you have something to prove by being perfect. It shows you aren't afraid of people discovering your weaknesses, and you understand that no one succeeds alone.

You know that failure isn't forever. You've learned that the only people who never fail are those who don't try. When you fail, you don't automatically assume that *you're* a failure. Instead, you embrace each failure as an opportunity to learn something—and then you move on.

You can tell the difference between drama and excitement. Remember the days when stable relationships were boring, and you quickly got tired of anyone who treated you as they should? If that kind of "drama" is a thing of the past, congratulations. If you prefer stability and depth to drama, you're succeeding.

You no longer care what other people think. You worry about what other people think only when you still feel like you have something to prove. Conversely, you know you've "made it" when you don't worry about that anymore—when you're true to yourself and your principles, and satisfied with your life. You know you've made it when you understand that other people's opinions are just that—opinions. They have no effect on reality. They don't change who or what you are.

You accept what you can't change and change what you can. There's a difference between pessimism and practicality. If there's a hurricane headed your way, there's nothing you can do to stop it. But once you accept that the hurricane is coming, you can start working to mitigate its effects. If your company downsizes and you get laid off, every moment you spend in denial just delays whatever is waiting over the horizon. You're able to move on only when you start exploring your options and making plans to change what you can. Taking responsibility for changing the things you don't like about your life is one of the biggest indicators of success.

LEAVING YOUR COMFORT ZONE

T.S. Eliot was clearly onto something when he asked, "If you aren't in over your head, how do you know how tall you are?" The very act of stepping outside your comfort zone is critical to your success and well-being. Our brains are wired such that it's difficult to take action until we feel at least some stress and discomfort. The chapter on beating stress discussed how your performance peaks when you're well out of your comfort zone. If you're too comfortable, your performance suffers from inaction, and if you move too far outside your comfort zone, you melt down from stress.

Peak performance and discomfort go hand in hand. Stepping outside your comfort zone makes you better, and it doesn't have to be as extreme as climbing Mount Everest. The everyday challenges push your boundaries the most. Step out of your comfort zone, and embrace these challenges.

Accomplish an "impossible" goal. Few things compare to the exhilaration of accomplishing something that you didn't think you were capable of. These achievements fall so far outside your comfort zone that they seem impossible. Maybe it's running a marathon or giving a keynote speech at a convention. These accomplishments are worth every bit of suffering you endure to achieve them, because once you finally do them, you feel invincible and carry that triumph with you forever.

Volunteer. It would be great if everyone volunteered for purely altruistic reasons, but we all have demands on our time and have to set priorities. The problem is that after a long workday, volunteering can get pushed down somewhere below watching Netflix. Volunteering is a powerful experience that feels good and expands your network at the same time. Have you ever met anyone who made volunteering a priority and wasn't changed for the better by the experience? Neither have I.

Practice public speaking. You've likely heard that the majority of people fear public speaking more than death. In fact, 74% of Americans have glossophobia (the fancy word for a fear of public speaking). So, yes, it's a challenge. It's also worth it. Whether you're addressing five people around a table or an audience of 5,000, becoming a better public speaker can be a huge boon to your career.

Talk to someone you don't know. Unless you're an extreme extrovert, or a politician, talking to new people probably makes you at least somewhat uncomfortable. Do it anyway. Social interaction is good for your mood (even when you don't like it), expands your network, exposes you to new ideas, and boosts your self-confidence.

Get up early. Unless you're a morning person, getting up earlier than usual can take you *way* out of your comfort zone. However, if you get up well before you have to start getting ready for work, it's worth it. It gives you an opportunity to collect your thoughts and mentally prepare yourself for the day ahead, rather than just dashing from one activity to another. It also gives you the opportunity to eat a good breakfast and exercise, both of which have well-known health benefits.

Bite your tongue. Sure, it can feel *so* good to unload on somebody and let them know what you really think, but that good feeling is temporary. What happens the next day, the next week, or the next year? It's human nature to want to prove that you're right, but it's rarely effective. The vast majority of the time, that means you should be biting your tongue.

TAKE YOUR BRAIN OFF AUTOPILOT

It's surprising how easy it is to lose sight of the important things in life. Busy schedules and regular routines tend to put your brain on autopilot. When things aren't going quite the way you'd like them to, it's often because you've lost focus on what really matters. But focusing on life's fundamental truths can be difficult, especially when they remind you that you're heading in the wrong direction.

The best things in life don't come easily, and failing to observe yourself carefully is a sure path to mediocrity and low emotional intelligence. I believe that Socrates said it best: "The unexamined life isn't worth living." Many of life's essential truths need repeating. We need reminders that help us stay focused on them. Keep these truths handy, and they're sure to give you a much-needed boost.

Great success is often preceded by failure. You will never experience true success until you learn to embrace failure. Your mistakes pave the way for you to succeed by revealing when you're on the wrong path. The biggest breakthroughs typically come when you're feeling the most frustrated and the most stuck. This frustration forces you to think differently, to look outside the box and see the solution that you've been missing. Success takes patience and the ability to maintain a good attitude even while suffering for what you believe in.

The first step is always the hardest. When you want to achieve something important, that first step will inevitably be daunting, even frightening. When you dare to make that first move, anxiety and fear dissipate in the name of action. People who dive headfirst into taking that brutal first step aren't any stronger than the rest of us. They've simply learned that it yields great results. They know that the pain of getting started is inevitable and that procrastination only prolongs their suffering.

Being busy does not equal being productive. Look at everyone around you. They all seem so busy—running from meeting to meeting and firing off emails. Yet how many of them are really producing, really succeeding at a high level? Success doesn't come from movement and activity. It comes from focus—from ensuring that your time is used efficiently and productively. You get the same number of hours in the day as everyone else. Use yours wisely. After all, you're the product of your output, not your effort. Make certain that your efforts are dedicated to tasks that get results.

You will always have less control than you want. There are too many extenuating circumstances in life to control every outcome. However, you can control how you react to things that are out of your control. Your reaction is what transforms a mistake into a learning experience and ensures that a victory doesn't send your ego through the roof. You can't win every battle, but with the right attitude, you can win the war.

You're living the life you've created. You are not a victim of circumstances. No one can force you to make decisions and take actions that run contrary to your values and aspirations. The circumstances you're living in today are your own—you created them. Likewise, your future is entirely up to you. If you're feeling stuck, it's probably because you're afraid to take the risks necessary to achieve your goals and live your dreams. When it's time to take action, remember that it's always better to be at the bottom of the ladder you want to climb than at the top of one you don't.

Good things take time. Success, above all, requires time and effort. Author Malcolm Gladwell suggested that mastery of anything requires 10,000 hours of tireless focus. Many successful people would agree. Consider Harry Bernstein, who dedicated his entire life to writing before he finally landed a best-seller at the age of 96. When you finally succeed, you realize that the journey was the best part of it.

Fear is the #1 source of regret. When it's all said and done, you'll lament the chances that you didn't take far more than you will your failures. Don't be afraid to take risks.

Your biggest problems are mental. Almost all our problems occur because we time travel: We go to the past and regret things we've done, or we go to the future and feel anxious about events that haven't even happened. It's all too easy to slip into the past or jet into the future. When you do, you lose sight of the one thing that you can actually control—the present.

Life is short. None of us is guaranteed tomorrow. Yet when someone dies unexpectedly, it causes us to take stock of our own life: what's really important, how we spend our time, and how we treat other people. Loss is a raw, visceral reminder of the frailty of life. It shouldn't be. Remind yourself every morning when you wake up that each day is a gift, and you're bound to make the most of the blessing you've been given. The moment you start acting like life is a blessing is the moment it will start acting like one. After all, a great day begins with a great mindset.

ASK YOURSELF THE RIGHT QUESTIONS

If you aren't achieving all that you'd hoped for, it's often the result of not asking yourself the right questions. Some questions are hard to confront because you're afraid you won't get the answer you want; others because you really don't want to know the answer. When Eric Schmidt was CEO of Google, he famously said, "We run this company on questions, not answers." Life runs on questions, not answers. You should be asking yourself regularly if you're headed in the right direction. Let's take a closer look at some of the tough questions you should ask yourself frequently.

How do people see me differently than I see myself?

Have you ever heard a recording of your voice and thought, "Is *that* what I really sound like?" Because of the way the sound of the voice travels through the human skull, we never hear ourselves the same way that everybody else hears us. The same is often true of the way we behave. We interpret our behavior in terms of how we think we come across, whereas everyone else sees the real thing.

A great way to gain this perspective is a 360° assessment. It gathers feedback from everyone you work with closely that is constructive, anonymous, and accurate. If you forego the 360° assessment and solicit feedback in person, make certain you ask for feedback that is specific, avoiding broad questions and generalizations. For example, you're more likely to get an honest and accurate answer to, "How well did I handle myself in the meeting when everyone disagreed with me?" than to, "Am I a good boss?" Be careful to show that you're receptive to the feedback. If you flip out or get defensive every time somebody speaks their mind, they're going to stop doing it.

What/whom did I make better today?

That's another way of saying, "Leave things better than you found them." Ending each day by asking yourself what or whom you made better is a great way to keep yourself grounded and focused on what really matters. Even when the answers are no one and nothing, asking yourself this question will keep you grounded and focused to do better the following day.

What haven't I taken the time to learn about?

It's a big world out there, and it's getting bigger all the time. Scientists have theorized that it once took 1,500 years for the accumulated knowledge in the world to double. Now, it takes only a year or two. Don't get left behind.

If I achieved all of my goals, how would I feel? What can I do to feel that way as I work to achieve them?

The ability to delay gratification in pursuit of your goals is one of the most fundamental prerequisites for success, but delaying gratification doesn't have to mean being miserable until you cross that finish line. You can achieve more—and have more fun doing it—if you let yourself feel some of that pride and pleasure along the way.

What do I want my life to be like in five years?

Lewis Carroll once said, "If you don't know where you're going, any road will take you there." The corollary is that once you have your destination in mind, you can plan your route. Five years is the perfect timeframe: It's not so far in the future that you can't imagine yourself there, but it's not so close that you can't do anything about it.

In what areas of my life am I settling?

When you settle, you accept less than you're capable of. Sometimes, we settle in dead-end jobs. Other times, we settle for unhealthy or unfulfilling relationships. If you don't ask yourself where and why you're settling, it's hard to stop.

What would I do if I wasn't scared?

From a survival perspective, fear has its purpose. It's what keeps us from sticking our hand in the washing machine or any of the million other things that could get us hurt or killed. However, fear tends to get carried away. Instead of keeping you safe, it keeps you from improving your life and living your dreams. Asking yourself what you're afraid of often makes it a lot less scary.

Am I being true to my values?

Do you ever get that nagging feeling that something is a little off in your life? This often happens when little habits creep up on you that violate your values. If spending quality time with your family is one of your primary values, but you keep staying late at work, there's a conflict. If you want that nagging little voice to go away, you have to do something about it.

Who has qualities that I aspire to develop?

When people have qualities that you admire, reflecting on these qualities and thinking about ways in which you can incorporate them into your repertoire is a great exercise. This also motivates you to spend more time around these individuals so that you can watch and learn.

What's stopping me from doing the things that I should be doing?

It's easy to shrug your shoulders and say, "I don't know what to do," but that's just an excuse. Most of the time, we know exactly what we should be doing. We just aren't willing to move the obstacles out of the way.

Will you be my mentor?

It's an intimidating question to ask, but few people will turn you down. Everyone likes being looked up to, and it feels good to share our knowledge with others.

BRINGING IT ALL TOGETHER

There's no sense in feeling like a failure because you think you should have a better job, a bigger house, or a nicer car. Real success comes from the inside, and it's completely independent of circumstances. Staying focused and asking yourself hard questions can be extremely uncomfortable, but it's good for your emotional intelligence. We don't learn and grow by sticking with what's comfortable. Staying in your comfort zone means stagnation. Just as an oyster only makes a pearl when it's irritated by a grain of sand, no one has ever accomplished anything remarkable when comfortable.

26

Make Your Workplace
a Better Place

It's tough to hold on to good employees, but it shouldn't be. Most of the mistakes that companies make are easily avoided. When you do make mistakes, your best employees are the first to go, because they have the most options. Far too many companies believe that a cutthroat pressure-cooker culture gets results. They think that the harder they crack that whip, the better people will perform. Cutthroat business culture is so prevalent that it's a cliché in our society, and the inspiration for countless TV shows and movies. The sad thing is that people relate to it on the screen because they've seen it first-hand.

But just because everybody seems to be doing it doesn't mean it works; it just makes it easier to stick your head in the sand and ignore the consequences. Make no mistake about it, the costs associated with treating people poorly are real. High-pressure cutthroat organizations spend 50% more on healthcare for their employees than organizations with a more positive, supportive environment. Cutthroat organizations are actually *less* productive because they experience significantly lower levels of employee engagement. Organizations with low levels of employee engagement have 40% lower earnings per share, are 18% less productive, and have 50% higher turnover.

If you can't keep your best employees engaged, you can't keep your best employees. Although this should be common sense, it isn't common enough. A survey by CEB found that one-third of star employees feel disengaged from their employer and are looking for a new job. According to the latest Gallup study, the level of disengagement people feel from their work has never been greater, and it doesn't matter if they work on-site, hybrid, or remote. "Improving life at work isn't rocket science, but the world is closer to colonizing Mars than it is to fixing the world's broken workplaces," said Gallup CEO John Clifton.

When you lose good employees, they don't disengage all at once. Instead, their interest in their jobs slowly dissipates. Michael Kibler, who has spent much of his career studying this phenomenon, refers to it as *"brownout."* Like dying stars, star employees slowly lose their fire for their jobs. "Brownout is different from burnout because workers afflicted by it are not in obvious crisis," Kibler said. "They seem to be performing fine: putting in massive hours, grinding out work while contributing to teams, and saying all the right things in meetings. However, they are operating in a silent state of continual overwhelm, and the predictable consequence is disengagement."

To prevent brownout and retain top talent, companies and managers should understand what they're doing that contributes to this slow fade. The following practices are the worst offenders, and you should abolish them if you're going to hang on to good employees.

They create a lot of stupid rules. Companies need to have rules (that's a given), but they don't have to be shortsighted and lazy attempts at creating order. Whether it's an overzealous attendance policy or restricting what people can place on their desks, even a couple of unnecessary rules can drive people crazy. When good employees feel like Big Brother is watching, they'll find someplace else to work. I understand the temptation. As TalentSmartEQ grew rapidly in the early years, so did our difficulty maintaining standards. There were many instances in which someone crossed a line, and we were tempted to respond with a new rule that applied to everyone. But that's where most companies blow it. In just about every instance, upon closer inspection, we realized that establishing a new rule would be a passive and morale-killing way to address the problem. The vast majority of the time, the problem needs to be handled one-on-one by the employee's manager. When companies create ridiculous and demoralizing rules to halt the outlandish behavior of a few individuals, it's a management problem. There's no sense in alienating your entire workforce because you don't know how to manage performance. It makes a bad situation that much worse.

They don't recognize accomplishments. It's easy to underestimate the power of a pat on the back, especially for top performers who are intrinsically motivated. Everyone likes kudos—none more so than those who work hard and give their all. Rewarding individual accomplishments shows that you're paying attention. Managers need to communicate with their people to find out what makes them feel good (for some, it's a raise; for others, it's public recognition) and then reward them for a job well done. For top performers, this will happen often if you're doing it right.

They restrict Internet use. There are certain sites that no one should visit at work, and I'm not talking about Facebook. But once you block pornography and the other obvious stuff, it's a difficult and arbitrary process to decide where to draw the line. Most companies draw it in the wrong place. People should be able to kill time on the Internet during breaks. When companies unnecessarily restrict people's Internet activity, it does more than demoralize those who can't check Facebook; it limits people's ability to do their jobs. Many companies restrict Internet activity so heavily that it makes it difficult for people to conduct online research. The most obvious example? Checking the Facebook profile of someone you just interviewed.

They treat everyone equally. Although this tactic works with schoolchildren, the workplace ought to function differently. Treating everyone equally shows your top performers that no matter how well they perform (and, typically, top performers are workhorses), they'll be treated the same as someone who barely manages to punch the clock.

They have ridiculous requirements for attendance, leave, and time off. Salaried employees are paid for the work they do, not the specific hours they sit at their desks. When you ding salaried employees for showing up five minutes late, although they routinely stay late and put in time on the weekend, you send the message that policies take precedence over performance. It reeks of distrust, and you should never put someone on salary you don't trust. Likewise, when companies are unnecessarily strict in requiring documentation for bereavement and medical leave, it leaves a sour taste in the mouths of employees who deserve better. After all, if you have employees who fake a death to miss a day's work, what does that say about your company?

They tolerate poor performance. It's said that in jazz bands, the band is only as good as the worst player; no matter how great some members may be, everyone hears the worst player. The same goes for a company. When you permit weak links to exist without consequence, they drag everyone else down, especially top performers.

They don't let people pursue their passions. Google mandates that employees spend at least 20% of their time doing "what they believe will benefit Google most." Although these passion projects have made major contributions to marquee Google products, such as Gmail and AdSense, their biggest impact is in creating highly engaged Googlers. Talented employees are passionate. Providing opportunities for employees to pursue their passions improves their productivity and job satisfaction, but many managers want people to work within a little box. These managers fear that productivity will decline if they let people expand their focus and pursue their passions. This fear is unfounded. Studies have shown that people who are able to pursue their passions at work experience flow, a euphoric state of mind that is five times more productive than the norm.

They ban mobile phones. If I ban mobile phones in the office, no one will waste time texting and talking to family and friends, right? Yeah, right. Organizations need to do the difficult work of hiring people who are trustworthy and who won't take advantage. They also need to train managers to deal effectively with employees who underperform and/or violate expectations (such as spending too much time on their phones). This is also hard work, but it's worth it. The easy, knee-jerk alternative (banning phones) demoralizes good employees who need to check their phones periodically due to pressing family or health issues or as an appropriate break from work.

They don't show people the big picture. It may seem efficient to simply send employees assignments and move on, but omitting the big picture is a dealbreaker for star performers. Star performers shoulder heavier loads because they genuinely care about their work, so their work must have a purpose. When they don't know what that is, they feel alienated and aimless. When they aren't given a purpose, they find one elsewhere.

They steal employees' frequent-flyer miles. If there's one thing that road-weary traveling employees earn, it's their frequent-flyer miles. When employers don't let people keep their miles for personal use, it's a greedy move that fuels resentment with every flight. Work travel is a major sacrifice of time, energy, and sanity. Taking employees' miles sends the message that you don't appreciate their sacrifice and that you'll hold on to every last dollar at their expense.

People don't help each other out. There's a big difference between delegating responsibility and abdicating it. A boss who abdicates responsibility thinks that it's your problem, not theirs, and that you alone are responsible for solving it. However, researchers have shown that managers who support their employees in tasks that they delegate produce better team players who are more willing to help others and are more committed to their jobs.

They make failed attempts at political correctness. Maintaining high standards for how people treat each other is a wonderful thing, as we live in a world that's rife with animosity and discrimination. However, employers have to know when and where to step in. Going on a witch hunt because someone says "Bless you" to another employee who sneezed (a real example) creates an environment of paranoia and stifled self-expression, without improving how people treat each other.

They shut down self-expression. Many organizations control what people can have at their desks. A life-size poster of a shirtless Jason Mo-

moa? I get it; that's a problem. But employers dictate how many photographs people can display, whether they can use a water bottle, and how many items they're allowed to place on their desks. Once again, it's the old "If I could just hire robots, I wouldn't have this problem" approach. The same goes for dress codes. They work well in private high schools, but they're unnecessary at work. Hire professionals, and they'll dress professionally. When someone crosses the line, their manager needs to have the skill to address the issue directly. Otherwise, you're making everyone wish they worked somewhere else because management is too inept to handle touchy subjects effectively.

They overwork people. Nothing burns out good employees quite like overworking them. It's so tempting to work your best people hard that managers frequently fall into this trap. Overworking good employees is often perplexing to them; it makes them feel as if they're being punished for their great performance.

They don't make things fun. Strong social connections are an integral part of a healthy workplace. People who have strong connections with their colleagues get sick less often, are less likely to become depressed, learn faster, remember more, and simply do a better job. If people aren't having fun at work, then you're doing it wrong. People don't give their all if they aren't having fun, and fun is a major protector against brownout. The best companies to work for know the importance of letting employees loosen up a little. The idea is simple: If work is fun, you'll not only perform better but also stick around for longer hours and an even longer career.

HOW SMART LEADERS FAIL THEIR COMPANIES

Most businesses are run by highly intelligent people, and when businesses fail, it's usually due to these smart leaders' boneheaded mistakes. Even when a product—or lack of one—is at the center of the spectacle, flawed thinking by very smart people is often what makes things fall apart. There are far too many examples to list them all, but among my favorites is Kodak, a company that invented and then sat on the technology for digital photography because its leadership was afraid it would disrupt their core business (they eventually went bankrupt). And then there's Xerox, a company that not only failed to capitalize on one of the most game-changing products in history—a desktop computer with a graphical user interface—but also let Apple employees visit the facility and copy their technology. I don't have to tell you how that one turned out!

It's easy and even comforting to assume these leaders weren't paying attention, because this reinforces the idea that such failures could never happen to us. But the truth is that these leaders were intelligent people with supremely impressive track records. You can bet they were paying attention. So, what happened? Sydney Finkelstein, a professor at Dartmouth's Tuck School of Business, spent six years searching for an answer to this question. He and his colleagues studied 51 of the business world's most notorious failures, interviewing CEOs and people at all levels. Finkelstein wanted to understand the inner workings of each business, explore the minds of key executives, and find out what led them to make disastrous decisions.

He and his team found that the poor decisions these smart leaders made were sometimes intentional and sometimes accidental, but they always followed a clear pattern of hubris that ensured even the most successful enterprise could be run into the ground. Here's what the leaders in Finkelstein's study had in common.

They viewed themselves, and their companies, as untouchable. There's nothing wrong with having lofty goals or a healthy sense of pride, but these leaders took their success for granted. They became so enamored with their ideas that they believed their competitors would never catch up, their circumstances would never change, and no disruptors would ever surface. These unrealistic expectations made failure inevitable. Leaders must continually question their positions, especially when they're on top.

They couldn't tell where they stopped and the company began.
The leaders in Finkelstein's study had high profiles and were obsessed with their company image. As a result, they were too busy being the face of the company to lead it effectively. This not only led to stagnation but also engendered dishonesty and corruption. A leader who sees a company as their own is more likely to hide anything that could tarnish that image, whether low numbers or faulty products.

They thought they were the smartest person in the room. Many intelligent leaders know quite well how smart they are. Their identities become so wrapped up in their intelligence that they believe input from others is unnecessary. They make decisions quickly and refuse to answer questions when there's a misunderstanding. Although this may fit the TV image of a strong leader, making split-second decisions with imprudence often leads to major mistakes. Your chance of failure is heightened when you don't want to know what other people think.

They surrounded themselves with yes-men and -women. Some leaders become so obsessed with loyalty that they expect mindless support for every decision they make. This alienates valuable employees and silences voices that could otherwise help the business succeed. When a leader begins to equate disagreement with disloyalty (or worse, the undermining of their authority), no one raises warning flags.

They drove past red flags and warning signs. Some leaders are so enamored with their personal visions that they're willing to drive the company off a cliff in pursuit of them. Many of these leaders solicit input and suggestions, but they just can't take their foot off the gas. Persistence is a great quality in a leader, but not if it means ignoring the facts.

They relied too much on what worked before. Evaluating your previous successes and failures can help a business thrive, but the past shouldn't be the driving force behind a company's future. Finkelstein's team found that many failed leaders took one pivotal moment in their careers and continually tried to repeat it, even when their previous strategies no longer made sense. Customer needs, technology, and the competitive landscape can change on a dime. For this reason, successful leaders are constantly adapting to their surroundings.

Finkelstein's research shows us that most business failures can be avoided. The smartest leaders look deeply at their own behavior to fix potential problems before it's too late.

WHY EVERYONE SHOULD HAVE UNLIMITED VACATION DAYS

Most of this chapter has focused on things that companies and leaders need to stop doing to make the workplace a better place. That's for good reason, as it's deeply needed. Still, I want to finish on a positive note with a powerful suggestion that few companies have put into practice—unlimited vacation days. Since 2004, Netflix employees have taken as many vacation days as they've wanted. They have the freedom to decide when to show up for work, when to take time off, and how much time it will take them to get the job done. This doesn't seem to have hurt Netflix one bit. Since instituting the policy, its market cap has grown as high as $300 billion.

However, just because there's flexibility at Netflix doesn't mean there's no accountability. Employees have to keep their managers in the loop, and they're expected to perform at a very high level. High performance is so ingrained in Netflix culture that they reward adequate performance with a generous severance package. Netflix employees have unlimited vacation time because no one is tracking their time. Instead of micromanaging how people get their jobs done, the leadership focuses only on what matters— results. They've found that giving people greater autonomy creates a more responsible culture. Without the distraction of stifling rules, employees are more focused and productive.

When Netflix still had the typical vacation policy, employees asked an important question: "We don't track the time we spend working outside the office (like emails we answer at home and the work we do at night and on weekends), so why do we track the time we spend off the job?" Management listened. They couldn't deny the simple logic behind the question.

Back in the industrial age, when people stood on the assembly line from 9 to 5, paying for time made sense. With advances in technology, however, that's no longer the case. People work when work needs to be done from wherever they are. There's really no such thing as "after hours" anymore. We're now operating in a participation economy, where people are measured and paid for what they produce. Yet when it comes to time off, we're still clinging to the vestiges of the industrial economy, in which people were paid for the time they spent on the job. This is a huge demotivator. Netflix realized this, and the company changed its policy to reflect the way that work actually gets done.

Although Netflix was one of the first notable American companies to institute an unlimited vacation policy, the idea didn't start there. Brazilian company Semco has been quietly offering unlimited vacation for more than 30 years. Ricardo Semler, the son of the company's founder, had a health scare when he was only 21 and realized that the schedule he was keeping was slowly killing him, and that if it could kill him, then it could kill his employees, too. So, he made the radical decision to do away with schedules, sick days, and vacation time. Contrary to the prevailing worry that productivity would plummet, Semler found that employees actually became more productive and fiercely loyal, and when the employees thrived, the company did, too. When Semler first instituted this policy in 1981, Semco was just a $4 million company. It's now worth more than $1 billion.

As successful as unlimited vacation policies have been, less than 1% of U.S. companies have adopted them. That's not hard to understand when you think about our workaholic culture. U.S. employees get less vacation time than workers in any country except South Korea. In fact, American companies aren't legally required to give any paid time off at all, whereas it's mandated in many other countries. Workers in the United Kingdom, for instance, are entitled to 28 paid days off per year (including national holidays).

In Austria, Denmark, Finland, France, Luxembourg, and Sweden, employees receive a mandated 25 days of paid leave, and in Brazil, workers get 30 paid vacation days each year plus 11 national holidays.

Companies defend their strict vacation policies with the belief that employees will take advantage of anything else. However, companies that have actually tried unlimited vacation policies have found the opposite to be true. Freedom gives people such a strong sense of ownership and accountability that, like business owners, many end up taking no vacation at all. Employers that have instituted unlimited vacation policies have also had to create policies that encourage people to actually take time off. Evernote, for example, gives employees $1,000 to spend on vacation, and FullContact gives employees a whopping $7,500. Because employees are hesitant to take time off, they have to submit receipts showing that the funds were spent on a vacation in order to be reimbursed.

Although workaholic employees might sound good on paper, that's not what smart companies want. Smart companies know that when employees take time off to recharge—especially when they have the freedom to take time when they need it—they come back even more creative and productive. Subsidizing that time off is money well spent. It's sad that we're still compensated according to an assembly-line mentality. We work from whenever and wherever necessary to get results, so it only makes sense that our compensation and benefits reflect that shift.

BRINGING IT ALL TOGETHER

If managers want their best people to stay, they should think carefully about how they treat them. Good employees are as tough as nails, and their talent gives them an abundance of options. Managers should make people want to work for them. If companies rethink their policies and remove or alter those that are unnecessary or demoralizing, we'll all have a more enjoyable and productive time at work.

So, what should you do if your work environment is cutthroat? Should you leave? Only you can answer that question. However, the mental and physical consequences are real. Even if you decide to stick it out because you think the potential payout is worth the short-term sacrifice, just be certain you're not sacrificing something you can't get back—your health.

27

Survive a Bad Boss

––––

The "bad boss" has become a comedic part of work culture, permeating movies and television, but when you actually work for a bad boss, there's nothing funny about it. Researchers at the Harvard Business School and Stanford University meta-analyzed the results of more than 200 studies to better understand the effects of stress in the workplace. They found that worrying about losing your job makes you 50% more likely to experience poor health and that having an overly demanding job makes you 35% more likely to have a physician-diagnosed illness. Job insecurity and unrelenting demands perfectly characterize the environment created by bad bosses, and the negative health effects measured by the Harvard and Stanford researchers are as bad as those seen in people who are exposed to significant amounts of second-hand smoke.

Bad bosses are more common than you think. The American Psychological Association reported that 75% of American workers identify their boss as the worst and most stressful part of their job, and 60% of U.S. workers would take a new boss over a pay raise. It's obvious that bad bosses have a disastrous impact on their employees' health and productivity, so what do people working for bad bosses do about it? Not much. While 27% of people working for a bad boss quit as soon as they secure a new job, and 11% quit without having secured a new job, an amazing 59% stay put. That's an alarming number of people who are living with overwhelming stress and experiencing the trickle-down effects this has on their sanity and health.

There are many theories as to why people keep working for bad bosses, ranging from Stockholm syndrome to company loyalty. Sometimes it's just "comfortable couch" syndrome, where putting in the effort to find a new job seems too overwhelming. The problem is that the longer you stay with a bad boss, the harder it becomes to convince yourself to leave, and the bigger the toll it takes on your mind, body, and family. That's why it's important to know how to recognize the signs of a bad boss early, before you're sucked in so deeply that it's hard to leave. Here are some critical things to watch out for.

Belittling. Sometimes, it's necessary for bosses to deliver feedback about your performance that isn't easy to hear. But some of them give you the strong impression that they enjoy it. They don't just give you important feedback; they relish the act of putting you in your place—even more so if they have an audience. Although you don't necessarily want a boss who can't deliver tough feedback, you definitely don't want to work for someone who takes pleasure in criticizing and blaming.

Temper tantrums. Like everyone else, bosses have bad days. Pressure might cause your boss to lose their temper, but that shouldn't be happening on a regular basis. If your boss flies off the handle anytime something doesn't go exactly the way they want it to, it's time to reconsider your employment. Whether they're directed at you, their bosses, or just the forces of nature, tantrums set a negative emotional tone that reverberates throughout your workplace. They make people timid and cautious. People stop speaking up and sharing their creative ideas because they're afraid they're going to get slapped back down. If you hear your boss yelling down the hall, and instead of thinking, "What in the world is going on?," you're thinking, "Here we go again," then maybe it's time to move on.

Unreasonable expectations. Some bosses see their employees the same way that young children see their teachers—as having no identity outside their work. They can't quite wrap their minds around the importance of family obligations, hobbies, or anything else outside the office that doesn't serve them. These are the bosses who expect you to put in unreasonable hours that serve little purpose. If you get the feeling that you're disappointing your boss every time you leave for the day, then you're working in an unhealthy environment.

Failure to lead by example. If there's one thing that drives almost all employees crazy, it's a boss who doesn't walk the talk. It's extremely difficult to feel inspired and to take your job seriously when the people who set the standards for you don't live up to those expectations themselves.

Unwilling to listen. When employees feel that their managers are approachable, supportive, and willing to listen, their performance improves. That feeling of connection leads to a willingness to experiment and take risks, which, in turn, leads to better outcomes. On the other hand, if conversations between managers and employees never extend beyond TPS reports, and any attempts to ask questions or offer suggestions are rebuffed, the work environment is probably toxic.

They don't care about people. More than half of the people who leave their jobs do so because of their relationship with their boss. Empathy matters. Does your boss really see you as a person and care about how you're doing, or are they only focused on how much work you churn out? Smart companies make certain that their managers know how to balance being professional with being human. These are the bosses who celebrate their employees' successes, empathize with those going through hard times, and challenge them even when it hurts. Bosses who fail to really care will always have high turnover rates. It's impossible to work for someone for eight-plus hours a day when they aren't personally involved and don't care about anything other than your output.

THE SEVEN TYPES OF BAD BOSSES

Bad bosses contaminate the workplace. Some do so obliviously, while others smugly manipulate their employees, using them as instruments for their own success. Regardless of their methods, bad bosses cause irrevocable damage to their companies and employees by hindering performance and creating unnecessary stress. Multiple studies have found that working for a bad boss increases your chance of having a heart attack by as much as 50%. Even more troubling is the number of bad bosses out there. Gallup research found that 60% of government workers are miserable because of bad bosses. In another study, 69% of U.S. workers compared bosses with too much power to toddlers with too much power. The comparisons don't stop there. Significant percentages of U.S. workers describe their bosses as self-oriented (60%), stubborn (49%), overly demanding (43%), and impulsive (41%). Most bosses aren't surprised by these statistics. A DDI study found that 64% of managers admit that they need to work on their management skills. When asked where they should focus their efforts, managers overwhelmingly say, "Bringing in the numbers," yet they are most often fired for poor people skills.

Although the best option when you have a bad boss is to seek other employment, this isn't always possible. People with high emotional intelligence know how to make the most of a bad situation. A bad boss doesn't deter them because they understand that success is simply the product of how well you play the hand you've been dealt. When that "hand" is a bad boss, they identify the type of bad boss they're working for and then use this information to neutralize their boss's behavior. The following are seven of the most common types of bad bosses and the habits that people with high emotional intelligence employ to survive them.

Tyrants

Tyrants resort to Machiavellian tactics and constantly make decisions that feed their egos. Their primary concern is maintaining power, and they coerce and intimidate others to do so. Tyrants think of their employees as a criminal gang aboard their ship. They classify people in their minds and treat them accordingly: High achievers who challenge tyrants' thinking are treated as mutinous. Those who support tyrants' achievements with gestures of loyalty find themselves in the position of first mate. Those who perform poorly are stuck cleaning the head and swabbing the decks.

How to neutralize a tyrant: A painful but effective strategy for tyrants is to present your ideas in a way that allows them to take partial credit. The tyrants can then maintain their egos without having to shut down your idea. Always be quick to give them some credit, although they are unlikely to reciprocate, because this will inevitably put you on their good side. Moreover, to survive a tyrant, you have to choose your battles wisely. If you practice self-awareness and manage your emotions, you can rationally choose which battles are worth fighting and which ones you should just let go. This way, you won't find yourself on latrine duty.

Micromanagers

These are bosses who make you feel like you're under constant surveillance. Micromanagers pay too much attention to small details, and their constant hovering makes employees feel discouraged, frustrated, and even uncomfortable. They thought your handwriting could use improvement, so they waited until you left work at 7:00 p.m. to throw away your pencils and replace them with the 0.9 mm lead mechanical pencils that have the "proper grip." They have even handed back your 20-page report because you used a binder clip instead of a staple.

How to neutralize a micromanager: Emotionally intelligent people appeal to micromanagers by proving themselves to be flexible, competent, and disciplined while staying in constant communication. Micromanagers are naturally drawn to the employees who produce work the way they envision. The challenge with micromanagers is grasping the "envisioned way." To do this, try asking specific questions about your project, check in frequently, and look for trends in the micromanager's feedback. Of course, this won't always work. Some micromanagers will never stop searching for something to over-analyze and micromanage. When this is the case, learn to derive your sense of satisfaction from within. Don't allow your boss's obsession with details to create feelings of inadequacy, as this will only lead to further stress and underperformance. Remember, a good report without a staple is still a good report. Despite your boss's focus on detail, they appreciate your work. They just don't know how to show it.

Inappropriate Buddies

This is the boss who's too friendly, and not in the fun, team-building sort of way. They're constantly inviting you to hang out outside work and engage in unnecessary office gossip. They use their influence to make friends at the expense of their work. They choose favorites and create divisions among employees, who become frustrated by the imbalance in attention and respect. They can't make tough decisions involving employees or even fire those who should be fired (unless they don't like them). Their office quickly becomes *The Office.*

How to neutralize an inappropriate buddy: The most important thing to do with this type of boss is to learn to set firm boundaries. Don't allow their position to intimidate you. By consciously and proactively establishing a boundary, you can take control of the situation. For example, you can remain friendly with your boss throughout the day but still not be afraid to say no to drinks after work. The difficult part here is maintaining consistency with your boundaries, even if your boss is persistent. By distancing yourself from your boss's behaviors that you deem inappropriate, you will still be able to succeed and even have a healthy relationship. It's important that you don't put up unnecessary boundaries that stop you from being seen as friendly. Having them see you as an ally will put you in a stronger position.

Robots

In the mind of robots, you are employee number 72 with a production yield of 84% and an experience level of 91. This boss makes decisions based on the numbers, and when they're forced to reach a conclusion without the proper data, they self-destruct. They make little or no effort to connect with their employees, and instead, look solely at the numbers to decide who is invaluable and who needs to go.

How to neutralize a robot: To succeed with robots, you need to speak their language. When you have an idea, make certain you have the data to back it up. The same goes for your performance—you need to know what they value and be able to show it to them if you want to prove your worth. Once you've accomplished this, you can begin trying to nudge them out of their antisocial comfort zone. The trick is to find ways to connect with them directly without being pushy or rude. Schedule face-to-face meetings and respond to some of their emails by knocking on their door. Forcing them to connect with you as a person, however so slightly, will make you more than a list of numbers and put a face to your name. Just because they're all about the numbers doesn't mean you can't make yourself the exception. Do so in small doses, however, because they're unlikely to respond well to the overbearing social type.

Visionaries

Their strength lies in their ideas and innovations. However, this entrepreneurial approach becomes dangerous when a plan or solution needs to be implemented, and they can't bring themselves to focus on the task at hand. When the time comes to execute their vision, they're already off to the next idea, and you're left to figure things out on your own.

How to neutralize a visionary: To best deal with this type, reverse their train of thought. They naturally take a broad perspective, so be quick to funnel things down into something smaller and more practical. To do so, ask a lot of specific questions that force them to rationally approach the issue and consider potential obstacles to executing their broad ideas. Don't refute their ideas directly, or they'll feel criticized. Instead, focus their attention on what it will take to realistically implement their plan. Often, your questions will diffuse their plans, and when they don't, they'll get them to understand—and commit to—the effort it's going to take on their part to help make it happen.

Incompetents

These bosses were promoted hastily or hired haphazardly and hold positions that are beyond their capabilities. Most likely, they are not completely incompetent, but they have people who report to them who have been at the company a lot longer and have information and skills they lack.

How to neutralize an incompetent: If you find yourself frustrated with this type of boss, it is likely because you have experience that they lack. It's important to swallow your pride and share your experience and knowledge, without rubbing it in their face. Share the information that this boss needs to grow into their role, and you'll become their ally and confidant.

Seagulls

We've all been there—sitting in the shadow of a seagull manager, who decided it was time to roll up their sleeves, swoop in, and squawk up a storm. Instead of taking the time to get the facts straight and work alongside the team to realize a viable solution, seagulls deposit steaming piles of formulaic advice and then abruptly take off, leaving everyone behind to clean up the mess. Seagulls interact with their employees only when there's a fire to put out. Even then, they move in and out so hastily—and put so little thought into their approach—that they make bad situations worse by frustrating and alienating those who need them the most.

How to neutralize a seagull: A group approach works best with seagulls. If you can get the entire team to sit down with the seagull and explain that their abrupt approach to solving problems makes it extremely difficult for everyone to perform at their best, this message is likely to be heard. If the entire group bands together and provides constructive, non-threatening feedback, the seagull will more often than not find a better way to work with their team. It's easy to spot a seagull when you're on the receiving end of their airborne dumps, but the manager doing the squawking is often unaware of the negative impact of their behavior. Have the group give the manager a little nudge, and things are bound to change for the better.

OVERCOMING TOXIC WORKING RELATIONSHIPS

At work, almost everyone has experienced a relationship that turned toxic. Whether the toxic relationship is with your boss or a coworker, they're a major drain on your energy, productivity, and happiness. In a study conducted by Georgetown University researchers, 98% of people reported experiencing toxic behavior at work. The study found that toxic relationships negatively influence employees and their organizations in eight notable ways:

1. 80% lost work time worrying about the incidents.
2. 78% said that their commitment to the organization decreased.
3. 66% said that their performance declined.
4. 63% lost work time avoiding the offender.
5. 47% intentionally decreased the time they spent at work.
6. 38% intentionally decreased the quality of their work.
7. 25% admitted to taking their frustration out on customers.
8. 12% said that they left their job because of it.

While the turnover from toxic relationships is costly, the real cost is the lost productivity and emotional distress experienced by people who are stuck in these relationships. We may not be able to control the toxicity of other people, but we can control how we respond to them, and this has the power to alter the course of a relationship. Before a toxic relationship can be neutralized, you have to understand what's making it toxic in the first place. Recognizing and understanding toxicity enables you to develop effective strategies for thwarting future toxic interactions. The following are the most common types of toxic relationships and strategies to help you overcome them.

Relationships that are passive aggressive. This type takes many forms in the workplace, from the manager who gives you the cold shoulder to the colleague who cc's emails to your boss. Passive aggression is deadly in the workplace, where opinions and feelings need to be placed on the table for progress to continue. When you find someone behaving passive aggressively toward you, you have to communicate the problem. Passive-aggressive types typically act the way they do because they're trying to avoid the issue at hand. If you can't bring yourself to open up a line of communication, you may find yourself joining in the mind games. Just remember, passive-aggressive types tend to be sensitive and to avoid conflict, so when you do bring something up, make sure to do so as constructively and harmoniously as possible.

Relationships that lack forgiveness and trust. It's inevitable that you're going to make mistakes at work. Some people get so fixated on other people's mistakes that it seems as if they believe they don't make mistakes themselves. You'll find that these people hold grudges, are constantly afraid that other people are going to do them harm, and may even begin nudging you out of important projects. If you're not careful, this can stifle upward career movement by removing important opportunities for growth. The frustrating thing about this type of relationship is that it takes just one mistake to lose hundreds of "trust points" but hundreds of perfect actions to get one trust point back. To win back their trust, it's crucial to pay extra-close attention to detail. Don't get frazzled by the fact that they will be constantly looking for mistakes. You have to use every ounce of patience while you dig yourself out of the subjective hole you're in. Remember, Rome wasn't built in a day.

Relationships that are idealistic. Idealistic relationships are those where we begin to hold people in too high a regard. When you think your colleague walks on water, the relationship becomes toxic because you don't have the boundaries you need in a healthy working relationship. For instance, you might overlook a mistake that needs attention or do work that violates your moral compass because you assume your colleague is in the right. This loss of boundaries is extremely toxic to you, and you have the power to set the relationship straight. No matter how close you may be to someone, or how great you think their work may be, you should remain objective. If you're the one people are idealizing, you should speak up and insist that they treat you the same way they treat everyone else.

Relationships that are one-sided. Relationships are supposed to be mutually beneficial. They have a natural give and take. In the workplace, this applies to relationships with people who report to you (they should be getting things done for you, and you should be teaching them) as well as with people you report to (you should be learning from them but also contributing). These relationships become toxic when one person gives a disproportionate amount, or one person only wants to take. It could be a manager who has to guide an employee through every excruciating detail or colleagues who find themselves doing all the work. If possible, the best thing to do with this type is to stop giving. Unfortunately, this isn't always possible. When it isn't, you need to have a frank conversation with them to recalibrate the relationship.

Relationships that are punitive. Punitive relationships are those in which one person punishes the other for behavior that doesn't align directly with their expectations. The major issue with punitive types is that their instinct is to punish without adequate communication, feedback, and understanding. This belittling approach creates conflict and bad feelings. To survive a punitive type, you must choose your battles wisely. Your voice won't be heard if you dive right into every conflict. They'll just label you as someone who is too sensitive.

Relationships built on lies. In these relationships, people get so caught up in looking good that they lose track of what's fact and what's fiction. Then, the lies pile up until they're the foundation of the relationship. People who won't give you straight answers don't deserve your trust. After all, if they're willing to lie to you, how can you ever really depend on them? When you remove trust from a relationship, you don't have a relationship at all. Building a relationship on lies is no different than building a house on a pile of sand. The best thing you can do is count your losses and move on.

BRINGING IT ALL TOGETHER

There are many different types of toxic relationships in the workplace. All of them will test your emotional intelligence skills. When you find yourself embroiled in one, it's worth the effort to evaluate things carefully and develop a course of action that will save your sanity and improve your career. If the toxic relationship is with your boss, things become considerably more complicated. You'll have your work cut out for you. Having a bad boss is more than just irritating—it can cause very real damage to your mental and physical health.

28

Learn Your Lesson

—

Our days are filled with a constant stream of decisions. Most are mundane, but some are so important that they can haunt you for the rest of your life. The sheer number of decisions we have to make each day leads to a phenomenon I've mentioned in previous chapters called decision fatigue, in which your brain actually tires like a muscle. A study at the University of Texas showed that even when our brains aren't tired, they can make it very difficult for us to make good decisions. When making a decision, instead of referencing the knowledge we've accumulated, our brains focus on specific, detailed memories. For example, if you're buying a new car and trying to decide if you should go for the leather seats, even though you know you can't afford them, your brain might focus on memories of the wonderful smell and feel of the leather seats in your brother's sports car when it should be focused on the misery you're going to experience when making your monthly car payments. Because you don't have memories of this yet, it's hard for your brain to contemplate.

Regardless of the magnitude of the decision, our brains make it hard for us to keep the perspective we need to make good decisions. Over time, these decisions add up, and when they're poor, they can lead to regret. Bronnie Ware spent her career as a palliative care nurse, working exclusively with people who were three to 12 months from death. She made a habit of asking them about their greatest regrets, and she heard the same five regrets repeatedly.

Examining these regrets now can help ensure that you make good, emotionally intelligent decisions and don't fall victim to them in your final days.

Regret 1: They wish they hadn't worked so hard.

Working hard is a great way to impact the world, to learn, to grow, to feel accomplished, and sometimes even to find happiness, but it becomes a problem when you work hard at the expense of the people closest to you. Ironically, we often work hard to make money for the people we care about, without realizing that they value our company more than money. The key is to find a balance between doing what you love and being with the people you love. Otherwise, you'll look back one day and wish you'd focused more on the latter.

Regret 2: They wish they had stayed in touch with their friends.

When you get caught up in your weekly routine, it's easy to lose sight of how important people are to you, especially those you have to make time for. Relationships with old friends are among the first things to fall off the table when we're busy. This is unfortunate because spending time with friends is a major stress buster. Close friends bring you energy, fresh perspectives, and a sense of belonging in a way that no one else can.

Regret 3: They wish they had expressed their feelings.

We're taught as children that emotions are dangerous and that they must be bottled up and controlled. This usually works at first, but boxing up your feelings causes them to grow until they erupt. The best thing you can do is put your feelings directly on the table. Although it's painful to initiate, it forces you to be honest and transparent. For example, if you feel as though you don't make enough money at work, schedule a meeting with your boss and propose why you think you're worth more. They will either agree with you and give you a raise or disagree and tell you what you need to do to become more valuable. However, if you do nothing and let your feelings fester, this will hinder your performance and prevent you from reaching your goal.

Regret 4: They wish they hadn't made decisions based on what other people think.

When you make decisions based on other people's opinions, two things tend to happen:

- You make poor career choices: There are too many people out there who studied for a degree they regret or even spent their lives pursuing a career they regret. Whether you're seeking parental approval or pursuing pay and prestige over passion, making a poor career choice is a decision that will live with you forever.

- You fail to uphold your morals: When you get too caught up in what your boss thinks of you, how much money you think your spouse needs to be happy, or how bad you will look if you fail, you are at high risk of violating your own morals. Your intense desires to make yourself look good and to please other people compromise your ability to stay true to yourself and, ultimately, to feel good.

Regret 5: They wish they had let themselves be happy.

When your life is about to end, all the difficulties you've faced suddenly become trivial compared to the good times. This is because you realize that, more often than not, suffering is a choice. Unfortunately, most people realize this far too late. Although we all inevitably experience pain, how we react to our pain is completely under our control, as is our ability to experience joy. Learning to laugh, smile, and be happy (especially when stressed) is a challenge at times, but it's one that's worth every ounce of effort.

PHRASES EMOTIONALLY INTELLIGENT PEOPLE NEVER UTTER AT WORK

There are some things you simply never want to say at work. These phrases carry special power: They have an uncanny ability to make you look bad, even when the words are true. Worst of all, there's no taking them back once they slip out. I'm not talking about shocking slips of the tongue, off-color jokes, or politically incorrect faux pas. These aren't the only ways to make yourself look bad. Often, it's the subtle remarks—the ones that paint us as incompetent and unconfident—that do the most damage. No matter how talented you are or what you've accomplished, certain phrases instantly change the way people see you and can forever cast you in a negative light. These phrases are so loaded with negative implications that they undermine careers in short order. So, make certain you never utter these emotionally unintelligent career killers.

"This is the way it's always been done."

Technology-fueled change is happening so fast that even a six-month-old process can be outdated. Saying "this is the way it's always been done" not only makes you sound lazy and resistant to change, but it could also make your boss wonder why you haven't tried to improve things on your own. If you really are doing things the way they've always been done, there's almost certainly a better way.

"He's lazy/incompetent/a jerk."

There is no upside to making a disparaging remark about a colleague. If your remark is accurate, everybody already knows it, so there's no need to point it out. If your remark is inaccurate, you're the one who ends up looking like a jerk. There will always be rude or incompetent people in any workplace, and chances are that everyone knows who they are. If you don't have the power to help them improve or fire them, then you have nothing to gain by broadcasting their ineptitude. Announcing your colleague's incompetence comes across as an insecure attempt to make you look better. Your callousness will inevitably come back to haunt you in the form of your coworkers' negative opinions of you.

"It's not fair."

Everyone knows that life isn't fair. Saying "it's not fair" suggests that you think life is supposed to be fair, which makes you look immature and naïve. If you don't want to make yourself look bad, you should stick to the facts, stay constructive, and leave your interpretation out of it. For instance, instead of saying the phrase above, you could say, "I noticed that you assigned Ann that big project I was hoping for. Would you mind telling me what went into that decision? I'd like to know why you thought I wasn't a good fit, so that I can work on improving those skills."

"No problem."

When someone asks you to do something or thanks you for doing something, and you tell them "no problem," you're implying that their request should have been a problem. This makes people feel as though they've imposed upon you. What you want to do instead is show people that you're happy to help. Say something like, "It was my pleasure" or "I'll be happy to take care of that." It's a subtle difference in language, but it has a huge impact on people.

"I think .../This may be a silly idea .../I'm going to ask a stupid question."

These overly passive phrases instantly erode your credibility. Even if you follow these phrases with a great idea, they suggest that you lack confidence, which makes the people you're speaking to lose confidence in you. Don't be your own worst critic. If you're not confident in what you're saying, no one else will be, either. And if you really don't know something, say, "I don't have that information right now, but I'll find out and get right back to you."

"I'll try."

Just like the word "think," "try" sounds tentative and suggests that you lack confidence in your ability to execute the task. Take full ownership of your capabilities. If you're asked to do something, either commit to doing it or offer an alternative, but don't say that you'll try, because it sounds like you won't try all that hard.

"That's not in my job description."

This often sarcastic phrase makes you sound as though you're only willing to do the bare minimum required to keep getting a paycheck, which is a bad thing if you like job security. If your boss asks you to do something that you feel is inappropriate for your position (as opposed to morally or ethically inappropriate), the best move is to complete the task eagerly. Later, schedule a conversation with your boss to discuss your role in the company and whether your job description needs an update. This ensures that you avoid looking petty. It also enables you and your boss to develop a long-term understanding of what you should and shouldn't be doing.

"It's not my fault."

It's never a good idea to cast blame. Be accountable. If you had any role—no matter how small—in whatever went wrong, own it. If not, offer an objective, dispassionate explanation of what happened. Stick to the facts, and let your boss and colleagues draw their own conclusions about who's to blame. The moment you start pointing fingers is the moment people start seeing you as someone who lacks accountability for their actions. This makes people nervous. Some will avoid working with you altogether, and others will strike first and blame you when something goes wrong.

"This will only take a minute."

Saying that something only takes a minute undermines your skills and gives the impression that you rush through tasks. Unless you're literally going to complete the task in 60 seconds, feel free to say that it won't take long, but don't make it sound as though the task can be completed any sooner than it can actually be finished.

"I can't."

"I can't" is "it's not my fault's" twisted sister. People don't like to hear "I can't" because they think it means "I won't." Saying "I can't" suggests that you're not willing to do what it takes to get the job done. If you really can't do something because you truly lack the necessary skills, you should offer an alternative solution. Instead of saying what you "can't" do, say what you "can" do. For example, instead of saying, "I can't stay late tonight," say, "I can come in early tomorrow morning. Will that work?" Instead of "I can't run those numbers," say, "I don't yet know how to run that type of analysis. Is there someone who can show me so that I can do it on my own next time?"

THINGS EMOTIONALLY INTELLIGENT PEOPLE NEVER REVEAL ABOUT THEMSELVES AT WORK

At work, sharing the right aspects of yourself in the right ways is an art form. Disclosures that feel like relationship builders in the moment can wind up as obvious no-nos with hindsight. The trouble is, you can't build a strong professional network if you don't open up to your colleagues. Doing so is tricky because revealing the wrong things can have a devastating effect on your career. You have to know where the line is and be careful not to cross it.

Emotionally intelligent people are adept at reading others, and this ability shows them what they should and shouldn't reveal about themselves at work. They know better than to reveal any of the following, because these things will send your career careening in the wrong direction.

Your political beliefs. People's political beliefs are too closely tied to their identities to be discussed without incident at work. Disagreeing with someone else's views can quickly alter their otherwise strong perception of you. Confronting someone's core values is one of the most insulting things you can do. Granted, different people treat politics differently, but asserting your values can alienate some people as quickly as it intrigues others. Even bringing up a hot-button world event without asserting a strong opinion can lead to conflict. People build their lives around their ideals and beliefs, and giving them your two cents is risky. Be willing to listen to others without inputting anything on your end. Political opinions are so deeply ingrained in people that challenging their views is more likely to get you judged than to change their minds.

How much money you make. Your parents may love to hear all about how much you're pulling in each month, but in the workplace, this only breeds negativity. It's impossible to allocate salaries with perfect fairness, and revealing yours gives your coworkers a direct measure of comparison. As soon as everyone knows how much you make, everything you do at work is considered against your income. It's tempting to swap salary figures with a buddy out of curiosity, but the moment you do, you'll never see each other the same way again.

That you hate your job. The last thing anyone wants to hear at work is someone complaining about how much they hate their job. Doing so labels you as a negative person who is not a team player. This brings down the morale of the group. Bosses are quick to catch on to naysayers who drag down morale, and they know that there are always enthusiastic replacements waiting just around the corner.

What you do in the bedroom. Whether your sex life is out of this world or lacking entirely, this information has no place at work. Such comments will get a chuckle from some people, but they make most uncomfortable, and even offended. Crossing this line will instantly give you a bad reputation.

What you think someone else does in the bedroom. A good 111% of the people you work with do not want to know that you bet they're tigers in the sack. There's no more surefire way to creep someone out than to let them know that thoughts of their love life have entered your brain. Anything from speculating on a colleague's sexual orientation to making a relatively indirect comment like, "Oh, to be a newlywed again," plants a permanent seed in the brains of all who hear it that casts you in a negative light. Keep your thoughts to yourself.

How wild you used to be. Your past can say a lot about you. Just because it's been many years since you did something outlandish or stupid doesn't mean people will believe you've developed impeccable judgment since then. Some behavior that might qualify as just another day in the typical fraternity (binge drinking, petty theft, and so on) shows everyone you work with that when push comes to shove, you have poor judgment and don't know where to draw the line. Many presidents have been elected despite their past indiscretions, but unless you have a team of handlers and PR types protecting and spinning your image, you should keep your unsavory past to yourself.

That you're job hunting. When I was a kid, I told my baseball coach that I would be quitting the team in two weeks. For the next two weeks, I found myself riding the bench. It got even worse after those two weeks when I decided to stay, as I became "the kid who doesn't even want to be here." I was crushed, but it was my own fault. I told him my decision before it was certain. The same thing happens when you tell people that you're job hunting. Once you reveal that you're planning to leave, you suddenly become a waste of everyone's time. There's also the chance that your hunt will be unsuccessful, so it's best to wait until you've found a job before you tell anyone. Otherwise, you'll end up riding the bench.

LEARN TO ENJOY BEING ALONE

We live in a world of constant contact—a place that's losing sight of the importance of being alone. Offices are abandoning cubicles in favor of shared desks and wide-open common spaces, and rather than sitting at desks working independently, schoolchildren are placed in groups. It seems that a never-ending "ping" has become our culture's omnipresent background noise, instantly informing us of every text, tweet, and notification. Even something as mundane as cooking dinner has become worthy of social sharing. One result of all this social connection is that many of us rarely have any time alone. Although we're told that this connectivity is a good thing and that being around other people is necessary for a fulfilled life, you can certainly have too much of a good thing. That's why the last lesson you'll learn in this chapter is that spending time alone is a good habit. In the words of Jean de La Bruyère, "All men's misfortunes spring from their hatred of being alone."

A study of 600 computer programmers at 92 companies found that although productivity levels were stable within each company, they varied greatly from one company to the next. The more productive companies had one thing in common: They ditched the ultra-hip open office in favor of private workspaces that provided freedom from interruptions. Of the top performers, 62% said they had adequate privacy at work, while only 19% of the worst performers shared that opinion. Among the low performers, 76% said they were often unnecessarily interrupted.

Solitude isn't just a professional plus; it's also good for your mental and emotional well-being. To get the most out of life, learn to enjoy spending time alone. The benefits of solitude are too numerous to catalog, but the following are some of the best.

You recuperate and recharge. All of us—even the most extroverted among us—need time to recuperate and recharge. There's nothing like spending time alone to make this happen. The peace, quiet, and mental solitude you experience when you're by yourself are essential to recovering from the stresses of daily living.

You can do what you want. As fun as it is to spend time with other people, it inevitably leads to compromise. You're constantly modifying your ideas to accommodate other people's interests. Being alone frees you up to do exactly what you want when you want. You can throw on whatever you feel like wearing, eat what you feel like eating, and work on projects that are meaningful to you.

It boosts your self-esteem. Enjoying your own company is a huge confidence booster. If you're bored and restless when you're by yourself, it's easy to start thinking that *you're* boring or that you need other people around to enjoy yourself. Learning to enjoy time alone boosts your self-esteem by confirming that you're enough.

You learn to trust yourself. Freedom is more than doing what you want; it's the ability to trust your gut and to think clearly, without any pressure or outside influence. Being alone helps you form a clear understanding of who you are, what you know, and what's right for you. It teaches you to trust yourself. When you're around others, even when you don't realize it, you monitor people's reactions to gauge the appropriateness of your own feelings and actions. When you're alone, it's all on you. You develop your own ideas and opinions without having them watered down by what anyone else thinks. Once you learn to enjoy being alone, you'll discover what you're truly capable of without the constraints of other people's thinking.

It increases your emotional intelligence. Self-awareness is the foundation of emotional intelligence, and you can't increase your EQ without it. Because self-awareness requires understanding your emotions and how you react to various people and situations, this necessitates careful self-reflection, which happens best when you're alone.

You appreciate other people more. Absence really does make the heart grow fonder. Time alone lets you see people in a whole new light, and it helps you develop a renewed sense of gratitude for who they are and what they do.

You get more done. It's said that "more hands make light work," and although that might be true when it comes to raking leaves, it's a completely different story with cognitive tasks. Even the effectiveness of brainstorming is more myth than reality. Researchers at Texas A&M found that group brainstorming hinders productivity due to "cognitive fixation." Cognitive fixation is the tendency for people working in groups to get stuck on other people's ideas, reducing their ability to come up with anything new, and the bigger the group, the more fixated everyone becomes. Spending time alone not only eliminates distractions but also ensures that you don't have trouble with "too many cooks."

BRINGING IT ALL TOGETHER

Emotionally intelligent people learn their lesson because they never stop learning. They learn from their mistakes, and they learn from their triumphs, and they're always changing themselves for the better. I hope the lessons in this chapter are as useful to you as they have been to me over the years. As I write them, I'm reminded of their power and my desire to use them every day.

29

Break the Bad Habits That Are Holding You Back

Have you ever tried to break a bad habit only to give up in frustration? The problem isn't that you're weak or that the bad habit is too ingrained. In all likelihood, you just gave up too soon. Researchers at University College, London, found that it takes 66 days for a new habit to form. Likewise, as long as a physical addiction isn't involved, it takes 66 days for you to shake a bad habit. But before you can develop the motivation to stick it out for that long, you should understand how bad habits form in the first place.

Bad habits are formed and reinforced via the *habit loop*. First, something triggers you to initiate an undesired behavior. Maybe you're feeling stressed, so you decide to numb out on Facebook for an hour or eat a whole bag of Flamin' Hot Cheetos. The trigger event is whatever puts this idea in your head. The second step is the behavior itself. Your brain says, "Sure, you deserve some Flamin' Hot Cheetos," so you dig in. The third step—and this part is crucial—is the reward. The behavior has to reward you in some way. That doesn't mean it's good for you or that it's smart, just that it does something that your brain likes. Numbing out on Facebook might help you forget your problems for a while, and we all know, all too well, the reward that comes from eating a bag of junk food. For better or worse, these rewards increase the likelihood that you'll repeat the behavior.

Once you repeat a behavior enough times, the habit loop becomes so automated that you don't even think about it anymore. Instead of making a conscious decision to procrastinate, you just automatically pull up Facebook as soon as you sit down at your desk, or you're digging into the Cheetos before you even realize that you're feeling stressed. Once a habit becomes automatic, it's a lot harder to break—and that's why you're probably failing if you're not giving yourself 66 days to wean yourself off it. Sixty-six days might seem like a long time, but there are specific stages that make the process feel much shorter. Let's look at them.

Days 1–10: Look Inward

It's usually pretty obvious which bad habits are causing the most problems in your life—the ones that keep coming up in performance appraisals or sparking arguments with your spouse. Once you've identified a habit to change, the real challenge lies in understanding your triggers. That can be harder than it sounds, especially if the habit has become so ingrained that you do it subconsciously. If you give it enough thought, you'll get to the bottom of it. Maybe you keep getting tickets for speeding, and you realize that you drive too fast when you leave work in a bad mood, or maybe you snack when you're stressed. Looking inward to explore the source of the habit you're trying to break makes breaking that habit possible. The first 10 days of trying to break the habit will provide substantial insight into its source, should you look.

Days 11–40: Spread the Word

Accountability is crucial for breaking bad habits. In this stage, you create a very vocal accountability network by telling everybody you can about the habit you're trying to break. The more vocal you are about it, the more likely people are to call you out when you slip up. Let them know that you really want them to say something. Just remember that you might have to keep reminding them—it's just as easy for them to forget and backslide as it is for you. Accountability feeds your efforts to avoid bad habits. Sure, you avoid them some on your own, but your efforts are turbocharged when you don't want the negative attention that comes with engaging in your bad habits. Before long, you've had enough practice avoiding them, and sometimes you don't even have to think about it.

Days 41–66: Mind Your Relapse Triggers

As you head for the home stretch, be ready to make some mistakes—it happens to everybody. Just be on the lookout for common threads running through those mistakes. If you tend to relapse in a certain situation, you'd be smart to avoid that trigger completely until you feel that your bad habit is really extinguished. In addition, keep an eye out for new or rare triggers that haven't popped up yet. Keeping new triggers from surprising you when it feels like you've kicked a habit is typically the difference between success and failure this late in the process.

Day 67: Reward Yourself

Sure, you could say that breaking the habit is its own reward, but why pass up an opportunity to celebrate? Just don't celebrate by indulging in the habit that you worked so hard to break! Rewarding yourself is critical because it reinforces the new habit loop you've created to replace and extinguish the bad habit. You've replaced your old negative responses to your triggers with positive new ones. Without a clear and apparent reward, your mind might lose the urge to follow through in the future. You should also use this opportunity to reflect on and select the next habit you're going to break.

THE BAD HABITS YOU MUST BREAK

Nothing sabotages your productivity quite like bad habits. Bad habits slow you down, decrease your accuracy, make you less creative, and stifle your performance. Ultimately, you are the sum of your habits. When you allow bad habits to take over, they dramatically impede your path to success. The challenge is that bad habits are insidious, creeping up on you slowly until you don't even notice the damage they're causing. I think Warren Buffet said it best: "Chains of habit are too light to be felt until they are too heavy to be broken."

Getting control of your bad habits is critical, and not just for productivity's sake. Breaking bad habits requires self-control—and lots of it. Self-control requires emotional intelligence. Research has indicated that it's worth the effort, as self-control has huge implications for success. University of Pennsylvania psychologists Angela Duckworth and Martin Seligman conducted a study in which they measured college students' IQ scores and levels of self-control upon entering university. Four years later, they looked at the students' grade point averages (GPAs) and found that self-control was twice as important as IQ in earning a high GPA. In addition, a University of Minnesota study found that people who exercise a high degree of self-control tend to be much happier than those who don't, both in the moment and in the long run.

The self-control required to develop good habits (and stop bad ones) also serves as the foundation for a strong work ethic and high productivity. Some bad habits cause more trouble than others. The following bad habits are the worst offenders. Shedding them will increase your productivity and allow you to enjoy the positive mood that comes with increased self-control.

Impulsively surfing the Internet. It takes you 15 consecutive minutes of focus before you can fully engage in a task. Once you do, you fall into a euphoric state of increased productivity called flow. Research has shown that people in a flow state are five times more productive than they would otherwise be. When you click out of your work because you get an itch to check the news, Facebook, a sport's score, or what have you, this pulls you out of flow. This means you have to go through another 15 minutes of continuous focus to reenter the flow state. Click in and out of your work enough times, and you can go through an entire day without experiencing high productivity.

Eating too much sugar. Glucose functions as the "gas pedal" for energy in the brain. You need glucose to concentrate on challenging tasks. With too little glucose, you feel tired, unfocused, and slow; too much glucose leaves you jittery and unable to concentrate. The tricky thing is that you can get your glucose any way you want, and you'll feel the same—at least initially. The difference lies in how long your productivity lasts. Donuts, soda, and other forms of refined sugar lead to an energy boost that lasts only 20 minutes, while oatmeal, brown rice, and other foods containing complex carbohydrates release their energy slowly, enabling you to sustain your focus.

Using multiple notifications. Multiple notifications are a productivity nightmare. Studies have shown that hopping on your phone and email every time they ping causes your productivity to plummet. Getting notified every time a message drops onto your phone or an email arrives in your inbox might feel productive, but it isn't. Instead of working at the whim of your notifications, pool all your emails/texts and check them at designated times (e.g., respond to your emails every hour). This is a proven, productive way to work. In addition to checking email on a schedule, productive people take advantage of features that prioritize messages by sender. They set alerts for their most important vendors and their best customers, and they save the rest until they reach a stopping point in their work. Some people even set up an autoresponder that lets senders know when they'll be checking their email again.

Putting off tough tasks. We have a limited amount of mental energy, and as we exhaust this energy, our decision-making and productivity decline rapidly. This is called decision fatigue. When you put off tough tasks until late in the day because they're intimidating, you save them for when you're at your worst. To beat decision fatigue, you should tackle complex tasks in the morning when your mind is fresh.

Letting toxic people live in your head rent free. There will always be toxic people who have a way of getting under your skin and staying there. Each time you find yourself thinking about a coworker or person who makes your blood boil, practice being grateful for someone else in your life instead. There are plenty of people out there who deserve your attention, and the last thing you want to do is think about the people who don't matter when there are people who do.

Hitting the snooze button. When you sleep, your brain moves through an elaborate series of cycles, the last of which prepares you to be alert at your wake-up time. This is why you sometimes wake up right before your alarm clock goes off—your brain knows it's time to wake up, and it's ready to do so. When you hit the snooze button and fall back asleep, you lose this alertness and wake up later, tired and groggy. Worst of all, this grogginess can take hours to wear off. So, no matter how tired you think you are when your alarm clock goes off, force yourself out of bed if you want to have a productive morning.

THE REAL HARM IN MULTITASKING

Multitasking is a bad habit that's so insidious and prevalent it's earned its own section in this chapter. You've likely heard that multitasking is problematic, but studies have shown that it kills your performance and may even damage your brain. Research conducted at Stanford University found that multitasking is less productive than doing a single thing at a time. The researchers showed that people who are regularly bombarded with several streams of electronic information cannot pay attention, recall information, or switch from one job to another as well as those who complete one task at a time.

But what if some people have a special gift for multitasking? The Stanford researchers compared groups of people based on their tendency to multitask and their belief that it helps their performance. They found that heavy multitaskers—those who multitask a lot and feel that it boosts their performance—were actually *worse* at multitasking than those who like to do a single thing at a time. The frequent multitaskers performed worse because they had more trouble organizing their thoughts and filtering out irrelevant information, and they were *slower* at switching from one task to another. Ouch.

Multitasking reduces your efficiency and performance because your brain can focus on only one thing at a time. When you try to do two things at once, your brain lacks the capacity to perform both tasks successfully. Researchers have also shown that in addition to slowing you down, multitasking temporarily lowers your IQ. A study at the University of London found that participants who multitasked during cognitive tasks experienced IQ score declines that were similar to what they'd expect if they had stayed up all night.

It was long believed that cognitive impairment from multitasking was always temporary, but new research suggests otherwise. Researchers at the University of Sussex in England compared the amount of time people spend on multiple devices (such as texting while watching TV) to MRI scans of their brains. They found that high multitaskers had less brain density in their anterior cingulate cortex, a region responsible for empathy as well as cognitive and emotional control. Although more research is needed to determine whether multitasking physically damages the brain (versus existing brain damage that predisposes people to multitask), it is clear that multitasking has negative effects. Neuroscientist Kep Kee Loh, the study's lead author, explained the implications: "I feel that it is important to create an awareness that the way we are interacting with the devices might be changing the way we think and these changes might be occurring at the level of brain structure."

If you're prone to multitasking, this is a bad habit you'll want to break—it clearly slows you down and decreases the quality of your work. Even if it doesn't cause brain damage, allowing yourself to multitask will fuel any existing difficulties you have with concentration, organization, and attention to detail. Multitasking in meetings and other social settings indicates low self- and social awareness, two emotional intelligence skills that are critical to success at work. If multitasking does damage your anterior cingulate cortex (a key brain region for EQ), as current research suggests, it will lower your EQ in the process. So, every time you multitask, you aren't just harming your performance in the moment; you may very well be damaging an area of your brain that's critical to your future success at work.

BRINGING IT ALL TOGETHER

You're not weak, stupid, or lazy if you have a hard time breaking bad habits. Psychological factors make this process challenging for everyone. The very science behind what makes habits hard to break also provides a research-supported method for breaking them. Focus on one habit at a time, follow the steps provided here and the timetable that goes with them, and your chances of success will go through the roof. By practicing self-control to break bad habits, you can simultaneously strengthen your self-control muscle and abolish nasty habits that have the power to hold you back. Some of the habits discussed here may seem minor, but they add up. Most amount to a personal choice between immediate pleasures and lasting ones. After all, the worst habit is losing track of what really matters to you.

30

Build Powerful New Success Habits

In Hans Christian Andersen's fable *The Red Shoes*, a young girl longs for a pair of pretty red shoes. She ultimately tricks the blind woman who cares for her into buying her a pair. Her love for the red shoes causes her to give them priority over the more important things in her life, and as often happens in fables, things go poorly for her. The shoes become stuck to her feet and force her to dance non-stop, to the point where she almost dies from exhaustion and starvation. We can scoff at the little girl's foolishness, but in real life, we often do the same thing—we chase after the things that we think will make us happy and don't realize that we're heading down a dangerous path. We don't always do this intentionally. We're driven in a given direction by our habits—small actions that we take each day, sometimes unconsciously. These little actions determine our direction in life.

When you focus on the right habits, no matter how small, you can see amazing changes over time. Your habits are the compound interest of self-improvement. Small changes may appear to make little to no difference until your habits accumulate and cross a critical threshold. That's when you experience a breakthrough and reap the full benefit of your efforts.

Habits are influenced by cues in your environment. For example, a study conducted by researchers at the University of Toronto found that simply seeing fast food logos makes people impatient and more likely to buy things impulsively. It's not that there's some intrinsic characteristic of fast food that makes people impatient. It's the habits we've come to associate with fast food—such as always being on the run, eating on the go, and the instant gratification of calorie-dense food—that bring out our impatience. When it comes to your habits, where you focus is what you'll get.

You should be very careful in choosing your pursuits, because your habits make you. Cultivating the right habits will take you where you want to go in life. The emotional intelligence habits that follow are a great start. They will help you lead a more meaningful and fulfilling life in which you cultivate the best within yourself.

Be biased toward action. If only we knew about all the great ideas that never came to fruition because people lacked the confidence to put them into action. Emotionally intelligent people confidently act on their ideas because they know that a failed idea is not a reflection of their ability; instead, they see it as a wonderful learning opportunity. This makes them eager to get going.

Seek composure. People who are composed constantly monitor their emotions. They understand their emotions well, and they use this knowledge in the moment to react with self-control to challenging situations. When things go downhill, they are persistently calm and frustratingly content (frustrating to those who aren't, at least). They know that no matter how good or bad things get, everything changes with time. All they can do is adapt and adjust to stay happy and in control.

Appreciate the here and now. Gratitude is fundamental to peace and happiness—not wealth, glamour, adventure, or fast cars, but simple appreciation for what you have. Just because you can't afford champagne and caviar doesn't mean that you never enjoy a meal. Hot dogs and beer on the back deck with your friends can taste just as good. So don't fool yourself into thinking that to be happy you need something that you don't have. The truth is that if you don't appreciate what you have now, you won't be able to appreciate the "good life" if you ever get it.

Realize that things aren't always as you perceive them to be. This goes along with appreciating the here and now. That person you envy because they seem to have the perfect life might be dealing with all kinds of problems behind closed doors. That "perfection" could be a total mirage. Your employer's decision to move the office might seem like a huge hassle when you first hear about it, but it could end up being one of the best things that ever happens to you. You're not omniscient and you're not a fortune-teller, so be open to the possibility that life might have some surprises in store, because what you see is not always what you get.

Stick to realistic goals. How many people start January by proclaiming, "I'm going to lose 30 pounds by March!"? Big, scary, crazy goals can be incredibly inspiring—until you fall short, and then, instead of inspiration, you're left with disappointment and guilt. Don't stop setting goals that push and challenge you, but try to stick within the bounds of reality. Small habits make big gains with time.

Expose yourself to a variety of people. There's no easier way to learn to think differently than spending time with someone whose strengths are your weaknesses or whose ideas are radically different from your own. This exposure sparks new ideas and makes you well rounded. This is why we see so many great companies with cofounders who are very different. Steve Jobs and Steve Wozniak at Apple were prime examples. Neither could have succeeded without the other.

Turn tedious tasks into games. Every job entails some degree of tedium. For most people, tedium leads to sloppy, rushed work. Emotionally intelligent people find ways to make the tedious interesting. By turning tedious work into a game, they challenge themselves and produce high-quality work, making things interesting in the process.

Start a collection of things that truly resonate with you. Have you ever come across a quote or a meme that so perfectly summed up your feelings that you wanted to keep it forever? When you come across things that resonate with you (whether it's something that expresses who you are or who you want to be), have a central place to keep those gems. It doesn't matter whether it's a spiral notebook, a bulletin board, or a folder on Evernote. Have a place to collect the things that matter so that you can revisit them regularly.

Get out and do something that reminds you who you are. We all joke about having "me" time, but what is that, really? It's making time for the activities that we feel most authentically ourselves doing. These are the times when all the masks are off, and we can just be. Whether it's going for a run or dancing around with your '80s favorites blaring at top volume, make time for those moments. They're incredibly rejuvenating.

THE PARADOXICAL HABITS OF WILDLY SUCCESSFUL PEOPLE

You know what they say about opinions—everybody has one. If you want to see that truth in action, Google "characteristics of successful people." Some of the results will undoubtedly point to the famous Marshmallow Study at Stanford, mentioned in a previous chapter, which demonstrated that the ability to delay gratification is a key component of success. The ability to delay gratification is important, but there's far more to it than that. Successful people are driven by personal growth. They focus on self-improvement and overcoming challenges. Successful people also play well with others. Successful people have other defining qualities. I could go on and on, but what's really happening here? Why are there so many different theories, complete with the science to back them up, about the traits that contribute to success? I think it's because most wildly successful people are complex—so complex that many of their defining qualities are paradoxical. Rather than an "either/or" set of static characteristics, they're more likely to demonstrate both. This is key to their success. The following are examples of what I'm referring to. These paradoxical habits are wildly effective. So effective that you should absolutely give them a try.

They're convergent and divergent thinkers. Convergent thinking is what's measured by IQ tests: rational thinking that typically results in a single right answer. Divergent thinking, on the other hand, is less precise. It's about generating ideas and asking questions that have no solid right or wrong answers. Both are important. No matter how high your IQ, you're not going to be successful if you can't think outside the proverbial box. On the other hand, you need rational thinking skills to correctly judge whether your ideas have merit. That's why this particular paradox is so important.

They're polite yet completely unafraid to rock the boat. Successful people are what I like to call "graciously disruptive." They're never satisfied with the status quo. They're the ones who constantly ask, "What if?" and "Why not?" They're not afraid to challenge conventional wisdom, but they don't disrupt things for the sake of being disruptive. They do it to make things better. Still, they're polite and considerate, and they don't draw attention to other people's mistakes just to humiliate them. However, that doesn't mean they sit back and let people wander in the wrong direction. They won't hesitate to speak up when it's time to change course.

They're naïve and smart. No one would argue that intelligence isn't an important part of success, but many successful people also have a childlike lack of awareness (or maybe it's a lack of respect for) of the type of constraints that other people blindly accept. They're not limited by what other people tell them is possible. This naiveté allows them to tackle problems from previously undiscovered angles.

They're both energetic and calm. Successful people seem to have limitless energy when it comes to doing the things they're passionate about, but they aren't frantic. They can keep that energy under control. They work hard and focus on the task at hand with devoted concentration, but they're so smooth that they make it look easy and fun. Some people are so energetic that they're hyperactive, unfocused, and constantly bouncing from one thing to another. Successful people know how to harness their energy so that it works in the service of progress and doesn't undermine it.

They're deeply passionate yet rational and objective about their work. Successful people are passionate about their work, but they don't let it skew their thinking. They have the ability to step back and look at their work with a critical eye and accept their mistakes. If it's a disaster, they'll admit it because they realize that it's better to try something different than to put out something subpar with their name on it. This sense of detachment also allows them to accept feedback from others without taking it personally.

They're ambiverts. Successful people are comfortable acting in ways that amplify their introversion and extraversion, depending on what the situation calls for. They can sit in the back of a conference room and silently listen to what's going on, or they can go up on stage, grab a microphone, and engage a huge crowd—and they look just as comfortable doing one as they do the other.

They're both humble and proud. Taking pride in your work is absolutely essential for success, but successful people know they wouldn't be where they are without the people who came before them and those they've worked with along the way. They know that they didn't achieve their success all on their own, and because they're okay with that, they don't have anything to prove. That's why so many incredibly successful people end up coming across as grounded and humble when you meet them in person.

They dream big but remain grounded. Successful people reach for the seemingly impossible, but they do so in a way that is actionable and realistic. While you may not know exactly how you're going to achieve your dream, you need to make progress, no matter how small the steps. For example, Elon Musk's goal at SpaceX is to "Occupy Mars." This is a big dream, but Musk keeps it realistic by engaging in regular steps that, someday, may get them there. SpaceX's ability to reuse rocket boosters is radically reducing the cost of space travel. It's a far cry from colonizing Mars, but it's an essential step in a very ambitious process.

THE UNUSUAL HABITS OF THE WORLD'S
MOST CREATIVE PEOPLE

I expend a huge amount of my time and energy writing books and articles. I've developed something of an obsession with some of history's most creative minds in the hope that I might learn tricks to expand my own creative productivity. Some of the things I've learned are more useful than others, and some are simply too weird to try. Steve Jobs, for example, routinely sat on toilets, dangling his bare feet in the water while he came up with new ideas, and Yoshiro Nakamatsu (the inventor of the floppy disk) dove deep underwater until his brain was deprived of oxygen and then wrote his ideas on an underwater sticky pad.

Weird ideas aside, I've developed a pretty good understanding of the habits of some of history's most creative minds. There's enough commonality among different people that I've distilled their habits into habits everyone can follow. Although their creativity was unique, the habits they used to help spark it were things we all can do. Six of these habits stand out because they have the power to change the way you think about creativity. Give them a try, and maybe you'll reach new levels of creative productivity.

1. Wake Up Early

Not all creative minds are morning people. Franz Kafka routinely stayed up all night writing, and William Styron (author of *Sophie's Choice*, among other best-sellers) woke up at noon every day and considered his "morning" routine to be staying in bed for another hour to think. However, early risers make up the clear majority of creative thinkers. The list of creative early risers ranges from Benjamin Franklin to Howard Schultz to Ernest Hemingway, although they didn't wake up early for the same reasons. Ben Franklin woke up early to plan his day, while Schultz used the time to send motivational emails to his employees. For many creative people, waking up early is a way to avoid distractions. Ernest Hemingway woke up at 5 a.m. every day to write. He said, "There is no one to disturb you and it is cool and cold and you come to your work and warm as you write." The trick to making getting up early stick is to do it every day and avoid naps. Eventually, you'll start going to bed earlier to make up for the lost sleep. This can make for a couple of groggy days at first, but you'll adjust quickly. Before you know it, you'll join the ranks of creative early risers.

2. Keep Your Day Job

Creativity flourishes when you're creating for yourself and no one else. Creativity becomes more difficult when your livelihood depends on what you create (and when you begin to think too much about what your audience will think of your product). Perhaps this is why so many successful and creative people held on to their day jobs. Many of them, like Stephen King, who was a schoolteacher, produced their breakout (and, in King's case, what many consider his very best) work while they still held a 9 to 5.

Day jobs provide more than the much-needed financial security to create freely. They also add structure to your day that can make your creative time a wonderful release. The list of successful, creative minds who kept their day jobs is long. Some notable individuals include Jacob Arabo, who started designing his own jewelry while working in a jewelry shop; William Faulkner, who worked in a power plant while writing *As I Lay Dying*; and composer Philip Glass, who worked as a plumber.

3. Exercise Frequently

There's plenty of evidence pointing to the benefits of exercise for creativity. Feeling good physically gets you in the right mood to focus and be productive. Exercise also forces you to have disconnected time (it's tough to text or email while working out hard), and this allows you to reflect on whatever it is you're working on. In a Stanford study, 90% of people were more creative after exercising. It's no surprise that so many creative and successful people build exercise into their daily routines. Kurt Vonnegut took walks into the nearby town, swam laps, and did push-ups and sit-ups, Richard

Branson runs every morning, and composers Beethoven and Tchaikovsky walked every day.

4. Stick to a Strict Schedule

It's a common misconception that in order to be creative, you should live life on a whim with no structure and no sense of needing to do anything. The habits of highly successful and creative people suggest otherwise. In fact, most creative minds scheduled their days rigorously. Psychologist William James described the impact of a schedule on creativity, saying that only by having a schedule can we "free our minds to advance to really interesting fields of action."

5. Learn to Work Anywhere, Anytime

Many people work in only one place, believing it's practically impossible for them to get anything done anywhere else. Staying in one place is actually a crutch; studies show that changing environments is beneficial to productivity and creativity. E.B. White, author of *Charlotte's Web*, said it well: "A writer who waits for ideal conditions under which to work will die without putting a word on paper." The same is true for any type of creative work. If you keep waiting until you're in the perfect place at the ideal time, the time will never come. Steve Jobs started Apple in his mom's garage, and J.K. Rowling wrote the first ideas for Harry Potter on a napkin on a train. When you have a creative idea, don't wait. Put it into action as soon as you can. Recording that spark of creativity may very well be the foundation of something great.

6. Learn that Creative Blocks Are Just Procrastination

As long as your heart is still beating, you have the ability to come up with new ideas and execute them. They may not always be great ones, but the greatest enemy of creativity is inactivity. Author Jodi Picoult summarized creative blocks perfectly: "I don't believe in writer's block. Think about it—

when you were blocked in college and had to write a paper, didn't it always manage to fix itself the night before the paper was due? Writer's block is having too much time on your hands. If you have a limited amount of time to write, you just sit down and do it. You might not write well every day, but you can always edit a bad page. You can't edit a blank page." Picoult's comment describes all creative activity—the only way to stay creative is to keep moving forward.

BRINGING IT ALL TOGETHER

The reason that there are so many different opinions on what traits are necessary for success—and the reason that so many contradict each other—is that successful people are complex. They have a wide variety of paradoxical habits that they call upon as needed, like a mechanic with a well-stocked toolbox. In my experience, you have to get intentional about your habits if you want to flourish. People who are truly successful use their emotional intelligence to focus on activities that address a variety of needs, not just immediate achievements. Stop chasing the things that you think will make you happy and successful, and start realizing that you are the sum of your habits.

31

Master Conflict

———

Simply put, your ability to handle moments of conflict has a massive impact on your success and sanity. Moments of conflict are inevitable in the workplace. Research by CPP, Inc. suggested that 85% of people experience conflict in the workplace, and the amount of time spent dealing with conflict has increased drastically over the last decade. Conflict typically boils down to moments when the stakes are high, emotions run strong, and opinions differ. How you handle these moments determines the amount of trust, respect, and connection you have with your colleagues. You cannot master these moments without a high degree of emotional intelligence.

When you're a nice person, conflict can be a real challenge. Not that mean people are any better at conflict; they just enjoy it more. This leads many of us to shy away from conflict. That's the wrong approach. Conflict is unavoidable, so it's important to be skilled at navigating it when it inevitably happens. Researchers at Columbia University showed that how you handle conflict can make or break your career. The researchers measured something scientifically that many of us have seen first-hand—people who are too aggressive in conflict situations harm their performance by upsetting and alienating their peers, while people who are too passive at handling conflict hinder their ability to achieve their goals because they fail to stand up for themselves.

The secret to effectively handling conflict is assertiveness—that delicate place where you get your needs met without bullying the other person into submission. Assertive people operate in the small space that lies between passivity and aggression (that is, they never lean too far in either direction). It's easy to think that nice people are too passive. Although that's often true, unchecked passivity can boil over into aggression. So, there are plenty of very nice people out there who have exhibited both extremes of the assertiveness spectrum. To be assertive, you need to learn to engage in healthy conflict. Healthy conflict directly and constructively addresses the issue at hand without ignoring or trivializing the needs of either party. The following habits will help you handle conflict assertively.

Consider the repercussions of silence. Sometimes, it's hard to muster the motivation to speak up when the likelihood is high that things will turn ugly. The fastest way to motivate yourself to act is to fully consider the costs of not speaking up—they're typically far greater than standing up for yourself. The trick is that you need to shift your attention from the headache that will come with getting involved to the things you stand to gain from your assertiveness.

Ask good questions until you get to the heart of the matter. Failing to understand the motive behind someone's behavior throws fuel on the fire of conflict, because it makes everything they do appear foolish and shortsighted. Instead of pointing out flaws, you should seek to understand where the other person is coming from. Try asking good questions, such as, *"Why did you choose to do it that way?" "What do you mean by that?" "Can you help me understand this better?"* Even when you don't see eye to eye, using questions to get at the underlying motive builds trust and understanding, both of which are conflict killers.

When you challenge, offer solutions. People don't like it when they feel as if you're attempting to take apart their idea right off the bat. When you challenge someone's idea but also offer a solution, you demonstrate that you want to work together to come up with a solution. This reinforces the value of their idea, even if it's full of holes. For example, you might say, "One potential problem that I see with your idea is ___. However, I think we can overcome this problem if we can just figure out a way to___." In this example, you aren't even providing the solution. You're just acknowledging that you're willing to work together to find one.

Say "and" instead of "but." The simple act of replacing the word "but" with "and" makes conflict much more constructive and collaborative. Say, for example, that your teammate John wants to use the majority of your budget on a marketing campaign, but you're worried that won't leave enough money for a critical new hire. Instead of saying, "I see that you want to use the money for marketing, but I think we need to make a new hire," say, "I see that you want to use the money for marketing, and I think we need to make a new hire." The difference is subtle, but the first sentence minimizes the value of his idea. The second sentence states the problem as you see it, without devaluing his idea, which then opens things up for discussion. Saying "and" makes the other party feel like you're working with them, rather than against them.

Use hypotheticals. When you assert yourself, you don't want it to look like you're poking holes in their idea (even when you are). Hypotheticals are the perfect way to pull this off. Telling someone, for example, "Your new product idea won't work because you overlooked how the sales team operates" comes across much more aggressively than suggesting the hypothetical, "How do you think our sales team will go about selling this new product?" When you see a flaw and present a hypothetical, you're engaging with the original idea and giving the other party a chance to explain how it might work. This shows that you're willing to hear the other person out.

THE FIVE MISTAKES THAT DERAIL ASSERTIVENESS

When people behave too aggressively or passively when dealing with conflict, they often begin by intending to be assertive. Along the way, they make mistakes that send their part of the interaction hurtling in a passive or aggressive direction. Five very common mistakes tend to do this. These mistakes often catch people by surprise, but you'll be ready for them. If you can avoid these mistakes, and use the alternative habits provided to address them, you'll remain assertive, and conflict will be much easier for you to deal with.

Mistake 1: Being Brutally Honest

You've suffered in silence long enough. Your colleague continues to park so close to your car that you have to enter through the passenger door. You've asked them to stop. After half a dozen more violations, you decide to do something about it. Clearly, they need to know what you think of their intentional disrespect. So you let them have it. You go right up to them and tell them what an inconsiderate jerk they are.

How to beat this? **Honesty without brutality.** From a young age, we're taught that we have to choose between telling the truth and keeping a friend—that the only options are brutality or harmony. With emotional intelligence, you can speak the truth without burning a bridge. Have you ever noticed how some conversations—even ones about very risky subjects—go very well? And others, even those about trivial things, can degenerate into combat? The antidote to conflict is not diluting your message. It's creating safety. Many people think the *content* of the conversation is what makes people defensive, so they assume it's best to just go for it and be brutally honest. It isn't. People don't get defensive because of the content—they get defensive because of the *intent* they perceive behind it. It isn't the truth that hurts—it's the malice used to deliver the truth. When you remove your emotions from your message, you can be honest without being brutal. In this case telling your colleague that you've asked them before not to park so close to your car, that they continue to do so, that it's a major inconvenience for you, and that you'd like them to stop is bound to get their attention and doesn't require an ounce of malice.

Mistake 2: Robotically Sharing Your Feelings

Some well-intentioned "communication" professionals suggest that when it's time to speak up, the diplomatic way to do so is to start by sharing your feelings. For example, you tell your parking-impaired colleague, "I feel rage and disgust." Somehow, that's supposed to help. It doesn't. People don't work this way. Robotically sharing your feelings only alienates, annoys, and confuses them.

How to beat this? **Start with the facts.** Our brains often serve us poorly during difficult conversations. To maximize cognitive efficiency, our minds store feelings and conclusions, but not the facts that created them. That's why, when you give your colleague negative feedback and they ask for an example, you often hem and haw. You truly can't remember. So you repeat your feelings or conclusions, but offer few helpful facts. Gathering the facts beforehand is the homework required to master conflict. Before opening your mouth, think through the basic information that helped you think or feel the way you do—and prepare to share it *first*.

Mistake 3: Defending Your Position

When someone takes an opposing view on a topic you care deeply about, the natural human response is "defense." Our brains are hardwired to assess for threats, but when we let feelings of being threatened hijack our behavior, things never end well. In conflict, getting defensive is a surefire path to failure.

How to beat this? **Get curious.** A great way to inoculate yourself against defensiveness is to develop a healthy doubt about your own certainty. Then, enter the conversation with intense curiosity about the other person's world. Give yourself the detective's task of discovering why a reasonable, rational, and decent person would think the way they do. As former Secretary of State Dean Rusk said, "The best way to persuade others is with your ears, by listening." When others feel deeply understood, they become far more open to hearing you.

Mistake 4: Blaming Others for Your Situation

Your boss tells you they'll go to bat for you for a promotion. You hear later that in the HR review they advocated for your colleague instead. You feel betrayed and angry. Certainly, your boss is the one responsible for your pain—right? The truth is, they're not the only one.

How to beat this? **Challenge your perspective.** When we feel threatened, we amplify our negative emotions by blaming others for our problems. Remember the anger funnel? You won't master conflict until you recognize the role you've played in creating your circumstances. Your boss may have passed you over, but they did so for a reason. Half your pain is the result of their betrayal; the other half is due to your disappointment over not performing well enough to win the promotion.

Mistake 5: Talking Yourself Out of Speaking Up

It's easy for conflict to fill you with dread. Under the influence of such stress, your negative self-talk takes over, and you obsess over all the bad things that might happen if you speak up. You conjure up images of conflict, retribution, isolation, and pain until you retreat into silence.

How to beat this? **Quantify the risks of not speaking up.** The fastest way to motivate yourself to step up to difficult conversations is to simply articulate the costs of not speaking up. People who consistently speak up aren't necessarily more courageous; they're simply more accurate. First, they scrupulously review what's likely to happen if they fail to speak up. Second, they ponder what might happen if they speak up and things go well. Finally (the order is important), they consider what may happen if the conversation goes poorly. Once they have an accurate understanding of the possibilities, saying something is their typical choice. The reward usually outweighs the risk.

BLUNDERS THAT LEAD TO VIRTUAL CONFLICT

We've all been on the receiving end of a scathing email, DM, or text, as well as their mysterious, vaguely insulting cousins. You know the messages I'm referring to. They don't need exclamation points or all caps to teem with anger and drip with sarcasm. Dressing someone down digitally is tempting because it's easy—you have plenty of time to dream up daggers that strike straight to the heart, and you lack the inhibition that's present when the recipient is staring you in the face. This type of virtual message is known as "flaming," and all such messages have a single thing in common—a complete and utter lack of emotional intelligence.

A survey sponsored by communications device manufacturer Poly found that 83% of today's workforce considers electronic communication more critical to their success than any other form of communication. Electronic communication has been a mainstay long enough that you'd think that we'd all be pros at using it by now. But we're human, and—if you think about it—we haven't mastered face-to-face communication either. Even the most likeable and well-mannered among us can still look like jerks when communicating virtually. Typing a message that comes across just like you do in person is a fine art. During a conversation, you adjust your tone, facial expression, gestures, and posture to fit the mood of what you're conveying. You do this because people tend to be much more responsive to *how* you say things than to *what* you actually say.

Text strips a conversation bare. It's efficient, but it turns otherwise easy interactions into messy misinterpretations. Without facial expressions and body posture to guide your message, people look at each word you type as an indicator of tone and mood. Most of the mistakes people make in their electronic messages are completely avoidable. The following bad habits lead to subtle mistakes and hidden blunders.

The Way-Too-Brief

All too often, the cause of a virtual conflict is an imbalance between the effort in the initial message and the effort in the response to that message. When someone types up a detailed paragraph outlining important issues, they expect you to respond carefully. Sending back "Got it" or "Noted" just doesn't do the trick. Without knowledge of your intent and tone, brief responses come across as apathetic and even sarcastic to the receiver. This is unfortunate because this is rarely the sender's intent. The best way to avoid being misinterpreted in a brief response is to share your intent. Even responding with "I'm a little busy but should be able to read it later this week" comes across much better than "Got it," which a lot of people will interpret as indifference.

The Compulsive CC and Reply All

CCing people all the time is one of the most annoying things you can do when communicating electronically. I'd say it's the most annoying, but this honor is bestowed on the excessive "Reply All." If someone sends an email to you and a bunch of other people, do you really think every recipient needs to get another email from you saying "thanks"? They don't, and when you do this, it sends people climbing up a wall. The trick for knowing when to CC someone is to treat your message as if it's an in-person meeting. The question then becomes, "Would it be necessary or helpful to have this person come to the meeting?" If the answer is no, then don't waste their time with a message. As for Reply All, just don't do it. Even if someone else in the thread Replies All, you're still annoying everyone to death when you join the fray. If you have something to say, it's better to send it directly (and privately) to the original sender and let them decide if the group should know about it, too.

The "URGENT" Subject Line

Subject lines that say "URGENT" or "ASAP" show complete disregard for the recipient. If your message is that urgent, pick up the phone and give the person a call. Even in the rare instance when a message is actually urgent, labeling it as such in the subject line is unnecessary and sets a strong, negative tone. The key to avoiding "URGENT" subject lines is twofold. First, if the issue is best dealt with in any form other than an electronic message, then that's how you should be dealing with it. Second, if this is not the case, then the issue lies in your ability to create a strong subject line. After all, people check their messages frequently, so as long as your subject line catches their eye, it will get the job done. Instead of labeling the message urgent, ask yourself why the message is urgent. The answer to this question is your new subject line. If a client needs an answer today, then simply make your subject line "Client needs response today." This maintains the sense of urgency without setting a rude, desperate tone.

The Debbie Downer

Sending messages that consistently tell people what they're doing wrong and what they shouldn't be doing really takes a toll. Even if you're trying to offer constructive criticism, you need to avoid negativity in your messages at all costs. Because people can't hear your tone directly, they read into the connotations of words and create a tone in their heads as they go along. Negatives become especially negative in electronic form. Whenever you find yourself using negative words like "don't," "can't," "won't," or "couldn't," turn them into positives. Making this change transforms the entire tone of the message. For example, instead of saying, "You can't complete reports like this in the future," say, "Next time you complete a report, please..." When you must deliver negative feedback, don't do it electronically. Just hop on the telephone or walk down the hall.

The Robot

It's easy to think of electronic communication as a way to get something done quickly, but when you do this to the extreme, you come across as inhuman. You wouldn't walk into someone's office and hand them a report to complete without acknowledging them somehow. Jumping straight into the nitty-gritty might seem like the most effective thing to do, but it leaves a lasting negative impression. Fixing this one is simple. Just take an extra second to greet the person you're writing to. You don't have to ask your recipient about their weekend. Just a simple acknowledgment of the individual as a human being is all it takes. This keeps the tone much more respectful than if you simply send assignments.

HABITS THAT QUIET VIRTUAL CONFLICT

The trickiest thing about electronic communication is making certain that people perceive your message the way you intend them to. You must be socially aware to pull this off. That is, be willing to take the time to consider how things look from your recipient's perspective before you hit "send." The reality is, we could all use a little help with this. The following five habits are proven methods for staying socially aware and keeping your emotions in check, so that you don't hit "send" while your emails, texts, DMs, and virtual chime-ins are still flaming.

Habit 1: Follow Honest Abe's First Rule of Netiquette

I know what you're thinking: *How could someone who died more than a century before the Internet existed teach us about message etiquette?* Well, in Lincoln's younger years, he had a bad habit of applying his legendary wit when writing insulting letters to, and about, his political rivals. But after one particularly scathing letter led a rival to challenge Lincoln to a duel, he learned a valuable lesson—*words impact the receiver in ways that the sender can't completely fathom.*

By the time he died, Lincoln had amassed stacks of flaming letters that verbally shredded his rivals and subordinates for their bone-headed mistakes. However, Lincoln never sent them. He vented his frustration on paper and then stuffed the sheet away in a drawer. The following day, the full intensity of his emotions having subsided, Lincoln wrote and sent a much more congenial and conciliatory letter. We can all benefit from learning to do the same with electronic communication. Your emotions are a valid representation of how you feel (no matter how intense), but that doesn't mean that acting on them in the moment serves you well. Go ahead and vent—tap out your anger and frustration on the keyboard. Save the draft and come back to it later when you've cooled down. By then, you'll be rational enough to edit the message and pare down the parts that burn, or—even better—rewrite the kind of message that you want to be remembered by.

Habit 2: Know the Limits of Virtual Humor

Some people show their displeasure with words typed in ALL CAPS and a barrage of exclamation points. Others, however, express dissatisfaction more subtly with sarcasm and satire. The latter is no less of a breakdown in the core emotional intelligence skill of self-management, and it can be even more dangerous because it's harder to detect when you're doing it. The sender can always convince themselves that the spite was just a little joke.

Although a little good-natured ribbing can sometimes help lighten face-to-face interaction, it's almost never a good idea to have a laugh at someone else's expense when communicating electronically. In-person interactions equip you with an arsenal of facial expressions and voice inflections to help you convey the right tone. Digitally, you don't have the same luxury. Your message can too easily be misinterpreted without your body language to help explain it, and you won't be there to soften the blow when your joke doesn't go over as intended. In the virtual world, it's best to err on the side of friendliness and professionalism. For those times when you absolutely cannot resist using humor, just make sure you're the butt of the joke.

Habit 3: Remember that People Virtually Are Still People

While entranced by the warm glow of a phone or computer screen, it's sometimes difficult to remember that a living, breathing human being will end up reading your message. Psychologist John Suler of Rider University found that when people are communicating virtually, they experience a "disinhibition effect." Without the real-time feedback between sender and receiver that takes place in face-to-face and telecommunication, we simply don't worry as much about offending people virtually. We don't have to experience the discomfort of watching someone else become confused, despondent, or angry because of something that we said. When these natural consequences are delayed, we tend to spill onto the screen whatever happens to be on our minds.

To avert such messages, you have to apply your social awareness skills. When you cannot physically see the other person's body language or hear the tone of their voice, picture the recipient in your mind and imagine what they might feel when reading your message as it's been written. The next time you receive a curt or outright rude message, put the brakes on before firing back a retort. Taking the time to *imagine* the sender and consider where they're coming from is often enough to extinguish the flames before they get out of control. Could the sender have misinterpreted a previous message that you sent to them? Could they just be having a bad day? Are they under a lot of pressure? Even when the other party is in the wrong, spending a moment on the other side of the screen will give you the perspective you need to avoid escalating the situation.

Habit 4: Let the Emojis Flow

Emojis have a mixed reputation in the business world. Some people and even organizations believe that smiley faces, winks, and other caricatures of digital emotion are unprofessional and undignified, and have no place outside a school hallway. When used properly, however, emojis can effectively enhance the desired tone of a message, as shown by a Dutch research team. The team led by Daantje Derks at the Open University of the Netherlands concluded that "to a large extent, emojis serve the same functions as actual nonverbal behavior." Considering that nonverbal behavior accounts for between 70% and 90% of a message when communicating face-to-face, it's time to ditch the stigma attached to emojis in a business setting. For those leery of dropping a winky face into your next work message, I'm not suggesting that you smile, wink, and heart eyes your way through every message you write. Just don't be afraid to use emojis when you want to be certain that the recipient understands the tone of your message.

Habit 5: Recognize When Online Chats Need to Become Offline Discussions

Managing online relationships will always be a somewhat difficult task for people built to communicate in person. However, they become substantially more difficult anytime emotions run strong. Significant, lengthy, and heated exchanges are almost always better taken offline and finished in person, or at least on the phone or a video chat. With so much communication via messaging and email these days, it can be hard to pull the trigger and initiate a face-to-face conversation when you sense that an interaction is becoming too heated or simply too difficult to do well online. Online technologies have become enormously useful for increasing the speed and efficiency of communication, but they have a long way to go before they become the primary source for creating and maintaining quality human relationships.

BRINGING IT ALL TOGETHER

Mastering conflict requires emotional intelligence. Emotionally intelligent people know how to craft their message in a conflict, whether they're naturally assertive or not. They take other people's feelings and perspectives into account while still asserting themselves. Of course, the only way to win an argument is never to have one in the first place. This is particularly true with virtual communication, where simple messages can be misconstrued and blown out of proportion. The habits in this chapter will help you face these challenging situations. Give them a try. You'll be amazed by the results.

32

Master Communication

———

When it comes to communication, we all tend to think we're pretty good at it. The truth is, even those of us who are good communicators aren't nearly as good as we think we are. This overestimation of our ability to communicate is magnified when we interact with people we know well. Researchers at the University of Chicago Booth School of Business put this theory to the test, and what they discovered is startling. In the study, the researchers paired participants with people they knew well and then with people they'd never met. The researchers discovered that people who knew each other well understood each other no better than people who'd just met! Even worse, the participants frequently overestimated their ability to communicate, and this was more pronounced with people they knew well.

"Our problem in communicating with friends is that we have an illusion of insight," said study coauthor Nicholas Epley. "Getting close to someone appears to create the illusion of understanding more than actual understanding." When communicating with people we know well, we make presumptions about what they understand—presumptions that we don't dare make with strangers. This tendency to overestimate how well we communicate (and how well we're understood) is so prevalent that psychologists have a name for it: closeness-communication bias. "The understanding, 'What I know is different from what you know' is essential for effective communication," said study lead Kenneth Savitsky, "but that insight can be elusive.

Some [people] may indeed be on the same wavelength, but maybe not as much as they think. You get rushed and preoccupied, and you stop taking the perspective of the other person."

You can't reach your full potential until you're a great communicator. Great communicators inspire people. They create a connection that is real, emotional, and personal. Great communicators forge this connection through an understanding of people and an ability to speak directly to their needs in a manner that they're ready to hear. The following habits will help you use your emotional intelligence to overcome communication bias and connect with people in a real and meaningful way. Apply these habits and watch your communication skills reach new heights.

Talk so people will listen. Great communicators read their audience (groups and individuals) carefully to ensure they aren't wasting their breath on a message that people aren't ready to hear. Talking so people will listen means you adjust your message on the fly to stay with your audience (what they're ready to hear and how they're ready to hear it). Droning on to ensure you've said what you wanted to say does not have the same effect on people as engaging them in a meaningful dialogue in which there is an exchange of ideas. Resist the urge to drive your point home at all costs. When your talking leads to people asking good questions, you know you're on the right track.

Listen so people will talk. One of the most disastrous temptations is to treat communication as a one-way street. When you communicate, you must give people ample opportunity to speak their minds. If you find that you're often having the last word in conversations, then this is likely something you should work on. Listening isn't just about hearing words; it's also about listening to the tone, speed, and volume of the voice. What is being said? Anything not being said? What hidden messages exist below the surface? When someone is talking to you, stop everything else and listen fully until the other person has finished speaking. When you're on a phone call, don't type an email. When you're meeting with someone, close the door and sit near the person so you can focus and listen. Simple behaviors like these will help you stay in the present moment, pick up on the cues the other person sends, and make it clear that you will really hear what they're saying.

Connect emotionally. Maya Angelou said it best: "People will forget what you said and did, but they will never forget how you made them feel." Your communication is impotent if people don't connect with it on an emotional level. This is hard for many people to pull off because they feel they need to project a certain persona. Let that go. To connect with people emotionally, you should be transparent. Be human. Show them what drives you, what you care about, what makes you get out of bed in the morning. Express these feelings openly, and you'll forge an emotional connection with everyone you encounter.

Read body language. Many people are pleasers, which makes it hard for them to say what's really on their minds. This is magnified when dealing with authority figures. No matter how good a relationship you have with your subordinates, you're kidding yourself if you think they're as open with you as they are with their peers. So, you must become adept at understanding unspoken messages. The greatest wealth of information lies in people's body language. The body communicates nonstop and is an abundant source of information, so purposefully watch body language during meetings and casual conversations. Once you tune into body language, the messages will become loud and clear. Pay as much attention to what isn't said as what is said, and you'll uncover facts and opinions that people are unwilling to express directly. Be certain to read the chapter on body language because it shows you specifically what to look for.

Prepare your intent. A little preparation goes a long way toward saying what you wanted to say and having a conversation achieve its intended impact. Don't prepare a speech; develop an understanding of what the focus of a conversation needs to be (in order for people to hear the message) and how you'll accomplish this. Your communication will be more persuasive and on point when you prepare your intent ahead of time.

Speak to each person in the room. In business, you often have to speak to groups of people. Whether it's a small team meeting or a company-wide gathering, you should develop a level of intimacy in your approach that makes each individual in the room feel as if you're speaking directly to them. The trick is to eliminate the distraction of the crowd so that you can deliver your message as if you were talking to one person. You want to be emotionally genuine and exude the same feelings, energy, and attention you would one-on-one (as opposed to the anxiety that comes with being in front of people). The ability to pull this off is the hallmark of great group communication.

Skip the jargon. At first, euphemisms surfaced in the workplace to help people deal with touchy subjects that were difficult to talk about. Before long, they morphed into corporate buzzwords that expanded and took over our vocabulary until our everyday conversations started sounding like they're taking place on another planet: "Listen, Ray, I don't have the bandwidth for it with everything that's on my plate, but ping me anyway because at the end of the day it's on my radar, and I don't want to be thrown under the bus because I didn't circle back around on this no-brainer." I understand the temptation. These phrases are spicy, and they make you feel clever ("*low-hanging fruit*" is a particular crutch of mine), but they also annoy the heck out of people. If you think you can use these phrases without consequences, you're kidding yourself. Most people overuse jargon and alienate others with their "business speak." Use jargon sparingly if you want to connect with people. Otherwise, you'll come across as insincere.

MASTER COMMUNICATORS ARE FABULOUS LISTENERS

Listening is a bit like intelligence—most everyone thinks they're above average, although that's impossible. And listening is a skill you want to be great at. A study conducted at George Washington University showed that listening can influence up to 40% of your job performance. There's so much talking happening at work that opportunities to listen well abound. We talk to provide feedback, explain instructions, and communicate deadlines. Beyond the spoken words, there's invaluable information to be deciphered through tone of voice, body language, and what *isn't* said. In other words, failing to keep your ears (and eyes) open could leave you out of the game.

Most people believe that their listening skills are where they need to be, even though they aren't. Researchers at Wright State University surveyed more than 8,000 people from different verticals, and almost all rated themselves as listening as well as or better than their coworkers. We know intuitively that many of them are wrong. Effective listening can be learned and mastered. Even if you find attentive listening difficult and, in certain situations, boring or unpleasant, that doesn't mean you can't do it. You just have to know what to work on. The following straightforward habits will get you there.

Put away distractions. It's impossible to listen well and monitor your phone at the same time. Even if you're able to do both things at once, you'll turn the other person off to your conversation, and they won't feel heard. When you commit to a conversation, focus all your energy on it. You'll find that conversations are more enjoyable and effective when you immerse yourself in them.

Practice reflective listening. Psychologist Carl Rogers used the term "reflective listening" to describe the listening strategy of paraphrasing the meaning of what's being said in order to make certain you've interpreted the speaker's words correctly. By doing this, you give the speaker the opportunity to clarify what they meant to say. When you practice reflective listening, don't simply repeat the speaker's words to them. Use your own words to show that you've absorbed the information.

Ask probing questions. People need to know that you're really listening, and the way you do that is by asking good questions. In addition to verifying what you've heard, you should ask questions that seek more information. Examples of probing questions are "What happened next?" and

"Why did he say that?" The key is to make certain that your questions really do add to your understanding of the speaker's words, rather than deflecting the conversation to a different topic.

Focus. When you're supposed to be listening, it's easy to get lost in your thoughts and fail to hear what's being said. Although that's not entirely true, because you hear the words but miss out on the meaning behind them. Focusing may seem like a simple suggestion, but it's not as easy as it sounds. Your thoughts can be incredibly distracting. To focus, listening has to become your number one priority during a conversation.

Use body language that shows you're engaged in the conversation. First, don't do anything that makes you look bored or distracted. No checking the clock, looking over your shoulder, or watching people walk down the hallway. Lean toward the speaker to show them that they have your whole attention. Use an enthusiastic tone when speaking, uncross your arms, and maintain eye contact. All of these forms of positive body language can make all the difference in a conversation because they show the speaker that you're fully engaged.

Reserve judgment. Good listeners are patient and open to new ideas. If you form strong opinions and judge what the speaker is saying, they'll pick up on this in your body language. Forming your opinions later isn't a problem. Forming them right there while the other person is still speaking is an issue because it shows that you're closed off to what they're trying to communicate. Having an open mind is crucial in the workplace, where approachability means access to new ideas and help. Listening without judgment doesn't mean that you condone someone's ideas or behavior; it simply means that you quit passing judgment long enough to truly understand what they're saying.

Keep your mouth shut. If you're not checking for understanding or asking a probing question, you shouldn't be talking. Not only does thinking about what you're going to say next take your attention away from the speaker, but hijacking the conversation shows that you think you have something more important to say. This means that you shouldn't jump in with solutions to the speaker's problems. It's human nature to want to help people, especially when it's someone you care about, but what a lot of us don't realize is that when we jump in with advice or a solution, we're shutting the other person down. It's essentially a more socially acceptable way of saying, "Okay, I've got it. You can stop now!" The effect is the same.

Practice active listening. The bulk of the good listening habits suggested here promote active listening. Active listening is a simple technique that ensures people feel heard, an essential component of good communication. To practice active listening:

- Spend more time listening than you do talking.

- Do not answer questions with questions.

- Avoid finishing other people's sentences.

- Focus more on the other person than you do on yourself.

- Focus on what people are saying right now, not on what their interests are.

- Reframe what the other person has said to make certain you understood them ("So, you're telling me that this budget needs further consideration, right?")

- Think about what you're going to say after someone has finished speaking—not while they're speaking.

- Ask plenty of questions.

- Never interrupt.

- Don't take notes.

BRINGING IT ALL TOGETHER

As you practice these communication habits, try to avoid biting off more than you can chew. Working on one to three at a time is sufficient. If you try to take on more than you can handle, you're not going to see as much progress as you would if you narrowed your focus. Once you become effective in one particular habit, take on another one in its place. Communication is a dynamic element of emotional intelligence that is intertwined with most of what you do each day. You'll have ample opportunity to improve your abilities in this critical skill. Life is busy, and it seems to whirl by faster every day. We all try to do a million things at once, and sometimes it works out. However, active, effective listening and communication aren't something you can do on the fly. They require conscious effort.

33

Beat Procrastination

Procrastination strikes everyone, and once it gets hold of you, it can be very difficult to shake it off. When you imagine a highly productive person, you likely think of someone who focuses effortlessly on the job and never succumbs to procrastination. You know, the type who can sit on the ground in a subway station with their laptop and still manage to get more done in an hour than you would in a day at the library. The truth is, ridiculously productive people face the same procrastination challenges as the rest of us. The difference is, they beat procrastination by using a calculated approach. First, they understand *why* they procrastinate, and then they apply strategies that beat procrastination before it takes hold. Anyone can follow this two-step, research-driven process to overcome procrastination.

You won't stop procrastinating until you first have a firm understanding of why you procrastinate. Research conducted by Joseph Ferrari at DePaul University showed that procrastination is more complicated than most people think. People tend to think of procrastination as coming from poor time management or laziness, but Ferrari's research showed that procrastination stems from negative emotions that hijack your mood. Once you're under the influence of these emotions, you can't bring yourself to work. You can't beat procrastination without emotional intelligence.

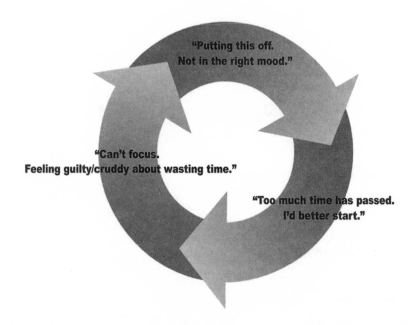

Instead of being lazy or disorganized, people usually put things off because they aren't in the right mood to complete the task. Doing so places you firmly inside the procrastination doom loop. Because you've decided that you aren't in the right mood to work, you distract yourself with other tasks (checking email, checking the news, cleaning your desk, talking to a coworker, etc.), and by the time you come up for air, you feel guilty for having wasted so much time. This only worsens your mood, and as the deadline draws closer, you feel worse than you did when you first put off the task. Procrastination affects everyone. It sneaks up on most people when they're feeling tired, off, or bored, but for some, procrastination can be a full-fledged addiction. They avoid all day the work that is right in front of them, only to go home and toil late into the night, frantically trying to finish what they could have easily completed before dinner.

The procrastination doom loop can be crippling, which is troubling, because studies have shown that procrastination magnifies stress, reduces performance, and leads to poor health. Psychologists at Case Western Reserve University conducted an interesting experiment in which they offered college students a date range instead of a single due date for their papers. The researchers tracked the date that the students turned in their papers and compared this date to their stress levels and overall health. Students who waited until the last minute to turn in their papers experienced greater stress and more health issues than others did. They also received worse grades on their papers and in the class overall than students who turned their papers in earlier. A study published by Bishop's University explored the link between chronic procrastination and stress-related health issues. The researchers found a strong link between procrastination and hypertension and heart disease, as procrastinators experienced greater amounts of stress and were more likely to delay healthy activities, such as proper diet and exercise.

Charles Dickens said, "Procrastination is the thief of time, collar him." We cannot expect to beat procrastination and improve our health and productivity until we're able to overcome the negative mental habits that lead us to procrastinate in the first place. To collar procrastination, you need to exit the doom loop by taking control of your mood. With the right habits in place, you can take the reins and get yourself in the mood to get things done. The following habits will help you make this happen.

Figure out why. When you aren't in the mood to work, procrastination is telling you something important. It could be something simple, such as needing to take a break or getting something to eat. It could also be something complex, such as you're carrying the team on your back or you're dissatisfied with your job. Whatever it is, instead of punishing yourself for procrastinating, take a moment to reflect and figure out *why* you're procrastinating. This could end up being the most productive step you take in conquering your task.

Focus on results. Chances are, you don't enjoy going to the dentist. Few people do. So, why do you go? It gets results. Your dentist is good at making your teeth and gums healthier and more appealing. You also go because the pain of having someone pick at your teeth for an hour is nowhere near the pain of a filling, an extraction, or a root canal. You go to the dentist because you know the process is worth it. The same mentality applies to a challenging task. While it may make you anxious to get started, don't focus on that. Just think of how great it's going to feel to get things done and how much worse you'll feel if you wait until the last minute and don't give it your best effort.

Jump right in, no matter what. Sometimes, it's really hard to get started on something, even when it's something you love to do. You might be staring at a blank Word document or standing on the beach on a cold winter morning. That first step is difficult, but once you get going (typing that first paragraph or taking off on that first wave), your mood improves dramatically. When you focus on how difficult and cruddy it is to get started, you discourage yourself from doing so. When you dive right in, no matter what, your mood quickly improves, which helps you stay on task.

Enjoy your progress. There's nothing quite like checking something off your to-do list. To keep yourself from procrastinating, you can experience this sense of accomplishment by carefully tracking your progress. Small victories keep you fired up and moving forward. Sometimes, crossing a few easy things off a list is all it takes to build up the motivation to tackle something big. Remember, it's not about doing small tasks to avoid big tasks; it's about including small tasks on your daily checklist to build up your confidence and momentum.

Get real. Setting unrealistic goals for your day is a great way to become discouraged and succumb to the negative moods that fuel procrastination. Setting realistic goals keeps things positive, which keeps you in the right mood to work.

Remove your obstacles. Before getting started on a task, take a moment to carefully consider the obstacles that might get in your way. Then develop a plan to ensure that they don't. For example, you might have instructions for a task in your email inbox, and if you don't do anything about it, you'll repeatedly go back to your inbox to look at them, only to get distracted by incoming emails. In this case, your management plan should be to get the instructions out of your inbox before you start working. By planning ahead, you can maintain your focus and avoid procrastination. After all, it's much harder to regain focus than to maintain it.

Work in the right environment. Even if you do everything else right, working in the wrong environment can make you succumb to procrastination. This means keeping yourself away from television, electronics, friends, and loud places. This isn't what works for everyone, but you should exercise discipline by working in the environment that's right for you.

Take control of your self-talk. Saying to yourself, "I'm not going to procrastinate. I will not procrastinate," virtually ensures that you *will* procrastinate. There's a classic study in which participants were told not to think about a white bear. It turns out that it's nearly impossible to avoid thinking about something that you tell yourself not to, as your mind gravitates toward the thing you're trying to avoid. The trick is to shift your attention to something completely different (and positive). Instead of telling yourself not to procrastinate, think about what you will do and how great it's going to feel to have completed it. This way, your mind fixates on the action you want to take instead of the behavior you're trying to avoid.

Forgive yourself. There's no point in beating yourself up when you slip up and procrastinate. You might think that punishing yourself will help you avoid procrastination in the future, but it actually has the opposite effect—beating yourself up sends you right back into the procrastination doom loop.

STOP MAKING EXCUSES

Procrastination is fueled by excuses. Excuses confirm and magnify the negative emotions that keep you in the procrastination doom loop. The final step in learning to exit the loop is knowing how to shut down excuses. The following are the most troubling excuses we use to help us procrastinate.

They're troubling because they're the most difficult excuses to conquer. For each one, there are preventative habits you can incorporate to overcome your procrastination and become productive, even when you don't feel like working.

"I don't know where to begin."

Paradoxically, we often find ourselves frozen like a deer in headlights when confronted with a difficult task. Moreover, much like deer, the best thing we can do is move in any direction fast. When a task is particularly difficult, you need all the time you're given to complete it. There's no sense in wasting valuable time by allowing yourself to be overwhelmed by the complexity of the task. The key is not to allow fear of the whole to stop you from engaging in the parts. When something looks too difficult, simply break it down. What can you accomplish in 60 minutes that will help you slay the beast? What can you do in 60 more minutes? Breaking your task into shorter periods (during which effort is guaranteed) allows you to move out of the "deer in headlights" frame of mind. Before you know it, you've accomplished something, and the task changes from way too hard to absolutely doable. When it comes to challenging tasks, inactivity is the enemy.

"There are too many distractions."

For most of us, getting started on a large project is a challenge. We stumble over all sorts of small, irrelevant tasks that distract us from the real assignment. We answer emails, make calls, and check the news online—anything to avoid the elephant in the room. When you find yourself avoiding a particularly sizeable task, slow down and visualize what will happen if you continue to put off the task. Distractions numb you by shifting your attention away from these consequences (a.k.a., away from reality). Reminding yourself what will happen if you continue procrastinating is a great way to make distractions less enchanting so that you can focus on your work.

"It's too easy."

Tasks that are too easy can be surprisingly dangerous, because when you put them off, it's easy to underestimate how much time they'll take to complete. Once you finally sit down to work on them, you discover you haven't given yourself enough time to complete them (or at least to complete them well). If a task is too easy, draw connections to the bigger picture, because these connections turn mundane tasks into a fundamental (and *do it now*) part of your job. For example, you might hate data entry, but when you think about the role the data plays in the strategic objectives of your department, the task becomes worthwhile. When the smaller, seemingly insignificant things don't get done or get done poorly, they have a ripple effect that's felt for miles.

"I don't like it."

Procrastination isn't always about a task being too easy or too hard. Sometimes, you just don't want to do it. It can be very hard to get moving on a task in which you're disinterested, much less despise. Unfortunately, there's no foolproof way to teach yourself to find something interesting, because certain things will never draw your attention. Rather than pushing these tasks to the side of your plate, make it a rule that you cannot touch any other project or task until you've finished the dreaded one. In this way, you're policing yourself by forcing yourself to "eat your vegetables before you can have dessert." When you do get started, you can always turn the task into a game. How can you achieve your task more efficiently? How can you change the steps of the process and still produce the same result? The task itself might not be fun, but the game can be.

"I don't think I can do it."

You're assigned a new project by your supervisor. In fact, it's one you've wished they would give you for a while. However, now that it's in your lap, you simply can't get started. You can't get past thoughts of failure: "What's going to happen if I blow it? How am I going to do this? Could I be fired over this?" It can reach a point where avoiding failure seems like the best possible option. After all, if you never engage in a project, you'll never fail. Right? Wrong. Procrastination itself is failure—failure to utilize your innate talents and abilities. When you procrastinate, you're failing to believe in yourself.

Remember when you were learning to drive and you could only look straight ahead, because if you looked at something off the road, you'd unwittingly turn the wheel in that direction? Worrying about everything that might go wrong if you fail has the same effect. It pulls you toward failure. You must shift your mind in a confident direction by focusing on all the positive things that will happen when you succeed. When you believe you can do something (and you visualize the positive things that will come from doing well), you equip yourself to succeed. This thought process gets your mind headed in the right direction. Worrying about everything that could go wrong only binds your hands. Break the chains, and get started!

BRINGING IT ALL TOGETHER

Procrastination is many people's biggest obstacle to high performance. It keeps you from performing your best. The key to beating procrastination is to understand that it's rooted in emotions. These emotions fuel a doom loop that keeps you procrastinating. You can't hope to beat procrastination without engaging your emotional intelligence. Once you do, the urge to procrastinate loses its strength. Fighting procrastination teaches us to fully engage in our work, become more creative with it, and, ultimately, get more done.

34

Accelerate Your Climb Up the Corporate Ladder

—

We all want to get ahead. However, even when it seems you're doing everything right (you're never late to work, rarely take a sick day, and always meet deadlines), promotions can be few and far between. You're putting the work in, so why aren't you getting rewarded? The answer is simple: You don't get promoted for fulfilling your boss's expectations. Your boss's expectations are the price of entry. Even if you're making a great effort and doing all that's asked of you, you won't stand out. You'll be seen as someone who completes the minimum requirements, and no one who builds a great career is seen this way.

The trick to advancing your career and getting paid more is to add value by making certain your contributions are worth more than you're paid. You want to go above and beyond so that you're seen as someone highly valuable—someone the organization can't live without. You should aim to exceed your boss's expectations so much that they feel like they're the smartest person in the world for hiring you. This isn't as hard as it sounds. In fact, you can blow your boss's mind and make it clear that you're ready for a raise in seven easy steps.

Step 1: Beyond developing the skills you need for your job, learn about your company's industry, competitors, latest developments, and challenges.

Professional development is important, but why stop there? If you really want to blow your boss's mind, soak up everything you can about your company and your industry. For example, if you're an IT developer, instead of simply learning the current best practices in coding, learn how those practices are being applied throughout your industry. Transferring your knowledge to the real-world context of your organization is a great way to add value. In addition to knowing how to do your job, it shows that you know why you're doing it and why it matters.

Step 2: Instead of always having the answer, pre-empt the question.

It's a good feeling when you can answer your boss's questions on the spot without shuffling through piles of paper or telling them you'll have to get back to them. But if you really want to blow their mind, pre-empt the question. Anticipate what they want to stay on top of, and send them regular updates. You'll save them time and energy, and they'll appreciate it as much as your enthusiasm.

Step 3: Instead of owning up to mistakes once they're discovered, bring them to light yourself.

Accountability is a lost art. Too many people try to cover up their mistakes, fearing the repercussions of admitting fault. Show your boss that you're not afraid to own up to your mistakes, and they'll be amazed. When you make a mistake, give your boss a simple heads-up and have a solution ready. Even better, tell them the steps you've taken to mitigate the problem. Everyone makes mistakes. You'll stand out by showing your boss that you're accountable, creative, and proactive when you inevitably make them.

Step 4: Instead of asking for training, do it on your own.

Typical career advice is to ask your boss to send you to classes and workshops to improve your skills. But we're not talking about what's typical; we're talking about blowing your boss's mind. Pursue training yourself on your own time. It doesn't have to be expensive; there are plenty of online courses available free or close to free. While everybody else is asking the boss to send them to training, you can tell your boss what you've already done, and your initiative will be rewarded. You'll save the company money, get ahead, and expand your skillset at the same time.

Step 5: Instead of doing what you're told, be proactive.

Anybody (well, almost anybody) can do what they're told. To blow your boss's mind, you have to be proactive. If you see a problem, fix it. If you see something that needs doing, do it. Put together a how-to guide for new hires, document your processes, and figure out where you can streamline them, or do whatever else you can think of to make a difference. Bosses appreciate vision more than anything. They love it when you see what could be useful to the company over the long term—and don't forget to tell your boss about it. It's only "kissing up" if you do it manipulatively or with the intention of making your coworkers look bad. There's absolutely nothing wrong with owning your accomplishments.

Step 6: Build relationships with other departments.

It's practically guaranteed that, at some point, your department will need help or input from another area. An excellent way to blow your boss's mind is to build relationships throughout the company. Person-to-person interactions are almost always more effective than department-to-department exchanges. You can make your boss's day by saying, "Why don't I take care of that for you? I know someone who can get that done for us right away."

Step 7: Be the calm one in a crisis.

Few things get your boss's attention like your ability to weather a storm. Whether it's conflict between people, everyone freaking out over a rule change, or what have you, make certain that you're the one who remains calm, composed, and in control of your emotions. Your composure and ability to think clearly during a crisis demonstrate leadership potential, and leaders get promoted.

A BIAS TOWARD PROMOTION

It's never too late to show your boss that you're worthy of a promotion. Maybe you've been in the same position for a few years and are ready to move up. Maybe your company is going through internal shuffling, and you're expecting your dream job to open up. Or maybe you've been disappointed a few too many times by other people being promoted ahead of you. Whatever the reason, make certain now that you're ready to move up. In other words, make certain your boss sees it that way. As Steve Martin said, "Be so good they can't ignore you."

Anthony Greenwald at the University of Washington has studied bias more than just about anyone, and his research findings have major implications for your ability to get promoted. His recent studies showed that unconscious workplace biases tend to stay constant, and bosses follow these biases, whether they're aware of them or not. "People are claiming that they can train away biases," Greenwald said. "[They're] making those claims without evidence."

When it comes to getting promoted, you want to present yourself in a way that feeds into the biases that bosses have about what makes someone promotable. You're already doing the hard work, so why not frame your effort in such a way that it increases your chances of obtaining the position you want? Although this probably sounds a bit manipulative, there are several straightforward things you can do to showcase your work and make certain that you're promotable. This is social awareness in action. The following five actions will appeal to your boss's inherent biases about promotability without you being disingenuous.

Stretch your boundaries. To get promoted, you have to go above and beyond. Taking on additional responsibilities without being asked is not only a great way to demonstrate your work ethic, energy, and skills, but it also lets your boss know that you're ready (and able) to expand your scope. When you take on more than the norm, your boss can't help but think that you're capable of a bigger role. This includes showing that you're willing to take risks by making innovative suggestions.

Don't be too irreplaceable. Most people fail at this. Of course, performing at your highest level, regardless of your position, is always the best idea. The key here is not to be seen as the only person capable of performing the necessary duties in the position that you want to move on from. If you do, your boss will conclude that promoting you isn't worth the trouble (and risk) of finding someone to replace you. The best way to find a balance between doing your best and showing that you're ready for more is by developing other people. As tempting as it is to hoard knowledge, don't. Instead, make certain that others know how to do important aspects of your job. Teaching is also a critical leadership skill. Thus, in addition to alleviating concerns about finding your replacement, you'll demonstrate that you can handle the responsibility that comes with a more advanced position.

Demonstrate emotional intelligence (EQ). You might be able to get away with being a temperamental genius in entry-level positions, but you'll never move past that without emotional intelligence. If you're the type who's prone to temper tantrums when things don't go your way, losing your cool when people cross you, yelling and storming out of rooms, or going silent during conflict, you're signaling to your boss that you don't want a promotion. No boss wants to be known as the one who promoted a short-fused person. Once you're promoted, your behavior is a reflection of the judgment of the person who promoted you. Show your boss that you have enough self-awareness to acknowledge your weaknesses and work on improving them. This will prove that you're capable.

Make certain you speak the company's language. As you move up in any company, your choice of language becomes increasingly important. It's no longer enough to simply be an expert at what you do; you have to demonstrate that you understand how the work you do serves the business. That means learning the vocabulary of the executive team and your boss. Whether that's KPIs, EBITDA, profit margin, market share, failure rate, or what have you, know what the terms mean and why they're important so that you can use them correctly when speaking with upper management. Speaking the right language will not only show that you're interested in more than your current role, but it will also demonstrate your intelligence and fit within the company.

Don't be afraid to ask for it. Not everybody wants to be promoted; some people are perfectly happy doing the same job for years. If you don't tell your boss otherwise, they may assume that you're one of them. When the time comes to show up in your boss's office and say, "I'm interested in a promotion," it's important that you have something specific in mind—if not a specific job title, then at least a clear idea of what the responsibilities might include and how this ties in with your career goals. And if the job requires skills you don't have, outline your plan for acquiring them.

You may not get the promotion you're aiming for. If that happens, ask for feedback, but stay away from sour grapes questions like, "Why did you pick him and not me?" In fact, don't talk at all about the person who got the promotion. Instead, ask which of the critical skills you lack and what you need to do to be ready for the next opportunity. Don't argue; just listen and ask thoughtful follow-up questions. However, make certain you follow through on the suggestions you're given. If your boss suggests things you can do to become more promotable, and you don't follow through, don't expect to be considered the next time around.

ABOVE ALL ELSE, BE EXCEPTIONAL

The further along you are in your career, the easier it is to mistakenly assume that you've made it and have all the skills you need to succeed. The tendency is to focus all your energy on getting the job done, and assume that the rest will take care of itself. Big mistake. Research from Stanford tells the story. Carol Dweck and her colleagues conducted a study of people who were struggling with their performance. One group was taught to perform better on a task on which they had performed poorly. The other group received a completely different intervention: For the task that they performed badly on, they were taught that they weren't stuck and that improving their performance was a choice. They were taught that learning produces physiological changes in the brain, just like exercise changes muscles. All they had to do was believe in themselves and make it happen.

When the performance of the two groups was reassessed several months later, the group that had been taught to perform the task better did even worse. The group that had been taught that they had the power to change their brains and improve their performance themselves improved dramatically. The primary takeaway from Dweck's research is that we should never stop learning. The moment we think that we are who we are is the moment we give away our unrealized potential. My favorite quote from Gandhi sums this up nicely: "Live as if you were to die tomorrow. Learn as if you were to live forever." Emotionally intelligent people never stop learning.

To accelerate your climb up the corporate ladder, you need to learn and grow and show everyone just how exceptional you are. Exceptional employees don't possess God-given traits; they rely on simple, everyday emotional intelligence habits that anyone can incorporate into their repertoire. Leaders don't need to search for these habits, either (although it doesn't hurt when you find them). Their duty is to help everyone on their team adopt these habits to become exceptional. The act of learning is just as important as what you learn. However, your time is finite, and you should dedicate yourself to learning habits that will yield the greatest benefit. These habits deliver the biggest payoff, both in terms of what they teach you and their tendency to keep the learning alive. The following habits fit the bill because they never stop paying dividends. They repeatedly show everyone just how exceptional you are.

Take initiative. Initiative is a habit that will take you far in life. In theory, initiative is easy (the desire to take action is always there), but in the real world, other things get in the way. There's a big difference between knowing what to do and being too scared or lazy to actually do it. That requires initiative. You have to take risks and push yourself out of your comfort zone until taking initiative is second nature.

Never satisfied. Exceptional employees have unparalleled convictions that things can always be better—and they're right. No one stops growing, and there is no such thing as "good enough" when it comes to personal improvement. No matter how well things are going, exceptional employees are driven to improve without forgetting to give themselves a healthy pat on the back.

Be judiciously courageous. Exceptional employees are willing to speak up when others are not, whether it's to ask a difficult (or "embarrassingly" simple) question or to challenge an executive decision. However, that's balanced with common sense and timing. They think before they speak and wisely choose the best time and place to do so.

Focus. Student pilots are often told, "When things start going wrong, don't forget to fly the plane." Plane crashes have resulted from pilots concentrating so hard on identifying the problem that they flew the plane into the ground. Eastern Airlines Flight 401 is just one example: The flight crew was so concerned about the landing gear being down that they didn't realize they were losing altitude until it was too late, despite alarms going off in the cockpit. Exceptional employees understand the principle of "just fly the plane." They don't get distracted by cranky customers, interoffice squabbles, or a switch to a different brand of coffee. They can differentiate between real problems and background noise; therefore, they stay focused on what matters.

Tolerate conflict with grace. Although exceptional employees don't seek conflict, they don't run away from it either. They're able to maintain their composure while presenting their positions calmly and logically. They're able to withstand personal attacks in pursuit of the greater goal and never use that tactic themselves.

Stay in control of your ego. Exceptional employees have egos. It's part of what drives them, but they never give their egos more weight than is deserved. They're willing to admit when they're wrong and willing to do things someone else's way, whether it's because the other way is better or it's important to maintain team harmony.

Delay gratification. One thing an exceptional employee never says is, "That's not in my job description." Exceptional employees work outside the boundaries of job descriptions. They're neither intimidated nor entitled. Instead of expecting recognition or compensation to come first, they forge ahead in their work, confident that they'll be rewarded for a job well done.

Recognize when things are broken and fix them. Whether it's a sticky desk drawer or an inefficient, wasteful process affecting the cash flow of the entire department, exceptional employees don't walk past problems. "Oh, it's been that way forever," simply isn't in their vocabulary. They see problems as issues to be fixed immediately; it's *that* simple.

Be accountable. If you're a manager trying to decipher a bungled report, "It's not my fault" is the most irritating phrase in the English language. Exceptional employees are accountable. They own their work, their decisions, and all of their results—good or bad. They bring their mistakes to management's attention rather than hoping no one will find out. They understand that managers aren't out to assign blame; they're out to get things done.

Be marketable. "Marketable" can mean many things. Inside the organization, it means "likeable." Exceptional employees are well liked by their coworkers. They have integrity and leadership skills (even if they're not in an official leadership position) that people respond to. Externally, this means they can be trusted to represent the brand well. Managers know they can send these employees out to meet with clients and prospects without worrying about what they'll say or do.

HOW TO WIN AT OFFICE POLITICS

With the endless cycle of media coverage, the frequent candidate faux pas, and all those awkward moments when friends and family force their political opinions upon us, it's no wonder that politics gets a bad rap. But we need it in some form. Politics is a necessary component of an open democratic system. The other kind of politics—office politics—are just as fraught with difficulty. Almost nobody likes dealing with office politics, and the people who do enjoy it are the ones you have to worry about. And just like regular politics, office politics is an unavoidable element of human behavior—bring people together and the jockeying begins.

A lot of the advice about how to handle office politics boils down to "just don't play," as if avoiding the political system in your office will protect you and your career. It won't. Saying you're not affected by office politics is like saying you're not affected by politics at large. It makes a difference even if you close your eyes and hope it goes away. The key to winning at office politics is to stop wishing it will go away and to start learning how to thrive in your workplace's political environment. You don't have to dive right into the seedy underbelly of office politics to win the game. You win by playing smart and knowing when and how it's worth getting involved.

First, learn the lay of the land. Whether you just started a new job or just realized that avoiding office politics is detrimental to your career, you have to begin by figuring out what's going on. Your office is full of allies and rivals, and if you watch and listen closely, you can get a pretty good sense of who's aligned with whom:

- Who has lunch together?

- Who gets invited to important meetings, and who doesn't?

- Who always seems to be the first to know about coming changes, and who always seems to be last to know?

- What are the hot buttons that get tempers boiling around here?

The answers to these questions define your political landscape. This doesn't mean that you should choose a side (that would be counterproductive), but it's smart to understand the rules, the players, and their strategies before you jump into the fray. Otherwise, you could find yourself unintentionally caught up in a long, simmering rivalry.

Next, build broad alliances. One of the smartest things you can do is build alliances throughout the company so that you'll have a foot in as many of the political camps as possible. If you accomplish this and show people across the board that they can rely on you, you'll stand a good chance of coming out ahead, no matter which political camp is currently "winning." You also won't be left out in the cold if a group of allies leaves the company.

Throughout the process, keep your eyes on your goal. Remind yourself, as many times as it takes, that you're not engaging in office politics for fun or being one of "them." You're doing it for two reasons: career success and job fulfillment. When you get caught up emotionally, you run the risk of making decisions you'll regret down the road. Gossiping, backstabbing, manipulating, and the rest are not needed to win at office politics. Keeping your eyes on the goal lets you develop and maintain a strategic approach to dealing with your workplace's unique political atmosphere.

Keep things win-win. Part of what gives office politics such a bad reputation is the perception that there's always a winner and a loser, and that you win only if your opponent limps off the battlefield, bloody and bruised. But done correctly, this isn't a zero-sum game. Navigating office politics works best when you follow the golden rule of negotiating: End with everybody feeling like they won. Instead of trying to defeat an opponent, spend that time and energy thinking about how you can both get what you want. This is how you play the game smart.

Never pit rivals against each other. One situation that everybody dreads is getting caught between two warring parties. In a situation like that, it's easy to tell each of them what they want to hear, even if that's just nodding in agreement when they bad-mouth each other. Fake allegiances are always exposed in the long run, and then neither of the people you were trying to impress will trust you again. Instead, steer your conversations back to the facts: What decisions need to be made? What are the next steps? What can I do to help improve this situation?

Stick to your principles without fail. Before taking any action that's fueled by office politics, ask yourself why you're doing it. If you're motivated by fear, revenge, or jealousy, don't do it. If it conflicts with your values and beliefs about fair behavior, it's better not to get involved.

Deciding to stay out of office politics altogether isn't an effective strategy. As long as it's going on around you, you're going to be affected by it. It's a lot better to be a competent, conscious player than to be a bystander or a pawn in the game. The key is to understand the players and the rules, and then to play the game in a way that aligns with your personal values and principles. Don't be fooled into compromising "just this once," because once is all it takes to lose control.

COMMON MISTAKES THAT WILL KILL YOUR CAREER

Sometimes accelerating your climb up the corporate ladder requires making sure you don't fall down. So many things can kill the careers of good, hard-working people. Honest mistakes often have hard-hitting consequences. We usually only hear about the more egregious examples, such as when Yelp employee Talia Jane became an Internet sensation for writing a blistering post criticizing the company's low pay and its CEO. To no one's surprise, she quickly found herself out of a job. Most people don't go down in a blaze of glory like Talia Jane; they kill their careers in subtle, decidedly undramatic ways. And it's a shame because it happens all the time. A survey by VitalSmarts found that 83% of people had seen someone make a blunder that had catastrophic results for their career, reputation, or business, and 69% admitted that they had done something that had damaged their careers:

- 31% said it cost them a promotion, a raise, or even a job.
- 27% said it damaged a working relationship.
- 11% said it destroyed their reputation.

These numbers show how damaging you can be to your own career if you're not careful. No matter how talented you are or what you've accomplished, certain behaviors instantly change the way people see you and forever cast you in a negative light. We've all heard of (or seen first-hand) people doing some pretty crazy things at work. The truth is, you don't have to throw a chair through a window or quit in the middle of a presentation to cause irreparable damage to your career. There doesn't have to be a single sickening moment when you realize that you just shoved your foot firmly in your mouth, either. Little things can add up over time and undermine your career just as much as (or more than) one huge lapse in judgment.

Study the list that follows so that you know which mistakes to avoid. If you stay aware of them, you can catch and control these mistakes before they creep up on you and kill your career. If you do make a mistake, remember you can't make the same mistake twice. The second time is not a mistake. It's a choice.

Over-promising and under-delivering. It's tempting to promise the moon to your colleagues and your clients, especially when you're honest and hardworking and believe you can do it. The problem is that there's no point in creating additional pressure that can make you look bad. If you promise to do something ridiculously fast, and you miss the deadline by just a little bit, you'll likely think that you did a good job because you still delivered quickly. But the moment you promise something to someone, they expect nothing less. You end up looking terrible when you fall short, which is a shame, because you could have done the same quality work in the same amount of time with great results if you'd just set up realistic expectations from the beginning. This is one of those situations in which perception matters more than reality. Don't deliberately undershoot your goals. Just be realistic about the results you can deliver so that you're certain to create expectations that you will blow out of the water.

Having an inflatable ego. Have you worked with someone who had a string of successes and started thinking that they were the be-all and end-all of superstardom? Success is great. It definitely boosts your career, and it feels really, really good. The problems start once you let success go to your head. You start thinking that success is going to last forever and that you're entitled to it. Never, ever be content with resting on your laurels. Once you start thinking that you're the cat's meow, you're setting yourself up for a very painful failure.

Being complacent. How long has it been since you proactively learned a new skill, reached out to your networking contacts, or even polished up your resume? If you can't remember, you might have become complacent, and complacency is a real career killer. It's what happens when you're just along for the ride and assume that nothing will ever change. We've seen enough disruption—technological and otherwise—over the last few years to realize that change is inevitable. If you're always too busy to learn something new or to expand your network, you've got your priorities mixed up. However, if you make continuous growth and development a priority, you'll be ready for whatever comes your way.

Fearing change. Fear of change is complacency's evil twin. It actively works to keep things the same. Things are changing too fast these days to latch on so tightly to the status quo, and the costs of doing so can be huge. Change is a constant part of our lives, both personally and professionally. It doesn't matter whether you think things should change or whether you prefer the old ways—change just is. You don't have to learn to love it, but you should learn to stop resisting it and start adapting.

Being negative. Sometimes, when you're feeling negative and down, your mood can leak out and affect other people, even if you don't intend it to. You were hired to make your boss's and your team's jobs easier, not harder. People who spread negativity through their department and complain about their work or other people complicate things for everyone else. If people always have to tiptoe around you to avoid dislodging that massive chip on your shoulder, they're unlikely to be willing to do it for very long.

Having low emotional intelligence (EQ). Everyone knows that you can get fired for being unable or unwilling to play nicely with others, but what trips up a lot of people is having a poorly developed poker face. If everyone can tell when you're bored or irritated or that you think something a colleague says is stupid, this will catch up with you. Emotional outbursts, belittling others, shutting coworkers down when they speak, having low self-awareness, and just generally being difficult are other ways that a lack of emotional intelligence will do great harm to your career.

Sucking up to your boss. Some people suck up to their boss and call it "managing up," but that isn't the case at all. Sucking up has nothing to do with a real relationship built on respect; it's sneaky and underhanded. Suck-ups try to get ahead by stroking the boss's ego instead of earning their favor. That doesn't go over well with colleagues who are trying to make it on merit. Yes, you want to bolster your relationship with your boss, but not by undermining your colleagues. That's the key distinction here. For a boss–employee relationship to work, it has to be based on authenticity. There's no substitute for merit.

Backstabbing. The name says it all. Stabbing your colleagues in the back, intentionally or otherwise, is a huge source of strife in the workplace. One of the most frequent forms of backstabbing is going over someone's head to solve a problem. People typically do this in an attempt to avoid conflict, but they end up creating even more conflict as soon as the victim feels the blade. Any time you make someone look bad in the eyes of their colleagues, it feels like a stab in the back, regardless of your intentions.

Misusing company supplies or resources. Many people don't think twice about taking a pack of printer paper home when they've run out or using the company's FedEx account to mail a last-minute holiday gift. However, in the eyes of your employer, this is stealing. Abusing company resources is a serious offense, even if the monetary value of the item doesn't add up to much. Catching you in the act can also be a good excuse if your boss is looking to fire you. It's a lot easier to document and justify firing someone for stealing than it is to fire them because they're just okay at their job.

Speaking on behalf of the company. This isn't just about sending out an unauthorized press release or venting on the company's Twitter account, because most people know that these types of things will get them fired. I'm talking about answering a question when a reporter sticks a microphone in your face or identifying yourself as an employee of the company when sharing your personal opinions online. This creates the perception that you're speaking as a representative of the company, even when you aren't trying to, and that's something that can definitely get you fired.

DON'T LET A BIG MISTAKE DERAIL YOUR CAREER

Most of us have experienced that sickening moment when you realize you've made a serious mistake. Perhaps it was a typo that threw off a financial forecast, or maybe you forgot to reserve a venue for an important meeting that's scheduled for the following day. The details are different for everybody, but at some point, we've all felt that rising tide of dread and panic. Mistakes and pressure are inevitable. The secret to getting past them is to use your emotional intelligence.

Researchers at Harvard Business School have shown that most of us go about staying calm the wrong way. People who welcome the challenge of a crisis—so much so that overcoming the challenge excites them—perform far better than those who try to force themselves to be calm. "People have a very strong intuition that trying to calm down is the best way to cope with their anxiety, but that can be very difficult and ineffective," said study author Alison Wood Brooks. "When people feel anxious and try to calm down, they are thinking about all the things that could go badly. When they are excited, they are thinking about how things could go well."

Staying composed, focused, and effective under pressure is all about your mentality. People who successfully manage crises are able to channel their emotions into producing the behavior that they want. In other words, they turn their anxiety into energy and excitement. This can't happen if you don't engage your logic. Yes, making a big mistake is embarrassing. You might get yelled at by your boss, and the mistake might even show up on your next performance appraisal, but in all likelihood, it's not going to result in you getting fired, losing your house, living out of your car, or any of the other catastrophic thoughts that fuel your anxiety and keep you from focusing.

If you struggle with putting things into perspective, ask yourself two simple questions: What's the worst thing that could happen as a result of this? Will this matter in five years? Your answers should stop cataclysmic thinking. You'll probably realize that you're panicking due to the anticipation of public embarrassment more than anything else. Once you get over that, you can build your confidence by picking up the pieces and making things better. Remind yourself: "There's more to me than this situation. One honest mistake won't define me."

Next, recognize that people are less focused on you than you think they are. It's easy to see yourself as the center of the maelstrom. You're embarrassed, and you're worried about your job. The more you feel judged by others, the more intense your anxiety. But your boss, and everyone else, will spend far less time worrying about you than they will about trying to improve a difficult situation, which is what you should be focusing on. Realize that they won't have much time to think about you until after the dust has settled, and by that time, you'll have become part of the solution.

Now, magnify your logic. Nothing helps you maintain the right frame of mind in a crisis like logical thinking. Once you've forestalled the panic, it's time to ask yourself important factual questions: What exactly happened? What are the possible repercussions? Is there still time to avoid the repercussions? If so, how? Who needs to be involved? If it's too late to head off the repercussions, what can be done to mitigate the damage? Don't let your mind run off with ridiculous self-accusations.

Finally, take action. Once you've figured out the facts and screwed your head on straight, it's time to own up to the situation. Putting off the hard work of cleaning up the mess just gives your sense of dread more power. Pouring your energy into making things better is both empowering and a wonderful distraction from any anxiety that might surface. Remember, getting excited by the challenge of rising from the ashes will improve your performance dramatically. To keep things humming, don't be so hard on yourself. Nobody's perfect. Even the most successful people make serious mistakes. Beating yourself up might be a tempting option, but it never accomplishes anything, and it certainly doesn't make you any calmer. Instead, focus your energy on the future and the things you can change.

BRINGING IT ALL TOGETHER

Promotions don't just happen, and they're not a guaranteed result of high performance. That's because you don't get promoted as a reward for what you've done. You get promoted because your boss thinks you have the potential to add more value in a larger role. The people who achieve the most are those who add the most value. Business is, after all, about making a profit. You want your boss and the company to know that they're getting a great return on the time and money they're investing in you.

Many people make the mistake of thinking that they can damage their careers only by making one huge misstep, but the reality is that it's usually not that dramatic. Some of the mistakes I've presented here may sound extreme and highly inconsiderate, but they tend to sneak up on you and are usually committed with good intentions. Use this chapter as a gentle reminder so that you can avoid making them. Nobody likes making mistakes. But no matter how big the mistake is, succumbing to panic isn't going to help. Giving in to catastrophic thinking undermines your ability to use your emotional intelligence to make good decisions and move forward effectively. Instead, use the strategies in this chapter to stay calm so that you can assess the situation, develop a plan, be accountable, and get busy making things right so you can move on.

35

Be Persuasive and Get Your Point Across

D o you ever feel like nobody takes you seriously at work? If so, you're not alone. More than 50% of people don't feel respected at work, according to a *Harvard Business Review* global survey of more than 20,000 employees. Maybe colleagues ignore your input in meetings. Perhaps they interrupt you or don't include you in important decisions. It's easy to blame that on a bad boss or a toxic work environment. In some cases, that's even true. But if you really want to be taken more seriously at work, you should start by looking in the mirror and doing what *you* can to increase your influence.

There are eight habits you can adopt right now to increase your credibility, get people to take you more seriously, and ensure that you get treated with the respect you deserve.

Don't let your statements sound like questions. One of the most common things people do to undermine their credibility is ending their sentences with a higher inflection than where they started. It's called "upspeak," and our brains are trained to interpret that pattern as a question. So, instead of delivering information, you end up sounding like you're asking if your own input is correct. And people notice. In a survey of 700 managers conducted by Pearson, 85% considered upspeak a sign of insecurity and emotional weakness, and 44% said they mark job candidates down by as much as a third for using upspeak. That's one habit you should break right now to give yourself an instant credibility boost.

Don't just give reports—tell stories. The most successful TED talks follow a magic formula—they are 75% stories and 25% data backing up those stories. Stories provide an emotional hook that helps people remember what you said, and they give you a platform for connecting your knowledge to the real world. There's a huge difference between memorizing mathematical formulas, for example, and being able to use them to calculate whether a particularly dangerous asteroid will hit us in our lifetime. Stories help people take you seriously because they demonstrate that you can apply what you know.

Encourage people to talk about themselves. When you first started dating, your mom probably encouraged you to get your dates to talk about themselves. Sure, it's good manners—and we all know that everybody likes to talk about themselves. But it turns out that there's a scientific basis for this. Your brain rewards you for self-disclosure. In fact, talking about yourself feels so good that it causes neurological changes in the brain. So, if you want people to pay attention to what you're saying, let them talk about themselves first. Once those "feel-good" neurotransmitters are flowing, and people start feeling connected to you, they're much more likely to take you and your contributions seriously.

Do your homework. One of the best ways to get people to take you seriously is to be prepared and know what you're talking about. Americans attend 11 million meetings every day, and unproductive meetings cost the U.S. economy $37 billion every year. Why are there so many unproductive meetings? Because people are unprepared. Don't be one of them. Whether it's a team meeting or briefing your boss, always take the time to prepare. Know what you want to say, be able to back up your opinions with data, and be prepared to answer questions two or three levels down.

Stay informed. The employee handbook for the tech company Valve states that the company looks for "T-shaped" employees: people who have a lot of broad knowledge layered on top of their primary area of expertise.

Do whatever it takes to keep up with what's going on in the world. It's particularly important to stay abreast of trends in science and technology, especially as they relate to business. You don't want to look like a deer in the headlights when somebody starts talking about how artificial intelligence is going to transform manufacturing.

Dress for success. Fair or not, we judge people on their appearance every single day. And it happens so fast—in about a tenth of a millisecond, according to researchers at Princeton—that we don't even realize we're doing it. We make inferences about a person's character and capabilities based on appearance. If your appearance is sloppy, for example, people are likely to subconsciously conclude that your work will be sloppy, too. Looking polished and well-groomed, however, creates the impression of responsibility and competence. That doesn't mean you have to rush out and blow your budget on a designer wardrobe. However, it does mean that you should show enough respect for yourself and for your colleagues to make a substantial effort.

Strike a power pose. If you assume an expansive pose (taking up more room by keeping your shoulders open and your arms wide), other people see you as more powerful. This is a hardwired human characteristic, as people who have been blind since birth throw their arms out in victory, although they've never seen someone do this. Moreover, power poses actually change our body chemistry. Researchers at Harvard found that after participants held a power pose for just two minutes, their testosterone levels rose by 20%, and their cortisol (the stress hormone) levels dropped. Power poses are a win-win: They make other people see you as more powerful, and they actually make you feel more powerful.

Be confident, but not too confident. No one is going to have confidence in you until you have confidence in yourself. But you have to balance that confidence with a little humility. Truly confident people aren't afraid to admit that they don't know everything—it doesn't make them feel threatened at all. In fact, the most confident people are eager to ask questions and learn. The best way to show your confidence is to own what you know and what you don't.

BE PERSUASIVE

Whether you're persuading your boss to fund your project or your preschooler to put their shoes on, persuasion is a skill that's instrumental to your success in life. Persuasive people have an uncanny ability to get you leaning toward their way of thinking. Their secret weapon is likeability. They get you to like more than their ideas; they get you to like *them*. Being persuasive requires being extremely skilled in the social side of emotional intelligence. People who possess these skills aren't just highly likeable and persuasive; they outperform those who don't by a large margin. I did some digging to uncover the key habits that emotionally intelligent people engage in that make them so persuasive. Here are the tricks of the trade that exceptionally persuasive people use to their advantage.

They know their audience. Persuasive people know their audience inside and out, and they use this knowledge to speak their audience's language. Whether it's toning down your assertiveness when talking to someone who is shy or cranking it up for the aggressive, high-energy type, everyone is different, and catching on to these subtleties goes a long way toward getting them to hear your point of view.

They aren't pushy. Persuasive people establish their ideas assertively and confidently, without being aggressive or pushy. Pushy people are a huge turn-off. The in-your-face approach starts the recipient backpedaling, and before long, they're running for the hills. Persuasive people don't ask for much, and they don't argue vehemently for their position because they know that subtlety is what wins people over in the long run. If you tend to come across as too aggressive, focus on being confident but calm. Don't be impatient and overly persistent. Know that if your idea is really a good one, people will catch on if you give them time. If you don't, they won't catch on at all.

They aren't mousy, either. On the other hand, presenting your ideas as questions or as though they need approval makes them seem flawed and unconvincing. If you tend to be shy, focus on presenting your ideas as statements and interesting facts for the other party to mull over. In addition, remove qualifiers from your speech. When you're trying to be persuasive, there's no room for "I think" or "It's possible that."

They respond rather than react. If someone criticizes a persuasive person for making a mistake, or if someone else makes a critical mistake, persuasive people don't react immediately and emotionally. They wait. They think. Then, they deliver an appropriate response. Persuasive people know how important relationships are, and they won't let an emotional overreaction harm theirs. They also know that emotions are contagious and that overreacting has a negative influence on everyone around them.

They form connections. People are much more likely to accept what you have to say once they have a sense of what kind of person you are. In a negotiation study, Stanford students were asked to reach agreement in class. Without instructions, 55% of the students successfully reached agreement. However, when students were instructed to introduce themselves and describe their backgrounds before attempting to reach agreement, 90% of the students did so successfully. The key is to avoid getting too caught up in the back and forth of the negotiation. The person you are speaking with is a person, not an opponent or a target. No matter how compelling your argument, if you fail to connect on a personal level, they will doubt everything you say.

They're pleasers. Persuasive people know how and when to stand their ground, yet they are constantly making sacrifices that help their cause. They are always giving in, giving ground, and doing things for other people that make them happy. Persuasive people do this because they know in the long run this wins people over. They know it's better to be successful than it is to be "right."

They acknowledge your point of view. An extremely powerful tactic of persuasion is to concede the point. Admit that your argument is not perfect. This shows that you are open-minded and willing to make adjustments instead of stubbornly sticking to your cause. You want your audience to know that you have their best interests at heart. Try using statements such as "I see where you're coming from" and "That makes a lot of sense." This shows that you're actively listening to what they're saying, and you won't just force your ideas on them. Persuasive people allow others to have their own opinions, and they treat these opinions as valid. They do this because it shows respect, which makes the other person more likely to consider their point of view.

They are proactive. Persuasive people don't wait for things like new ideas and new technologies to find them; they seek those things out. These early adopters always want to anticipate what's next. They're persuasive because they see what's coming, and they see what's coming because they intentionally look for it. Then, they spread the word.

They paint a picture. Researchers have shown that people are far more likely to be persuaded by something that has visuals that bring it to life. Persuasive people capitalize on this by using powerful visual imagery. When actual images aren't available or appropriate, these people tell vivid stories that breathe life into their ideas. Good stories create images in the minds of recipients that are easy to relate to and hard to forget.

BE POWERFUL

Power gets a bad rap, but only because people pursue it for the wrong reasons. When power is pursued for the right reasons, it can be a tremendous force for good. Niccolò Machiavelli spread the belief that people can become powerful only by exploiting the worst aspects of human nature. One of his teachings was, "A wise ruler ought never to keep faith when by doing so, it would be against his interests." Machiavelli was essentially saying that you're an idiot if you keep your promises or stick to your values when you'd benefit more by breaking them. We hear this not only from Machiavelli but also from plenty of voices in our own era, such as Robert Greene, who said, "The key to power is the ability to judge who is best able to further your interests in all situations." It's no wonder so many people think that the only way to get power is to be a jerk.

Fortunately, Machiavelli and Greene had something in common: They were both wrong. Researchers at UC Berkeley have shown that when it comes to power, nice guys finish first. The researchers found that the most powerful people (according to ratings from their peers) were those who were the most considerate and outgoing. They also found that those who were the most Machiavellian—using things like gossip and manipulation to gain power—were quickly identified and isolated, and ended up with no power at all. Studies like these are rehabilitating power's bad rap. Power isn't inherently evil, and it isn't inherently bad to seek power. Without power, you can't accomplish anything—good or evil. Even those who want nothing more than to make the world a better place can't do so without exerting personal power. It's the abuse of power and the underhanded things people do to achieve it that cause problems.

Powerful people have a lot in common. Their pursuit of excellence is driven by nine habits, which you can employ and watch your power and influence expand.

They don't wait for a title to lead. It's important not to confuse power with authority. The right title can give you authority, but it can't give you power. However, you don't need a title to be powerful. You can lead without being a boss, and you can have a powerful influence on your workplace and community without a title.

They think for themselves. Powerful people aren't buffeted by the latest trends or by public opinion. They form their opinions carefully based on the facts. They're more than willing to change their minds when the facts support it, but they aren't influenced by what other people *think*, only by what they *know*.

They focus only on what really matters. Powerful people aren't distracted by trivialities. They're able to cut through the static and clutter, focus on what matters, and point it out to everyone else. They speak only when they have something important to say, and they never bore people with idle banter.

They inspire conversation. When powerful people speak, their words spread like ripples in a pond. Influencers inspire *everyone* around them to explore new ideas and think differently about their work. That is the definition of power.

They know their strengths and weaknesses. People who get seduced by power and, therefore, start abusing it are often blind to their own weaknesses. To become truly powerful, you have to see yourself as you really are and position yourself to use your strengths for the greater good. That means taking a clear-eyed look at your strengths *and* your weaknesses and owning them completely.

They grow and leverage their networks. Those who grow power in the Machiavellian way don't bother with people who aren't useful to them. People see this coming a mile away, and it doesn't win any friends. Truly powerful people know how to make lasting connections. Not only do they know a lot of people, but they also get to know their connections' connections. More importantly, they add value to everyone in their network. They share advice and know-how, and they make connections between people who should get to know each other.

They believe. Powerful people always expect the best. They believe in their own power to achieve their dreams, and they believe that others share that same power. They believe that nothing is out of reach, and that belief inspires those around them to stretch for their own goals. They firmly believe that one person can change the world.

They ask for help when they need it. It's easy to mistakenly assume that powerful people never ask for help from anybody. Asking for help when you don't know the answer or can't do it all by yourself is not a sign of weakness; it's a sign of strength. It sends the message that you're not so insecure that you put your ego above the mission. It takes a tremendous amount of humility to admit that you need assistance. Asking for assistance is critical because there's nothing worse than trucking down the wrong path because you're too embarrassed or proud to admit that you don't know what you're doing.

They do it *now.* Way back in 1894, Orison Swett Marden made an important point: "Don't wait for extraordinary opportunities. Seek common occasions, and make them great. Weak men wait for opportunities. Strong men make them." If you put off growing your power until the right opportunity comes along, it's never going to happen. Powerful people stop making excuses and just start. You know what you believe in, you know who you are, and you know what you want to become, so act like it. Yes, it will be uncomfortable at times, and yes, some people will tell you you're doing it wrong, but the only way to be persuasive, achieve power, and use it for good is to get out there and do it.

BRINGING IT ALL TOGETHER

Boris Yeltsin once said, "You can make a throne of bayonets, but you can't sit on it for very long." Forget everything you've heard about power, because in the end, nice guys really do win. Whether you call it power or influence, it's okay to want it, and it's okay to have it. You just have to pursue it and use it with integrity, which won't happen without emotional intelligence. If you feel like you don't get the respect you deserve at work, nobody can change that but you. Sometimes, people don't take you seriously because of little things that you don't even realize you're doing. And that's something you can fix.

36

Avoid Integrity Traps

W hat makes you happy at work? Maybe you have a great boss who gives you the freedom to be creative, rewards you for going the extra mile, and helps you reach your career goals. Maybe you have none of the above and are updating your resume as we speak. It's pretty incredible how often you hear managers complaining about their best employees leaving, and they really do have something to complain about—few things are as costly and disruptive as good people walking out the door. But managers tend to blame their turnover problems on everything under the sun while ignoring the crux of the matter: People don't leave jobs; they leave managers.

Over the years, we've watched in horror as leaders who lack integrity have destroyed businesses time and again. But the real tragedy happens when regular leaders, who are otherwise great, sabotage themselves day after day with mistakes that they can't see but are obvious to everyone else. In most cases, slight and often unintentional gaps in integrity hold leaders, their employees, and their companies back. Despite the leaders' potential, they harm their employees and themselves.

Fred Kiel did the difficult job of quantifying the value of a leader's integrity for his book *Return on Character*, and his findings are fascinating. Over a seven-year period, Kiel collected data on 84 CEOs and compared employee ratings of their behavior to company performance. Kiel found that high-integrity CEOs had a multiyear return of 9.4%, while low-integrity CEOs had a yield of just 1.9%. What's more, employee engagement was 26% higher in organizations led by high-integrity CEOs. Kiel described high-integrity CEOs this way: "They were often humble. They appeared to have very little concern for their career success or their compensation. The funny point is that they all did better than the self-focused CEOs with regard to compensation and career success. It's sort of ironic." Kiel added, "Companies who try to compete under the leadership of a skilled but self-focused CEO are setting themselves up to lose."

Kiel's data is clear: Companies perform better under the guidance of high-integrity leadership. Every leader has the responsibility to hone their integrity. This requires a great deal of emotional intelligence. Many times, there are integrity traps that tend to catch well-meaning leaders off guard. These traps are often driven by lapses in emotional intelligence. By studying these traps, you can sharpen the saw and keep your integrity high.

Fostering a cult of personality. It's easy for leaders to get caught up in their own worlds, as there are many systems in place that make it all about them. These leaders identify so strongly with their leadership roles that instead of remembering that the only reason they're there is to serve others, they start thinking, "It's my world, and we'll do things my way." Being a good leader requires remembering that you're there for a reason, and that the reason certainly isn't to get your way. High-integrity leaders not only welcome questioning and criticism but insist on it.

Dodging accountability. Politicians are notorious for refusing to be accountable for their mistakes, and business leaders do it, too. Even if only a few people (instead of millions) see a leader's misstep, dodging accountability can be incredibly damaging. A person who refuses to say "the buck stops here" really isn't a leader at all. Being a leader requires being confident enough in your own decisions and those of your team to own them when they fail. The very best leaders take the blame but share the credit. A boss who is too proud to admit a mistake or who singles out individuals in front of the group creates a culture that is riddled with fear and anxiety.

It's impossible to bring your best to your work when you're walking on eggshells. Instead of pointing fingers when something goes wrong, good managers work collaboratively with their team and focus on solutions. They pull people aside to discuss slip-ups instead of publicly shaming them, and they're willing to accept responsibility for mistakes made under their leadership.

Frequent threats of firing. Some managers use threats of termination to keep you in line and to scare you into performing better. This is a lazy and shortsighted way of motivating people, and it lacks integrity. People who feel disposable are quick to find another job where they'll be valued and receive the respect they deserve.

Holding people back. As an employee, you want to bring value to your job, and you do so with a unique set of skills and experience. So, how is it that you can do your job so well that you become irreplaceable? This happens when managers sacrifice *your* upward mobility for *their* best interests. If you're looking for your next career opportunity, and your boss is unwilling to let you move up the ladder, your enthusiasm is bound to wane. Taking away opportunities for advancement is a serious morale killer.

Management may have a beginning, but it certainly has no end. When blessed with a talented employee, a manager should keep finding areas in which the employee can improve to expand their skill set and further their career. The most talented employees want feedback (more so than the less talented ones), and it's a manager's job to keep it coming. Otherwise, people become bored and complacent.

Lacking self-awareness. Many leaders think they have sufficient emotional intelligence. Often, they are proficient in some emotional intelligence skills, but when it comes to understanding themselves, they are woefully blind. It's not that they're hypocrites; they just don't see what everyone else sees. They might play favorites, be tough to work with, or receive criticism badly. They think that because they don't have angry outbursts, their emotional intelligence isn't an issue, but everyone else knows that it is.

Forgetting that communication is a two-way street. Many leaders also think that they're great communicators, not realizing that they're communicating in only one direction. Some pride themselves on being approachable and easily accessible, yet they don't really hear the ideas that people share with them. Some leaders don't set goals or provide context for the things they ask people to do, while others never offer feedback, leaving people wondering if they're more likely to get promoted or fired.

Not firing poor performers. Sometimes, whether it's because they feel sorry for an employee or simply because they want to avoid conflict, leaders dodge making the really tough decisions. Although there's certainly nothing wrong with being compassionate, real leaders know when it's just not a good fit, and they understand that they owe it to the company and to the rest of the team to let someone go.

Hiring and promoting the wrong people. Good, hardworking employees want to work with like-minded professionals. When managers don't do the hard work of hiring good people, it's a major demotivator for those stuck working alongside them. Doing so is lazy, and it's a dereliction of duty that shows a lack of integrity. Promoting the wrong people (because they're the manager's favorites) is even worse. When you work your tail off only to get passed over for a promotion that's given to someone who glad-handed their way to the top, it's a massive insult. No wonder it makes good people leave.

Succumbing to the tyranny of the urgent. The chapter on productivity introduced you to the tyranny of the urgent. This is what happens when leaders spend their days putting out small fires. They take care of what's dancing around in front of their faces and lose focus on what's truly important—their people. Your integrity as a leader hinges on your ability to avoid distractions that prevent you from putting your people first.

Micromanaging. You see this mistake most often in people who have recently worked their way up through the ranks. They still haven't made the mental shift from doer to leader. Without something tangible to point to at the end of the day, they feel unproductive, not realizing that productivity means something different for a leader. As a result, they micromanage to the point of madness and fall off schedule. An important part of a leader's integrity rests on giving people the freedom to do their jobs.

Going back on their commitments. Making promises to people places you on the fine line that lies between making them very happy and watching them walk out the door. When you uphold a commitment, you grow in the eyes of your employees because you prove yourself to be trustworthy and honorable (two very important qualities in a boss). But when you disregard your commitment, you come across as slimy, uncaring, and disrespectful. After all, if the boss doesn't honor their commitments, why should everyone else?

BRINGING IT ALL TOGETHER

The bad news is that these mistakes are as common as they are damaging. The good news is that they're really easy to fix once you're aware of them. People tend to think of integrity as an all-or-nothing thing, but there is great subtlety in how people view your integrity, especially if you're a leader. You'll likely never make huge gaffes when it comes to your integrity, but you might slip up in smaller yet still important ways if you're not careful. Let emotional intelligence be your guide.

37

Create True Work-Life Balance

The typical workday is long enough as it is, and technology is making it even longer. When you finally get home from a full day at the office, your mobile phone rings off the hook, and emails drop into your inbox from people who expect immediate responses. Although most people claim they disconnect as soon as they get home, research says otherwise. A study conducted by the American Psychological Association found that more than 50% of us check our work email before and after work hours, throughout the weekend, and even when we're sick. Even worse, 44% of us check our work email while on vacation.

A Northern Illinois University study showed just how bad this level of connection really is. The study found that the expectation that people need to respond to emails during off-work hours produces a prolonged stress response, which the researchers named "telepressure." Telepressure ensures that you're never able to relax and truly disengage from work. This prolonged state of stress is terrible for your health. In addition to increasing your risk of heart disease, depression, and obesity, stress decreases your cognitive performance.

We need to establish boundaries between our personal and professional lives. When we don't, our work, our health, and our personal lives suffer. Responding to emails during off-work hours isn't the only area in which you should set boundaries. You should make a critical distinction between what belongs to your employer and what belongs to you and you only. The following items are yours. If you don't set boundaries around them and learn to say no to your boss, you're giving away something that has immeasurable value.

Your family. It's easy to let your family suffer for your work. Many of us do this because we see our jobs as a means of maintaining our families. We have thoughts such as, "I need to make more money so that my kids can go to college debt free." Although these thoughts are well-intentioned, they can burden your family with the biggest debt of all—a lack of quality time with you. When you're on your deathbed, you won't remember how much money you made for your spouse and kids. You'll remember the memories you created with them.

Your sanity. While we all have our own levels of sanity, you don't owe a shred of it to your employer. A job that takes even a small portion of your sanity is taking more than it's entitled to. Your sanity is difficult for your boss to keep track of. You have to monitor it on your own and set good limits to keep yourself healthy. Often, it's your life outside work that keeps you sane. When you've already put in a good day's (or week's) work, and your boss wants more, the most productive thing you can do is say no, and then go and enjoy your friends and hobbies. This way, you return to work refreshed and de-stressed. You certainly can work extra hours if you want to, but it's important to say no to your boss when you need time away from work.

Your health. It's difficult to know when to set boundaries around your health at work because the decline is so gradual. Allowing stress to build up, losing sleep, and sitting all day without exercising all add up. Before you know it, you're rubbing your aching back with one hand and your zombie-like eyes with the other, and you're looking down at your belly. The key is not to let things sneak up on you. The way you do that is by maintaining a routine. Think about what you need to do to keep yourself healthy (taking walks during lunch, not working weekends, taking your vacations as scheduled, etc.), make a plan, and stick to it, no matter what. If you don't, you're allowing your work to overstep its bounds.

Your contacts. Although you do owe your employer your best effort, you certainly don't owe them the contacts you've developed over the course of your career. Your contacts are a product of your hard work and effort, and although you might share them with your company, they belong to you.

Your identity. Your work is an important part of your identity, but it's dangerous to allow it to become your whole identity. You know you've allowed this to go too far when you reflect on what's important to you, and work is all that (or most of what) comes to mind. Having an identity outside of work is about more than just having fun. It also helps you relieve stress, grow as a person, and avoid burnout.

Your integrity. Sacrificing your integrity causes massive amounts of stress. Once you realize that your actions and beliefs no longer align, it's time to make it clear to your employer that you're not willing to do things their way. If that's a problem for your boss, it might be time to part ways.

ARE YOU BURNING OUT?

Even the best jobs can lead to burnout. The harder you work and the more motivated you are to succeed, the easier it is to get in over your head. The prevalence of burnout is increasing as technology further blurs the line between work and home. New research from the American Psychological Association and the National Opinion Research Center at the University of Chicago reported the following:

- 48% of Americans experienced increased stress over the past five years.

- 31% of employed adults have difficulty managing their work and family responsibilities.

- 53% said work leaves them "overtired and overwhelmed."

A Society for Human Resource Management (SHRM) poll found that "burnout from my current job" was one of the top reasons people quit. Burnout can get the better of you even when you have great passion for your work. Arianna Huffington experienced this first-hand when she almost lost an eye from burnout. She was so tired at work that she passed out, hitting her face on her desk. She broke her cheekbone and had to get four stitches *on* her eye. Arianna reflected, "I wish I could go back and tell myself that not only is there no trade-off between living a well-rounded life and high performance, performance is actually improved when our lives include time for renewal, wisdom, wonder and giving. That would have saved me a lot of unnecessary stress, burnout and exhaustion."

Burnout often results from a misalignment of input and output: You get burnt out when you feel like you're putting more into your work than you're getting out of it. Sometimes, this happens when a job isn't rewarding, but more often than not, it's because you aren't taking care of yourself. Before you can treat and even prevent burnout, recognize the following warning signs so that you'll know when it's time to take action.

Cognitive difficulties. Research shows that stress hammers your prefrontal cortex, the part of your brain responsible for executive function. Executive function impacts your memory, decision-making abilities, emotional control, and focus. When you notice that you're making silly mistakes, forgetting important things, having outbursts of emotion, or making poor decisions, you're likely burning out.

Difficulty with work and personal relationships. Stress bleeds over into everything you do, particularly how you interact with people. Even when you feel that you're keeping your stress under control at work, it can rear its ugly head at home. Often, it's your relationships that suffer. Stress makes many people more likely to snap at others, lose their cool, and become involved in silly, unnecessary conflicts. Others are more inclined to withdraw and avoid the people they care about.

Fatigue. Burnout often leads to exhaustion because of the toll that stress takes on your mind and body. The hallmarks of burnout fatigue are waking up with no energy after a good night's sleep, drinking large amounts of caffeine to get you through the day, or having trouble staying awake at work.

Health problems. Burnout has a massive, negative impact on your physical and mental health. Whether you're experiencing back pain, depression, heart disease, or obesity, or you're just getting sick a lot, consider the role your work plays in this. You'll know when burnout is affecting your health, and you'll have to decide whether your approach to work is worth the consequences.

Negativity. Burnout can turn you very negative even when you're usually a positive person. If you find yourself focusing on the downside of situations, judging others, and feeling cynical, it's clear that negativity has taken hold, and it's time for you to do something about it.

Decreased satisfaction. Burnout almost always leads to a nagging sense of dissatisfaction. Projects and people who used to get you excited no longer do so. This dip in satisfaction makes work very difficult, because no matter what you're putting into your job, you don't feel like you're getting much out of it.

Lost motivation. We begin jobs in a honeymoon phase, seeing everything through rose-colored glasses. When you're in this phase, motivation comes naturally. When you're burnt out, you struggle to find the motivation to get the job done. You may complete tasks, and even complete them well, but the motivation that used to drive you is gone. Instead of doing work for the sake of the work itself, your motivation stems from fear—of missing deadlines, letting people down, or getting fired.

Taking your work home with you. You know that sickening feeling when you're lying in bed thinking about all the work that you didn't get done and hoping that you didn't miss something important? When you can't stop thinking about work when you're at home, it's a strong sign that you're burning out.

Performance issues. People who burn out are often high achievers, so when their performance begins to slip, others don't always notice. It's crucial to monitor your slippage. How were you performing a month ago? Six months ago? A year ago? If you see a dip in your performance, it's time to determine if burnout is behind it.

Poor self-care. Life is a constant struggle against the things that feel good momentarily but aren't good for you. When you experience burnout, your self-control wanes, and you find yourself succumbing to temptations more easily. This is largely due to the way that stress compromises your decision-making and self-control and partially due to lower levels of confidence and motivation.

FIGHTING BURNOUT

If you recognize many of these symptoms in yourself, don't worry. Fighting burnout is a simple matter of self-care and emotional intelligence. You need good ways to separate yourself from your work so that you can recharge and find balance. The following habits will help you set boundaries and recover from burnout.

Disconnect. Disconnecting is the most important burnout strategy on this list. If you can't find time to remove yourself electronically from your work, then you've never really left work. If taking the entire evening or weekend off from handling work emails and calls isn't realistic, try designating specific times to check on emails and respond to voicemails. For example, on weekday evenings, you might check emails once after dinner, and on the weekend, you might check your messages on Sunday morning before everyone is up. Scheduling such specific and short blocks of time alleviates stress without completely sacrificing your availability.

Schedule relaxation. It's just as important to plan your relaxation time as it is to plan when you work. Even scheduling something as simple as "read for 30 minutes" benefits you greatly. Scheduling relaxing activities makes certain they happen as well as gives you something to look forward to.

Pay attention to your body's signals. It's easy to think that a headache is the result of dehydration, that a stomachache is the result of something you ate, and that an aching neck is from sleeping on it wrong, but that's not always the case. Often, aches and pains are an accumulation of stress and anxiety. Burnout manifests in your body, so learn to pay attention to your body's signals so that you can nip burnout in the bud. Your body is always talking, but you have to listen.

Get organized. Much of the stress we experience on a daily basis doesn't stem from having too much work; it stems from being too disorganized to handle the work effectively. When you take the time to get organized, the load feels much more manageable.

Take regular breaks during the workday. Physiologically, we work best in spurts of 60 to 90 minutes, followed by 15-minute breaks (more on that later). If you wait until you feel tired to take a break, it's too late—you've already missed the window of peak productivity and tired yourself unnecessarily in the process. Keeping to a schedule ensures that you work when you're the most productive and that you rest during times that would otherwise be unproductive.

Lean on your support system. It's tempting to withdraw from other people when you're feeling stressed, but they can be powerful allies in the war against burnout. Sympathetic family and friends are capable of helping you. Spending time with people who care about you helps you remove yourself from the stresses of work and reminds you to live a little and have fun.

DITCH THE TRADITIONAL EIGHT-HOUR WORKDAY

The eight-hour workday is an outdated and ineffective approach to work. If you want to be as balanced and productive as possible, you need to let go of this relic and find a new approach. The eight-hour workday was created during the industrial revolution as an effort to cut down on the number of hours of manual labor workers were forced to endure on the factory floor.

This breakthrough was a more humane approach to work 200 years ago, but it has little relevance for many people today. Like our ancestors, we're expected to put in eight-hour days, working in long, continuous blocks of time, with few or no breaks. Heck, most people even work right through their lunch hour! This antiquated approach to work isn't helping us; it's holding us back.

A study conducted by the Draugiem Group used a computer application to track employees' work habits. Specifically, the application measured how much time people spent on various tasks and compared this to their productivity levels. In the process of measuring people's activity, they stumbled on a fascinating finding: The length of the workday didn't matter much. What mattered was how people structured their day. In particular, people who were religious about taking short breaks were far more productive than those who worked longer hours. The ideal work-to-break ratio was 52 minutes of work followed by 17 minutes of rest. People who maintained this schedule had a unique level of focus in their work. For roughly an hour at a time, they were 100% dedicated to the task they needed to accomplish. They didn't check Facebook "real quick" or get distracted by emails. When they felt fatigue (again, after about an hour), they took short breaks, during which they completely separated themselves from their work. This helped them to dive back in refreshed for another productive hour of work.

People who have discovered this magic productivity ratio crush their competition because they tap into a fundamental need of the human mind: Your brain naturally functions in spurts of high energy (roughly an hour) followed by spurts of low energy (15–20 minutes). For most of us, this natural ebb and flow of energy leaves us wavering between focused periods of high energy, followed by far less productive periods when we tire and succumb to distractions. The best way to beat exhaustion and frustrating distractions is to be intentional about your workday. Instead of working for an hour or more and then trying to battle through distractions and fatigue when your productivity begins to dip, take this as a sign that it's time for a break.

Real breaks are easier to take when you know they're going to make your day more productive. We often let fatigue win because we continue working through it (long after we've lost energy and focus), and the breaks we take aren't *real* breaks (checking your email and watching YouTube doesn't recharge you the same way taking a walk does). The eight-hour workday can work for you if you break your time into strategic intervals. Once you align your natural energy with your effort, things begin to run much more smoothly. The following four habits will get you into that perfect rhythm.

Break your day into hourly intervals. We naturally plan what we need to accomplish by the end of the day, the week, or the month, but we're far more effective when we focus on what we can accomplish right now. Beyond getting you into the right rhythm, planning your day around hour-long intervals simplifies daunting tasks by breaking them into manageable pieces. If you want to be a literalist, you can plan your day around 52-minute intervals if you like, but 60 minutes works just as well.

Respect your hour. The interval strategy works only because we use our peak energy levels to reach an extremely high level of focus for a relatively short amount of time. When you disrespect your hour by texting, checking emails, or doing a quick Facebook check, you defeat the entire purpose of the approach.

Take *real* rest. In the study conducted by the Draugiem Group, they found that employees who took more frequent rests than the hourly optimum were more productive than those who didn't rest at all. Similarly, those who took deliberately relaxing breaks were better off than those who, when "resting," had trouble separating themselves from their work. Getting away from your computer, your phone, and your to-do list is essential to boost your productivity and sanity. Breaks such as walking, reading, and chatting are the most effective forms of recharging because they take you away from your work. On a busy day, it might be tempting to think of dealing with emails or making phone calls as breaks, but they aren't, so don't give in to this line of thought.

Don't wait until your body tells you to take a break. If you wait until you feel tired to take a break, it's too late—you've already missed the window of peak productivity. Keeping to your schedule ensures that you work when you're the most productive and that you rest during times that would otherwise be unproductive. Remember, it's far more productive to rest for short periods than to keep working when you're tired and distracted.

BRINGING IT ALL TOGETHER

Having balance between your work and your personal life requires boundaries. Saving your sanity in a stressful job requires boundaries. Success and fulfillment also depend on your ability to set good boundaries. Once you can do this, everything else just falls into place. It's good to understand the signs of burnout so that you can use your emotional intelligence to do something about it. If these strategies for fighting burnout don't work for you, then the problem might be your job. The wrong job can cause burnout that can't be stopped. In that case, decide what's more important: your work or your health.

Research Report: The Latest Discoveries in Emotional Intelligence

By Maggie Sass, Ph.D.

Since TalentSmartEQ released the Emotional Intelligence Appraisal® test in 2003, much has happened in the field of emotional intelligence. Millions of people have obtained a snapshot of their emotional intelligence and a roadmap to EQ development, which provides what many other emotional intelligence assessments cannot—the *what* and *how* of EQ. Learning what doesn't come naturally or what may sit in your blind spots can be easier when paired with a personalized development plan of strategies to get you started. We've found over two decades that the Emotional Intelligence Appraisal® enables people to translate their new EQ knowledge into better decision-making, improved leadership and teamwork, stronger relationships, and healthier and more successful organizations. We've learned from you, our readers, and the thousands of people we've worked with that there is great interest in the latest emotional intelligence trends. This report includes EQ trends from our research and EQ research conducted by others around the world.

When Daniel Goleman first popularized the idea of emotional intelligence in the mid-1990s, a large initial research focus concentrated on whether EQ could be learned. One of the differentiators between EQ and personality or IQ is that EQ can be taught and developed. A 2019 meta-analysis of EQ training examined 76 published and unpublished studies (pre-post measurement design and treatment-control group design) between 2000 and 2016. The 4,312 participants included managers, nurses, police officers, sales professionals, teachers, retail staff, and undergraduate and graduate students. Analysis across all studies—regardless of design—suggested a robust positive effect of training on the participants' emotional intelligence scores.

This is great news for organizations that are planning initiatives based on EQ training and allocating organizational time and resources to this effort. What does the research show that increased emotional intelligence actually does for people and companies? Among the various outcomes shown in research over the past two decades, some of the most interesting include emotional intelligence's relationship with personal well-being, relationship quality, leadership performance, life satisfaction, income, feedback-seeking behavior, and individual and team performance.

In one study that used a treatment–control group design, 132 participants were randomly assigned to either an emotional competence intervention or a control group. The intervention included structured training on the capacity to identify one's own and others' emotions, the capacity to understand, express, and manage emotions, as well as the capacity to use emotions to enhance thinking and actions. Results showed that the intervention group demonstrated an increase in their emotional competence compared to the control group but also showed lower cortisol (the stress hormone) secretion, better well-being, and improved relationship quality.

An article in the *Journal of Applied Psychology* showed that higher emotional intelligence scores predicted more successful management of workplace relationships and better leadership skills. Additional studies presented in that article showed initial evidence for the predictive validity of an emotional intelligence test for life satisfaction, academic achievement, and income. This last outcome is in line with our previous research suggesting that people with high EQ make more money—$29,000 more per year, on average—than those with low EQ.

One study showed that a leader's growth mindset and interpersonal identity were important elements of their humility, which directly impact-ed the work performance of those who worked for them. Many leadership researchers argue that, generally, most employees have a net negative emo-tional experience with their bosses. However, this study showed that by demonstrating humility, leaders can increase their direct reports' positive emotional experiences, which in turn enhances their performance.

A study of 212 professionals across organizations and industries showed that employees with higher emotional intelligence displayed higher team ef-fectiveness and job performance in jobs characterized by high managerial work demands. The effect of emotional intelligence was found even after controlling for IQ, personality, emotional labor job demands, job complexi-ty, and demographic control variables.

FUTURE OF WORK: EMOTION-CENTRIC JOBS

In the early 2000s, emotional intelligence was just finding its footing in re-search and public domains. In the decades since, emotional intelligence has become a mainstay on "Top Skills" lists needed for the future of work. A *Harvard Business Review* study that examined 5,000 job descriptions from 2000 to 20017 showed that C-suite openings have increasingly emphasized the importance of social and emotional skills and deemphasized operation-al expertise. What we have seen over the last couple of decades is that the world of work is constantly shifting, driven by growth, VUCA (volatility, uncertainty, complexity, ambiguity), digital transformation, and increasing interest in inclusion, equity, and well-being. These and other changes are usually accompanied by emotions, making it essential that we equip people with the social and emotional skills necessary to be successful as we navigate the changes, and as new forms of work take shape. *The Future of Jobs Report* put out by the World Economic Forum lists emotional intelligence skills as two of the eight skills forecasted to be important by more than 90% of or-ganizations.

As more people and organizations begin grappling with the impact of automation, AI, and other technologies on the future of work, it could be argued that rather than trying to compete with technology, we should lean in to doing the things that only humans can do. As Kevin Roose put it, "when we try to do our jobs, we should be trying to do them as humanly as possible." A large part of that is emotional intelligence. Consider what many working parents learned about the value of school, particularly teachers, during the lockdowns of the COVID-19 pandemic. Teachers are responsible for materials development, lesson design, test construction, and grading— all things that could potentially be automated by technology. However, so much of what makes a great teacher is the ability to be *human* with children. Teachers read a child's energy and mood and can sense when something is off with a student. Good teachers listen deeply and help students navigate situations with their own feelings and with other children. They ask important questions. The best teachers guide students in discovering what they're great at. As organizations, industries, and professions continue to shift and evolve with the changing landscape of the world of work, it will be important to think differently about how emotions and emotional intelligence can serve us and potentially help us solve some of society's biggest challenges.

IS EQ MORE ESSENTIAL IN CERTAIN PROFESSIONS?

Data from the EQ scores of TalentSmartEQ's Emotional Intelligence Appraisal® were examined by profession. The results of a one-way ANOVA revealed statistically significant differences in the average EQ scores of various professions. Profession explained the greatest amount of variation across all other demographic variables, including gender, age, and job level.

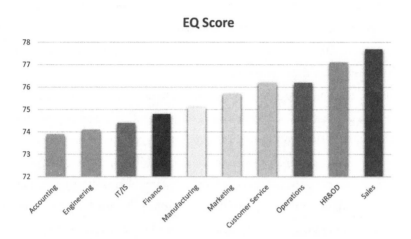

Differences in EQ scores between individuals in manufacturing, marketing, customer service, and operations were insignificant. The EQ scores for accounting, engineering, IT/IS, and finance were insignificantly different from one another but statistically lower than those for the rest of the job functions. HR&OD and sales positions were highest in EQ and were statistically different from the others. However, there may be a difference between statistical significance and *practical significance*. Consider that among these 10 professions, the means ranged from 73.9 to 77.7, a gap of only 3.8 points.

Some researchers have suggested that emotional intelligence is less significant, if not harmful, in work in which emotions seem less vital. Adam Grant doubled down on this notion: "If you are fixing my car or doing my taxes, I'd rather you didn't pay too much attention to my emotions." The argument that individuals in technical roles shouldn't need emotional intelligence is shortsighted at best and harmful at worst. The flawed assumption is that high EQ would make them *less* capable in their jobs. Grant clearly misunderstands how people use emotional intelligence for their benefit. Having high EQ doesn't mean people over-prioritize emotions; it means they are considered part of the overall decision-making process and managed appropriately for the most effective solution in the moment. If you're my mechanic, I want you to be present and focused, not distracted and careless because you're overwhelmed emotionally and having a bad day. The same goes for my accountant. Of course, for both of them, being attuned to my emotions is a bonus when I'm the one having a bad day.

We know that emotional intelligence is a skill that can be learned. Some professions, such as HR, provide ample opportunities for people to develop their EQ skills. Other roles, such as accounting, engineering, and IT, may not have as many opportunities to practice EQ skills, and their performance metrics may not be as directly connected. Organizations might consider the potential ramifications of this situation. As organizations have become larger, more complicated, and more matrixed, very few jobs can be done—much less done well—without interacting effectively with other people. It would behoove organizations to consider the interpersonal expectations of all roles—not instead of functional skills but as an additional toolkit that aids in conflict management, effective communication, and the development of cooperative working relationships that drive results.

EQ STRENGTHS AND IMPROVEMENT AREAS

Client feedback over the years inspired us to enhance our Emotional Intelligence Appraisal® by balancing the focus and including a section on the highest emotional intelligence scores with additional strategies for maximizing those strengths. This addition has inspired research in areas that could be considered collective natural emotional intelligence strengths.

Our research has shown that the item rated highest by individuals responding to the assessment reflects how much they can be counted on (an average score of 5.34 out of 6.00). Most people say they can always or almost always be counted on. This is good news. Researchers have shown that accountability can lead to increased productivity, better performance, and increased trust in teams, which results in more transparent conversations and collaboration. Organizational cultures that emphasize accountability have been shown to reduce engagement in unethical or risky behavior. Interestingly enough, self-perception doesn't always match reality. When we compare self-scores with the scores given by supervisors, direct reports, and peer rater groups in the 360 version of the Emotional Intelligence Appraisal®, all rater groups give lower average ratings on this item than the individuals give themselves. Inherently, we may evaluate ourselves based on our intentions and impact, while others tend to evaluate us based solely on impact. If you really want to be counted on, make it a habit to check in with people and ask their opinions about this. If your assessment is different from theirs, recalibrate, ask for suggestions about how to improve, and start with small habit changes.

Few words create as much emotional response as the word *feedback*. Perhaps surprisingly, the second highest average item on our survey is about being open to feedback, with 71.2% of people indicating that they are always or almost always open to feedback. In addition, there is self and other agreement. There is no statistically significant difference between how people and their supervisors, direct reports, or peers evaluate their openness to feedback. This matters, because research published in the *Harvard Business Review* showed that of 51,896 executives, those who ranked at the bottom 10% in asking for feedback were rated in the 15th percentile in overall leadership effectiveness, while leaders in the top 10% for feedback were rated at the 86th percentile for leadership effectiveness.

Although external events such as global pandemics and economic calamities are responsible for a portion of the challenges in our lives, we have at least a small part in creating the bulk of the difficulties we encounter. Data from the Emotional Intelligence Appraisal® shows that one of the areas in which people score the lowest is recognizing the role they play in creating the difficult circumstances they encounter (70% of survey respondents said they could be doing a better job at this). In reality, we almost always have a hand in at least some part of the challenges we're experiencing, whether it is how we think about the experience or actively behave in ways that make situations worse. However, research suggests that many of us struggle to accept blame when bad things happen. No matter the situation, more things are within your control or influence than you may realize.

From Stoic philosophers to physicists, U.S. presidents to marketing experts, spiritual leaders to motivational speakers, everyone has an opinion, mindset, or strategy for change. And although change is something humans have been confronting and managing for millennia, we still seem to struggle. Our research shows that only 13.3% of us consistently embrace change early on. From an emotional intelligence standpoint, the ability to embrace change and be an early adopter allows you to be more flexible and open to new possibilities. Research suggests that openness to change creates positive emotions and job satisfaction, the ability to implement successful strategic initiatives, and greater career success.

Our final finding is connected to regret. Regret is the unpleasant feeling associated with some action or inaction that leads to a state of affairs that you wish were different. In our research, 50% of survey respondents said that, at least some of the time, they do things that they regret when they're upset. This is a clear area of improvement for most people, as regret is the type of pressure that when paired with rumination quickly turns molehills into mountains and creates an unnecessary emotional burden.

Your unique Emotional Intelligence Appraisal® score profile will give you insight into which of the emotional intelligence skills are your strengths and weaknesses. You may find that your scores are very different from what we see on average. This insight is invaluable as you work to increase your EQ. To access our previous findings, stay up to date with EQ research, and glean insights into related topics, follow Dr. Travis Bradberry on LinkedIn and visit the TalentSmartEQ website at www.talentsmarteq.com/eqtrends.

Notes

1. The Power of Emotional Intelligence

Daniel Goleman (1995). *Emotional Intelligence: Why It Can Matter More Than IQ.* New York: Random House.

https://www.vox.com/2016/5/24/11723182/iq-test-intelligence

http://scottbarrykaufman.com/wp-content/uploads/2016/03/Dumfart-Neubauer-2016.pdf

Travis Bradberry; Jean Greaves (2009). *Emotional Intelligence 2.0.* San Diego: TalentSmart.

Adrian Furnham, "Trait emotional intelligence and happiness." *Social Behavior & Personality* 31 (2003).

Benjamin Palmer, et al., "Emotional intelligence and life satisfaction." *Personality and Individual Differences* 33 (2002).

https://www.dispatchhealth.com/blog/how-depression-affects-your-immune-system/

Shankar Vedantam, "Stress Found to Weaken Resistance to Illness", *Washington Post* (December 22, 2003)

Joel B. Finkelstein, "Ability to Cope With Stress May Play a Role in Cancer Progression." *Health Behavior News Service* (Dec. 1, 2002).

"Animal Research Suggests That Stress May Increase Risk of Uterine Cancer." *Wake Forest University Medical Center Press Release* (Jul. 9, 2004).

Study on the role of emotional coping skills in breast cancer recovery by Barbara Andersen et al. in the *Journal of Clinical Oncology* reported by the Associated Press (Sep. 2004).

Research linking emotional coping skills to recovery from heart disease presented by Bishop et al. (2002, Nov.). AHA Scientific Sessions, Chicago.

Also Gruen, W. (1975). Effects of brief psychotherapy during the hospitalization period on the recovery process in heart attacks. *Journal of Consulting and Clinical Psychology, 43*(2), 223–232.

Research linking emotional intelligence, stress and mental health was conducted at the University of Wollongong in Australia by Dr. Joseph Ciarrochi and colleagues, "Emotional intelligence moderates the relationship between stress and mental health." *Personality and Individual Differences* 32 (2002).

Emotional intelligence scores have strong ties to alcohol and drug use, poor relationships with others, and abnormal coping behavior, such as aggressive and delinquent acts. A study from The University of Southern California, Institute of Health and Disease Prevention serves as an illustrative example: Dennis R. Trinidad, "The association between emotional intelligence and early adolescent tobacco and alcohol use." *Personality and Individual Differences* 32 (2002).

3. Beat Stress and Stay Calm

https://news.yale.edu/2012/01/09/even-healthy-stress-causes brain-shrink-yale-study-shows

https://www.cnn.com/2020/06/07/health/negative-thinking-dementia-wellness/index.html

https://www.ncbi.nlm.nih.gov/pmc/articles/PMC4911781/

https://elife.elifesciences.org/content/2/e00362

https://health.ucdavis.edu/medicalcenter/features/2015-2016/11/20151125_gratitude.html

http://greatergood.berkeley.edu/pdfs/GratitudePDFs/6Emmons-BlessingsBurdens.pdf

http://ftp.iza.org/dp8129.pdf

4. Make Yourself Even More Likeable

http://psycnet.apa.org/index.cfm?fa=buy.optionToBuy&id=1968-13734-001

https://www.researchgate.net/publication/228198319_Internal_Auditors%27_Use_of_Interpersonal_Likability_Arguments_and_Accounting_Information_in_a_Corporate_Governance_Setting

https://hbr.org/2013/05/im-the-boss-why-should-i-care

http://www.pewresearch.org/fact-tank/2014/02/03/6-new-facts-about-facebook/

https://scholar.google.com/citations?user=BbxU8lwAAAAJ&hl=en

http://foster.uw.edu/research-brief/emotional-leaders-is-positivity-or-sincerity-more-effective/

5. Neutralize Toxic People

https://www.washingtonpost.com/wellness/2022/04/26/inner-workings-stress-how-it-affects-your-brain-body/

https://www.pnas.org/doi/pdf/10.1073/pnas.1320040111

https://www.researchgate.net/profile/Sebastian_Pohlack/publication/5384642_Differential_amygdala_activation_to_negative_and_positive_emotional_pictures_during_an_indirect_task/links/0c9605188bbdf861c9000000.pdf

https://www.npr.org/transcripts/193483931

6. Increase Your Happiness

http://pages.ucsd.edu/~nchristenfeld/Happiness_Readings_files/Class%203%20-%20Brickman%201978.pdf

https://www.psychologytoday.com/intl/blog/how-happiness/200805/what-influences-our-happiness-the-most

http://www.rjews.net/v_rotenberg/genes-of-happiness.pdf

http://citeseerx.ist.psu.edu/viewdoc/download?doi=10.1.1.607.6024&rep=rep1&type=pdf

http://sonjalyubomirsky.com/papers-publications/

http://www.happinessresearchinstitute.com/

https://www.psychologytoday.com/blog/bouncing-back/201106/the-no-1-contributor-happiness

www.nytimes.com/2013/04/21/fashion/happiness-inc.html?pagewanted=all&_r=2

https://personal.eur.nl/veenhoven/Pub2000s/2008d-full.pdf

http://www.psychologie.uni-heidelberg.de/ae/allg/mitarb/ms/Isen_2001.pdf

https://www.researchgate.net/publication/235275530_Exercising_at_work_and_self-reported_work_performance

http://greatergood.berkeley.edu/pdfs/GratitudePDFs/6Emmons-BlessingsBurdens.pdf

https://hbr.org/2012/01/positive-intelligence

http://citeseerx.ist.psu.edu/viewdoc/download?doi=10.1.1.471.1586&rep=rep1&type=pdf

http://science.sciencemag.org/content/319/5870/1687

https://hbr.org/2012/01/positive-intelligence

http://psycnet.apa.org/psycinfo/2014-38834-001/

http://www.apa.org/monitor/dec02/selfesteem.aspx

https://marketing.wharton.upenn.edu/mktg/assets/File/Venkatraman_paper_Neuron2009.pdf

http://www.ncbi.nlm.nih.gov/pubmed/16162447

http://www.ncbi.nlm.nih.gov/pubmed/24577108

http://www.happinessresearchinstitute.com/

https://www.psychologytoday.com/blog/bouncing-back/201106/the-no-1-contributor-happiness

www.nytimes.com/2013/04/21/fashion/happiness-inc.html?pagewanted=all&_r=2

http://www.theatlantic.com/health/archive/2011/04/the-poison-of-unhappiness/236967/

https://www.psychologytoday.com/blog/how-happiness/200805/what-influences-our-happi-ness-the-most

http://faculty-gsb.stanford.edu/aaker/pages/documents/ThePsychologyofHappiness.pdf

http://www.fastcoexist.com/3043858/world-changing-ideas/the-science-of-why-you-should-spend-your-money-on-experiences-not-thing

http://www.webmd.com/balance/features/can-money-buy-happiness

http://www.news.cornell.edu/stories/2013/01/feel-happier-talk-about-experiences-not-things

http://papers.ssrn.com/sol3/papers.cfm?abstract_id=1496117

http://www.ncbi.nlm.nih.gov/pubmed/24136970

http://www.psychwiki.com/dms/wiki/uploadedfiles/other/Puetz2006.pdf

https://www.sciencedaily.com/releases/2012/10/121001084132.html

7. Increase Your Confidence

https://www.sciencedaily.com/releases/2012/10/121018103214.htm

http://jpepsy.oxfordjournals.org/content/early/2012/09/28/jpepsy.jss084.abstract

https://www.sciencedaily.com/releases/2012/10/121001084132.htm

https://www.psychologytoday.com/blog/beautiful-minds/201112/confidence-matters-just-much-ability

http://www.sciencedirect.com/science/article/pii/S1041608007000052

8. Increase Your Mental Strength

https://www.sas.upenn.edu/~duckwort/images/Grit%20JPSP.pdf

http://www.uark.edu/ua/yangw/PSED/erc_code.pdf

9. Know When You're Being Lied To

http://psycnet.apa.org/psycinfo/2002-01693-008

http://www.leannetenbrinke.com/uploads/2/1/0/4/21049652/ten_brinke_stimson___carney_2014.pdf

https://www.ncbi.nlm.nih.gov/pubmed/21707129

http://journals.sagepub.com/doi/abs/10.1207/s15327957pspr1003_2

10. Develop a Growth Mindset

http://citeseerx.ist.psu.edu/viewdoc/download?doi=10.1.1.583.9142&rep=rep1&type=pdf

https://profiles.stanford.edu/carol-dweck?tab=publications

https://ppc.sas.upenn.edu/people/martin-ep-seligman

http://www.bestyears.com/expectations.html

http://www.lscp.net/persons/dupoux/teaching/JOURNEE_AUTOMNE_CogMaster_2011-12/readings_deontology/Rosenthal_1994_interpersonal_expectancy_effects_a_review.pdf

http://etd.lsu.edu/docs/available/etd-0409103-084327/unrestricted/Landry_dis.pdf

https://journals.sagepub.com/doi/abs/10.1177/17456916211059817

http://cpl.psy.msu.edu/wp-content/uploads/2011/12/Moser_Schroder_Moran_et-al_Mind-your-errors-2011.pdf

11. Clean Up Your Sleep Hygiene

https://www.urmc.rochester.edu/news/story/3956/to-sleep-perchance-to-clean.aspx

https://sleepfoundation.org/media-center/press-release/lack-sleep-affecting-americans-finds-the-national-sleep-foundation

https://www.cdc.gov/niosh/emres/longhourstraining/caffeine.html

https://www.ncbi.nlm.nih.gov/pmc/articles/PMC3777290/

http://www.ncbi.nlm.nih.gov/pmc/articles/PMC3060715/

http://www.ncbi.nlm.nih.gov/pmc/articles/PMC3927626/

http://diabetes.diabetesjournals.org/content/early/2014/06/18/db14-0513

http://www.prnewswire.com/news-releases/national-sleep-survey-pulls-back-the-covers-on-how-we-doze-and-dream-184798691.html

http://www.dailymail.co.uk/health/article-2701058/How-cold-bed-help-lose-weight-Body-burns-fat-help-warm-sleep.html

12. Read Body Language Like a Pro

https://dash.harvard.edu/bitstream/handle/1/9547823/13-027.pdf?sequence=1

http://ambadylab.stanford.edu/pubs/2006Ambady.pdf

http://www.ncbi.nlm.nih.gov/pmc/articles/PMC2084277/

http://publik.tuwien.ac.at/files/PubDat_238053.pdf

Gerard Nierenberg; Henry Calero (1994). *How to Read a Person Like a Book*. New York: Barnes and Noble Publishing.

https://www.sciencedirect.com/science/article/abs/pii/S0092656612000608

https://sites.lsa.umich.edu/chang-lab/publications/

https://deepblue.lib.umich.edu/bitstream/handle/2027.42/85293/nataalie.pdf?sequence=1

https://www.ncbi.nlm.nih.gov/pmc/articles/PMC6869607/

https://pubmed.ncbi.nlm.nih.gov/10909881/

https://news.ua.edu/2001/08/study-suggests-firm-handshakes-and-good-impressions-really-do-go-hand-in-hand/

https://jeffconte.sdsu.edu/publication.html

https://bigthink.com/surprising-science/researchers-discover-why-its-hard-to-maintain-eye-contact-while-talking-with-someone/

http://www.kaaj.com/psych/smorder.html

13. Maintain a Positive Attitude

http://www.massgeneral.org/psychiatry/assets/published_papers/Peterson-1988.pdf

https://www.researchgate.net/publication/12631151_Optimists_vs_Pessimists_Survival_Rate_Among_Medical_Patients_Over_a_30-Year_Period

http://psycnet.apa.org/index.cfm?fa=buy.optionToBuy&id=1997-42747-004

http://psych415.class.uic.edu/Readings/Segerstrom,%20optimism,%20mood,%20immune%20status,%20JPSP,%201998.pdf

http://www.mindresources.net/marketing/website/profilingtools/MetLifeCaseStudyMRSSS.pdf

https://health.ucdavis.edu/medicalcenter/features/2015-2016/11/20151125_gratitude.html

http://www.womenandlanguage.org/OJS/index.php?journal=wandl&page=article&op=view&path%5B%5D=41

http://www.fastcompany.com/3040672/how-to-be-a-success-at-everything/why-complaining-may-be-dangerous-to-your-health

14. Be Utterly Authentic

http://www.hbs.edu/faculty/Publication%20Files/Moral%20Virtue_7caef67d-e4c7-4b38-88c7-b98da81826a5.pdf

http://pom.sagepub.com/content/39/1/123

15. Increase Your Self-Control

https://www.ncbi.nlm.nih.gov/pmc/articles/PMC5626575/

http://www.apa.org/helpcenter/willpower.aspx

https://news.ufl.edu/articles/2017/05/the-surprising-way-self-control-shapes-how-we-feel-about-our-choices.html

https://education.ufl.edu/cognitive-behavioral-research-group/publications/

http://personality-project.org/revelle/syllabi/classreadings/psp825804.pdf

http://www.ncbi.nlm.nih.gov/pubmed/16484496

http://www.theatlantic.com/magazine/archive/2014/05/the-confidence-gap/359815/

https://www.ncbi.nlm.nih.gov/pubmed/16455864

https://hbr.org/2014/08/why-women-dont-apply-for-jobs-unless-theyre-100-qualified

17. Unlock the Power of Your Personality

http://www.ncbi.nlm.nih.gov/pubmed?cmd=Retrieve&list_uids=16367029&dopt=AbstractPlus

https://journals.sagepub.com/doi/abs/10.1177/0956797612463706

http://www.hsperson.com/pdf/JPSP_Aron_and_Aron_97_Sensitivity_vs_I_and_N.pdf

18. Increase Your Intelligence

https://www.ncbi.nlm.nih.gov/pmc/articles/PMC3607395/

http://pss.sagepub.com/content/early/2011/10/03/0956797611416999.abstract

http://www.slate.com/articles/health_and_science/science/2015/04/do_smart_people_worry_more_iq_is_correlated_with_anxiety.html

http://www.sciencedirect.com/science/article/pii/S0028393200001342

http://onlinelibrary.wiley.com/doi/10.1111/cdev.12272/full

https://www.psychologytoday.com/sites/default/files/attachments/95822/humor-predicts-mating-success.pdf

https://onlinelibrary.wiley.com/doi/abs/10.1002/ejsp.2026

https://www.businessinsider.com/graphs-persuade-win-arguments-2014-10

https://www.sciencedirect.com/science/article/abs/pii/S1057740812000927

https://pubmed.ncbi.nlm.nih.gov/17312315/

https://www.thejuryexpert.com/2013/03/the-glasses-stereotype-revisited/

https://www.sciencedirect.com/science/article/abs/pii/S0022103112000200

http://emilkirkegaard.dk/en/wp-content/uploads/Shane-Frederick-Cognitive-Re%EF%AC%82ection-and-Decision-Making.pdf

http://www4.ncsu.edu/~jlnietfe/Metacog_Articles_files/West,%20Meserve,%20%26%20Stanovich%20%282012%29.pdf

https://news.stanford.edu/2009/08/24/multitask-research-study-082409/

19. Make Smart Decisions

https://zuckermaninstitute.columbia.edu/decision-making

https://blogs.lse.ac.uk/management/2016/05/30/does-regular-physical-activity-help-us-make-better-decisions/

http://www.ncbi.nlm.nih.gov/pubmed/9036851

http://www.ncbi.nlm.nih.gov/pubmed/16484496

https://www.caltech.edu/about/news/experimental-economists-find-brain-regions-govern-fear-economic-unknown-1080

20. Crush Cognitive Biases

http://amosyang.net/wp-content/uploads/2012/11/physicalappearanceandwages.pdf

https://faculty.fuqua.duke.edu/~charvey/Research/Working_Papers/W101_A_corporate_beauty.pdf

http://ctl.yale.edu/sites/default/files/basic-page-supplementary-materials-files/science_facultys_subtle_gender_biases_favor_male_students.pdf

http://www.hoplofobia.info/wp-content/uploads/2015/08/Yamagishi_Implications-for-Risk-Communication.pdf

http://papers.ssrn.com/sol3/papers.cfm?abstract_id=1463018

21. Make Your Relationships Last

Nan Silver; Gottman, John (1999). *The Seven Principles for Making Marriage Work*. New York: Three Rivers Press.

Gottman, John; Joan Declaire (2001). *The Relationship Cure: A Five-Step Guide for Building Better Connections with Family, Friends, and Lovers*. New York: Crown Publishers.

https://www.johngottman.net/research/

22. Become a Great Leader

https://www.barna.com/research/the-different-impact-of-good-and-and-bad-leadership/#.V-6zTrX8G75

http://oser.state.wi.us/docview.asp?docid=6939

http://www.huffingtonpost.com/david-rock/how-leaders-fail_b_4221596.html

https://www.shrm.org/ResourcesAndTools/hr-topics/technology/Pages/JobSeekersWantGrowth.aspx

http://www.informl.com/where-did-the-80-come-from/

Zenger, J. H., Folkman, J., & Edinger, S. K. (2009). *The Extraordinary Leader: Turning Good Managers into Great Leaders*. McGraw Hill.

http://bmcpublichealth.biomedcentral.com/articles/10.1186/1471-2458-11-642

http://www.bmj.com/content/332/7540/521

http://www.ncbi.nlm.nih.gov/pubmed/24047248

https://www.randstadusa.com/about/news/randstad-us-employee-engagement-study-reveals-how-bosses-can-become-workplace-heroes/

http://onlinelibrary.wiley.com/doi/10.1111/j.1540-5885.2009.00344.x/abstract

http://faculty.virginia.edu/haidtlab/articles/vianello.galliani.2010.elevation-at-work.pub081.pdf

23. Increase Your Productivity

https://www.apa.org/topics/research/multitasking

https://www.microsoft.com/en-us/research/publication/a-diary-study-of-task-switching-and-interruptions/

https://pubmed.ncbi.nlm.nih.gov/20548057/

http://stephenshapiro.com/disorganization-costs/

http://www.simplyproductive.com/2012/03/time-management-statistics/

http://www.prevention.com/weight-loss/effects-skipping-meals

http://www.ncbi.nlm.nih.gov/pubmed/18649490

https://www.ncbi.nlm.nih.gov/labs/articles/26881317/

https://www.ncbi.nlm.nih.gov/pmc/articles/PMC4323230/

https://hbr.org/2014/05/create-a-work-environment-that-fosters-flow

24. Practice Mindfulness

http://www.ncbi.nlm.nih.gov/pubmed/24705269

http://pom.sagepub.com/content/37/2/125.short?rss=1&ssource=mfr

http://www.northeastern.edu/cos/2013/04/release-can-mindfulness-make-you-a-more-compassionate-person/

25. Get Motivated

http://www.strayer.edu/sites/default/files/businessinsider_strayer.pdf

Gladwell, M. (2008). *Outliers: The Story of Success.* New York, NY: Little, Brown.

26. Make Your Workplace a Better Place

http://ftp.iza.org/dp8129.pdf

https://hbr.org/2015/01/prevent-your-star-performers-from-losing-passion-in-their-work

https://www.gallup.com/workplace/468233/employee-engagement-needs-rebound-2023.aspx?utm_campaign=syndication&utm_medium=rss&utm_source=google

https://hbr.org/2010/05/how-to-keep-your-top-talent?cm_sp=Topics-_-Links-_-Read%20These%20First

http://faculty.virginia.edu/haidtlab/articles/vianello.galliani.2010.elevation-at-work.pub081.pdf

http://webuser.bus.umich.edu/janedut/Compassion/Contours%20of%20compassion%20final%20copy%20in%20JOB.pdf

Kiel, F. (2015). *Return on Character: The Real Reason Leaders and Their Companies Win.* Boston, MA: Harvard Business Review Press.

http://www.apa.org/research/action/control.aspx

http://www.gallup.com/poll/181289/majority-employees-not-engaged-despite-gains-2014.aspx

https://www.apa.org/pubs/journals/releases/bul-1316803.pdf

https://www.stcloudstate.edu/humanresources/_files/documents/supv-brown-bag/employee-engagement.pdf

http://www.gallup.com/businessjournal/182792/managers-account-variance-employee-engagement.aspx

Finkelstein, S. (2003). *Why Smart Executives Fail: And What You Can Learn from Their Mistakes.* New York, NY: Portfolio.

27. Survive a Bad Boss

https://www.hbs.edu/faculty/Pages/item.aspx?num=50306

https://www.hbs.edu/faculty/Pages/item.aspx?num=50305

https://hbr.org/2022/06/stressed-sad-and-anxious-a-snapshot-of-the-global-workforce

https://www.apa.org/pubs/reports/work-well-being/compounding-pressure-2021

https://www.webmd.com/heart-disease/news/20081124/having-a-bad-boss-is-bad-for-the-heart

https://www.prnewswire.com/news-releases/bad-boss-behaviors-rise-up-to-50-says-five-year-comparative-study-63685702.html

http://ww2.valdosta.edu/~mschnake/PearsonPorath2005.pdf

https://hbr.org/2013/01/the-price-of-incivility/

28. Learn Your Lesson

Ware, B. (2011). *The Top Five Regrets of the Dying - A Life Transformed by the Dearly Departing.* San Diego, CA: Hay House.

https://www.ncbi.nlm.nih.gov/pubmed/11138768

https://www.washingtonpost.com/blogs/post-leadership/post/why-brainstorming-doesnt-work/2011/04/01/gIQAock7cM_blog.html

https://kansasreflections.wordpress.com/2012/01/30/the-importance-of-alone-time-solitude-and-innovation/

29. Break the Bad Habits That Are Holding You Back

http://onlinelibrary.wiley.com/doi/10.1002/ejsp.674/abstract

http://onlinelibrary.wiley.com/doi/abs/10.1111/jopy.12050

http://www.pnas.org/content/106/37/15583.full

https://www.researchgate.net/publication/277608926_Individual_differences_in_glucose_facilitation_of_cognitive_function

https://news.stanford.edu/2009/08/24/multitask-research-study-082409/

https://www.eurekalert.org/pub_releases/2014-09/uos-bsr092314.php

https://www.eurekalert.org/news-releases/467495

30. Build Powerful New Success Habits

http://www.apa.org/monitor/jan01/positivepsych.aspx

https://www.sciencedaily.com/releases/2010/03/100325151345.htm

http://www.ncbi.nlm.nih.gov/pubmed/5010404

http://www.ncbi.nlm.nih.gov/pubmed/9686450

http://www.cell.com/neuron/abstract/S0896-6273(09)00489-9

http://psycnet.apa.org/psycinfo/2014-14435-001/

http://papers.ssrn.com/sol3/papers.cfm?abstract_id=1496117

http://www.ncbi.nlm.nih.gov/pubmed/24136970

http://www.psychwiki.com/dms/wiki/uploadedfiles/other/Puetz2006.pdf

https://www.sciencedaily.com/releases/2012/10/121001084132.html

31. Master Conflict

https://img.en25.com/Web/CPP/Conflict_report.pdf

https://www.themyersbriggs.com/en-US/Programs/Conflict-at-Work-Research

http://www.columbia.edu/~da358/publications/ames_flynn_assertiveness.pdf

https://www.networkcomputing.com/networking/executives-demand-communications-arsenal

https://www.researchgate.net/publication/8451443_The_Online_Disinhibition_Effect

https://journals.sagepub.com/doi/abs/10.1177/0894439307311611

32. Master Communication

http://news.uchicago.edu/article/2011/01/20/couples-sometimes-communicate-no-better-strangers-study-finds#sthash.i76Wm6c9.dpuf

Kramer, R. (1997). *Leading by listening: An empirical test of Carl Rogers's theory of human relationship using interpersonal assessments of leaders by followers.* Doctoral dissertation, The George Washington University.

Haney, W. V. (1979). *Communication and interpersonal relations.* Homewood, IL: Irwin.

33. Beat Procrastination

http://users.ugent.be/~wbeyers/scripties2012/artikels/Ferrari%20&%20Olivette_1994.pdf

http://www.apa.org/news/press/releases/2010/04/procrastination.aspx

http://pss.sagepub.com/content/8/6/454.abstract

http://link.springer.com/article/10.1007%2Fs10865-015-9629-2

34. Accelerate Your Climb Up the Corporate Ladder

https://faculty.washington.edu/agg/bytopic.htm

http://www.nature.com/scitable/forums/women-in-science/growth-mindset-research-studies-19947999

https://www.hyperisland.com/community/news/hyper-island-executive-study

http://www.prnewswire.com/news-releases/pink-slips-of-the-tongue-vitalsmarts-study-reveals-the-top-five-one-sentence-career-killers-300232156.html

https://newsroom.accenture.com/subjects/client-winsnew-contracts/accenture-research-finds-career-capital-is-key-to-success.htm

https://www.hbs.edu/faculty/Pages/item.aspx?num=45869

https://hbr.org/2013/11/how-to-make-use-of-your-anxiety-for-positive-results

35. Be Persuasive and Get Your Point Across

https://hbr.org/2014/11/half-of-employees-dont-feel-respected-by-their-bosses

https://www.dailymail.co.uk/sciencetech/article-2538554/Want-promotion-Dont-speak-like-AUSSIE-Rising-pitch-end-sentences-make-sound-insecure.html

https://dash.harvard.edu/bitstream/handle/1/9547823/13-027.pdf?sequence=1

https://www.gsb.stanford.edu/faculty-research/working-papers/schmooze-or-lose-social-friction-lubrication-e-mail-negotiations

http://www.ncbi.nlm.nih.gov/pubmed/22869334

http://www.ncbi.nlm.nih.gov/pmc/articles/PMC1647299/

http://www.wsj.com/articles/SB10001424052748704407804575425561952689390

36. Avoid Integrity Traps

Kiel, F. (2015). *Return on Character: The Real Reason Leaders and Their Companies Win.* Harvard Business Review Press.

37. Create True Work-Life Balance

http://www.apaexcellence.org/assets/general/2013-work-and-communication-technology-survey-final.pdf

https://www.ncbi.nlm.nih.gov/pubmed/25365629

http://cwfr.la.psu.edu/news/news15.htm

http://activepause.com/stress/statistics.htm

http://www.ncbi.nlm.nih.gov/pubmed/534670

https://www.apa.org/topics/healthy-workplaces/employee-control-stress

http://www.statisticbrain.com/startup-failure-by-industry/

Research Report: The Latest Discoveries in Emotional Intelligence

Better decision-making, improved leadership and teamwork, stronger relationships–at and outside of work– and at scale, healthier and more successful organizations: Unpublished data from End of Program surveys (2009-current) and client feedback about the impact of the Emotional Intelligence Appraisal and the TalentSmartEQ EQ training program.

"Top Skills" lists needed for the future of work: Future of Jobs Report 2020 (World Economic Forum, 2020). Online at: https://www.weforum.org/reports/the-future-of-jobs-report-2020; Forbes - The Skills You Need To Succeed in 2020. Online at: https://www.forbes.com/sites/ellevate/2018/08/06/the-skills-you-need-to-succeed-in-2020/?sh=64e0485f288a

Harvard Business Review study of C-suite jobs from Raffaella Sadun, Joseph Fuller, Stephen Hansen, and PJ Neal. The C-Suite Skills That Matter Most. *Harvard Business Review* July-August 2022.

2019 meta-analysis of EQ training in Mattingly, V. and Kraiger, K. (2019). Can Emotional Intelligence be Trained? A Meta-analytical Investigation. *Human Resources Management Review* 29.

Emotional competence training increased emotional competence scores compared to the control group but also showed lower cortisol (the stress hormone) secretion, better wellbeing, and improved relationship quality in Kotsou, I., Nelis, D., Grégoire, J., & Mikolajczak, M. (2011).

Emotional plasticity: Conditions and effects of improving emotional competence in adulthood. *Journal of Applied Psychology*, 96(4), 827–839. https://doi.org/10.1037/a0023047

Higher emotional intelligence scores predicted more successful management of relational situations in the workplace and likely leadership, life satisfaction, academic achievement, and income in Katja Schlegel and Marcello Mortillaro, "The Geneva Emotional Competence Test (GECo): An Ability Measure of Workplace Emotional Intelligence." *Journal of Applied Psychology* 104, no. 4 (April 2019): 559–80. doi:10.1037/apl0000365.supp (Supplemental).

On average $29,000 more per year than those with low EQs in Travis Bradberry and Jean Greaves, *Emotional Intelligence 2.0*. TalentSmart: San Diego. *(2009)*.

2015 study showed that a leader's mood was a factor in feedback seeking behavior by direct reports in Liu, W., Tangirala, S., Lam, W., Chen, Z., Jia, R. T., & Huang, X. (2015). How and when peers' positive mood influences employees' voice. *Journal of Applied Psychology*, 100(3), 976–989. https://doi.org/10.1037/a0038066

A leader's growth mindset and interpersonal identity were important elements for their humility in Wang, L., Owens, B. P., Li, J. (Jason), & Shi, L. (2018). Exploring the affective impact, boundary conditions, and antecedents of leader humility. *Journal of Applied Psychology*, 103(9), 1019–1038. https://doi.org/10.1037/apl0000314

Study of 212 professionals across organizations and industries showed employees with higher emotional intelligence displayed higher team effectiveness and job performance in Farh, C. I. C. C., Seo, M.-G., & Tesluk, P. E. (2012). Emotional intelligence, teamwork effectiveness, and job performance: The moderating role of job context. *Journal of Applied Psychology*, 97(4), 890–900. https://doi.org/10.1037/a0027377

Kevin Roose as quoted in his February 2021 Ted Talk The value of your humanity in an automated future. Online at: https://www.ted.com/talks/kevin_roose_the_value_of_your_humanity_in_an_automated_future

Value of Teachers during COVID-19: Adapted from blog article published February 2021 on TalentSmartEQ.com by Maggie Sass, Ph.D. Online at: https://www.talentsmarteq.com/blog/great-resignation-the-future-of-work/

Adam Grant, *Think Again*. New York: Penguin Random House. (2021).

Original research on Emotional Intelligence and Profession found in Travis Bradberry and Jean Greaves, The Emotional Intelligence Appraisal: Technical Manual (2013).

Previous research on what creates hard times from Travis Bradberry and Jean Greaves, *Emotional Intelligence 2.0*. TalentSmart: San Diego (2009).

Resilience research – area people score lowest in: Comes from data analysis of the Emotional Intelligence Appraisal database (Self-Survey Edition) 2009-2021 consisting of 109, 800 respondents.

Perception of negative emotions: Willroth, E. C., Young, G., Tamir, M., & Mauss, I. B. (2023). Judging emotions as good or bad: Individual differences and associations with psychological health. Emotion. https://doi.org/10.1037/emo0001220.supp (Supplemental)

Difference between pressure and stress from Derek Roger and Nick Petrie Work Without Stress: Building a Resilient Mindset for Lasting Success, (McGraw-Hill, 2017).

Rumination and anxiety in Van der Velden, A. M., Kuyken, W., Wattar, U., Crane, C., Pallesen, K. J., Dahlgaard, J., ... & Piet, J. (2020).

A systematic review of mechanisms of change in mindfulness-based cognitive therapy in the treatment of recurrent major depressive disorder. *Clinical Psychology Review*, 76, 101834; Rumination and sleep in Pires, G. N., Bezerra, A. G., Tufik, S., & Andersen, M. L. (2016).

Conscious and unconscious perseverative cognition: Is a large part of prolonged physiological activity due to unconscious stress? *Journal of Psychosomatic Research*, 117, 70-74.

Rumination and gastrointestinal issues in Kinsinger, S. W., & Ballou, S. (2020). The Role of Psychological Factors in Gastrointestinal Disorders: Beyond the Brain-Gut Axis. *Current Treatment Options in Gastroenterology*, 18(1), 65-831.

Rumination and chronic pain in Gauthier, N., Thibault, P., & Sullivan, M. J. (2017). Perseverative cognition and chronic pain: A meta-analytical review. *Journal of Pain*, 18(11), 1321-1329.

Openness to change is related to positive emotions and job satisfaction: Ng, T. W., & Feldman, D. C. (2015). Affective fit in response to organizational change: The interplay between dispositional affect and affective climate. *Journal of Applied Psychology*, 100(4), 1159-1168. doi: 10.1037/a0038541.

Openness to change is related to the ability to implement successful strategic initiatives: Thorgren, S., & Wincent, J. (2019). Strategic initiative implementation: The role of CEO openness to change. *Journal of Business Research*, 98, 190-199. doi: 10.1016/j.jbusres.2018.12.029.

Openness to change is related to greater career success: Bindl, U. K., Parker, S. K., & Totterdell, P. (2017). Openness to change, work enjoyment, and proactive personality: A cross-lagged analysis. *Journal of Vocational Behavior*, 98, 115-126. doi: 10.1016/j.jvb.2016.11.004

Process these emotions more deeply and can typically remember them more vividly than positive emotions: Baumeister, R. F., Bratslavsky, E., Finkenauer, C., & Vohs, K. D. (2001). Bad is stronger than good. *Review of General Psychology*, 5(4), 323-370; Rozin, P., & Royzman, E. B. (2001).

Negativity bias, negativity dominance, and contagion. *Personality and Social Psychology Review*, 5(4), 296-320; Ito, T. A., Larsen, J. T., Smith, N. K., & Cacioppo, J. T. (1998).

Negative information weighs more heavily on the brain: The negativity bias in evaluative categorizations. *Journal of Personality and Social Psychology*, 75(4), 887-900.

Accountability can lead to increased productivity: Karakowsky, L., & Gowan, M. A. (2010). The role of accountability in job performance: Implications for management development. *Management Decision*, 48(6), 834-847; increased trust on teams: Weng, Q., McElroy, J. C., Morrow, P. C., & Liu, R. (2010).

The effects of accountability on trust and conflict in virtual teams. *International Journal of Human-Computer Studies*, 68(12), 856-867; better performance: Marchiondo, L. A., González-Mulé, E., & Riggio, R. E. (2017).

The impact of accountability on the relationship between transformational leadership and follower performance. *Journal of Leadership & Organizational Studies*, 24(3), 366-377; transparent conversations and collaboration: De Cremer, D., & Van Knippenberg, D. (2002). How do leaders promote cooperation? The effects of charisma and procedural fairness. *Journal of Applied Psychology*, 87(5), 858-866.

Harvard Business Review on feedback of 51,896 executives in Jack Zenger and Joseph Folkman, Overcoming Feedback Phobia: Take the First Step, *Harvard Business Review* (December 16, 2013).

Take Your EQ Habits to the Next Level

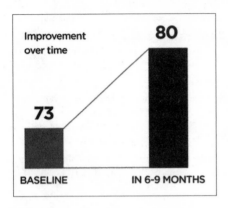

Improvement over time

80

73

BASELINE   IN 6-9 MONTHS

Our clients find that with continued practice, training, and coaching, they can increase their EQ by an average of 7 points over 6-9 months. Research has shown that increasing your EQ can lead to better wellbeing, healthier relationships, improved leadership skills, increased life and work satisfaction, stronger academic achievement, and more effective individual and team performance.

Take EQ Habits to Your Organization

Strong EQ Habits go beyond an individual. EQ habits can also serve as a foundation for addressing critical challenges your organization might face.

In fact, integrating EQ Habits into the workplace can provide a competitive advantage by improving the outcomes that are critical to your organization's performance and culture:

- More effective leadership
- More inclusive cultures
- Higher productivity
- Improved collaboration
- Better decision-making
- Greater resilience
- Stronger communication

TalentSmartEQ offers training programs to help individuals, teams and organizations utilize proven and practical approaches to teach emotional intelligence habits—through online, in-person and virtual delivery methods.

- **Foundational programs** to provide essential EQ skills to individuals at all levels.

- **Leadership training** for leaders and managers to access a 360-degree view of their EQ competency skills.

- **Team training programs** designed for intact teams and executive teams to improve productivity, communication, and collaboration.

The ROI on EQ

EQ training at the organizational level can have an immediate impact on the metrics that matter:

Leaders at one of the largest U.S. not-for-profit healthcare systems experienced a:
- **93%** improvement in their ability to handle conflict effectively.
- **57%** improvement in their ability to deal effectively with change.
- **54%** improvement in their ability to communicate clearly and effectively.

Engineers at a Fortune 200 defense contractor experienced a:
- **40%** improvement in their ability to handle change effectively.
- **26%** improvement in the quality of their relationships with their coworkers

Why TalentSmartEQ?

TalentSmartEQ is the world's premier provider of emotional intelligence development, training, assessments, certification, and coaching. We have spent over 20 years focused on emotional intelligence research and skill development.

Our proven and powerful approach to EQ development is based on decades of research and assessments taken by millions worldwide.

2 million+
assessments

75%
Fortune 500 served

2 million+
books sold

35+ countries
25+ languages

CLIENT TESTIMONIALS

"Best training our company has ever had. I will never view a customer the same. This has helped with my relationships at home and my life."
—**Program Participant and Warehouse Employee from a National Furniture Retailer**

"Invaluable in identifying strengths and opportunities to improve your EQ. It helped me to apply direct strategies, improving my approach to work and my relationships each day."
—**Program Participant, Executive at a Global Financial Company**

"One of the most valuable events in my professional training life...Thank you!"
—**Certified Trainer from an Energy & Utilities Organization**

"This program relates to real-life work experiences. It resonates with all types of personalities and employees, and it's totally universal across all levels and functions."
—**Leadership Executive at Multi-National Retail Client**

"The best, most impactful class our team has had the pleasure to teach!"
—**Talent Development Leader at Division of a National Defense Organization**

Additional Resources

TalentSmartEQ offers complimentary EQ resources including: articles, white papers, live webinars, and the Better EQ newsletter that covers the latest trends in workplace learning. You can subscribe for free at: **www.talentsmarteq.com**.

Interested in bringing Emotional Intelligence Habits to your organization? Please visit us at www.talentsmarteq.com or contact us at 888.818.SMART.

www.talentsmarteq.com